The Personal
Wealth
Coach

Jeff McClure

The Personal Wealth Coach

Copyright© 2003 by Jeffrey W. McClure

Cover Design by Ryan Meyers

ISBN: 0-9741858-5-X

Published by

TurnKey
press·

2525 W Anderson Lane, Suite 540
Austin, Texas 78757

Tel: 512.407.8876
Fax: 512.478.2117

Bill —

I cannot tell you how much I appreciate your faith in our economy and our system and for the great contributions you have made to it!

JJ McDe

August 14, 2003

*To Lisa, Bonnie, Molly, and Michael for their
unending loving support. To Bette and Ray
for giving me this opportunity*
MRF

*To Cstephani, Rebekah and my parents
for the patience and gentle lessons
that sustain me every day*
THS

Notice

Obstetrics is an ever-changing field. Standard safety precautions must be followed, but as new research and clinical experience broaden our knowledge, changes in treatment and drug therapy become necessary or appropriate. Readers are advised to check the product information currently provided by the manufacturer of each drug to be administered to verify the recommended dose, the method and duration of administration, and contraindications. It is the responsibility of the treating physician relying on experience and knowledge of the patient to determine dosages and the best treatment for the patient. Neither the Publisher nor the editor assumes any responsibility for any injury and/or damage to persons or property.

The Publisher

Contributors

MANUEL ALVAREZ, MD
Chairman, Department of Obstetrics and Gynecology, Hackensack University Medical Center, Hackensack, New Jersey
Acute Renal Failure in the Obstetric Intensive Care Patient

THOMAS M. BAJO, MD
Associate Director of Critical Care, Good Samaritan Regional Medical Center, Phoenix, Arizona
Cardiopulmonary Resuscitation of the Pregnant Patient

JAMES BERNASKO, MD
Department of Obstetrics, Gynecology, and Reproductive Services, The Mount Sinai Medical Center, New York, New York
Acute Renal Failure in the Obstetric Intensive Care Patient

GEORGE BRAITBERG, MB, BS
Senior Associate, Department of Clinical Pharmacology and Therapeutics, University of Melbourne, Melbourne; Director of Emergency Medicine, Austin and Repatriation Medical Centre, Melbourne, Australia
Poisoning in Pregnancy

CRISTINA CARBALLO, MD
Clinical Lecturer, Pediatrics, Department of Pediatrics, University of Arizona College of Medicine, Tucson, Arizona; Neonatologist, Neonatal Specialists, Ltd., Phoenix Children's Hospital, Phoenix, Arizona
Neonatal Evaluation, Resuscitation, and Survival

LINDA R. CHAMBLISS, MD
Director, Maternal-Fetal Medicine, Department of Obstetrics and Gynecology, Maricopa Medical Center, Phoenix, Arizona
Human Immunodeficiency Virus Infection and Pregnancy

STEVEN L. CLARK, MD
Professor, Department of Obstetrics and Gynecology, University of Utah School of Medicine, Salt Lake City; Director, Intermountain Health Care Perinatal Centers, LDS Hospital, Salt Lake City, Utah
Amniotic Fluid Embolism

WILLIAM H. CLEWELL, MD
Clinical Professor of Obstetrics and Gynecology, University of Arizona College of Medicine, Tucson, Arizona; Associate Director, Obstetrics and Gynecology Residency, Good Samaritan Regional Medical Center, Phoenix; Partner, Phoenix Perinatal Associates, Phoenix, Arizona
Hypertensive Emergencies in Pregnancy

STEVEN C. CURRY, MD
Associate Professor of Clinical Medicine, Department of Medicine,

University of Arizona College of
Medicine, Tucson, Arizona; Director,
Department of Medical Toxicology,
Good Samaritan Regional Medical
Center, Phoenix, Arizona
Poisoning in Pregnancy

LISA A. DADO, MD
Partner, Valley Anesthesia
Consultants, Phoenix; Good
Samaritan Regional Medical Center,
Phoenix Children's Hospital, St.
Joseph's Medical Center, Phoenix,
Arizona
*Anesthesia for the Obstetric Patient
with Complications*

GARY A. DILDY, MD
Assistant Professor, Department of
Obstetrics and Gynecology,
University of Utah, Salt Lake City,
Utah; Director, Perinatal Center,
Utah Valley Regional Medical
Center, Provo, Utah
Amniotic Fluid Embolism

JOHN P. ELLIOTT, MD
Clinical Professor of Obstetrics and
Gynecology, University of Arizona
College of Medicine, Tucson,
Arizona; Co-Director, Maternal-Fetal
Medicine, Good Samaritan Regional
Medical Center, Phoenix; Medical
Director for Maternal Transport,
Samaritan Air Evacuation, Phoenix;
Partner, Phoenix Perinatal
Associates, Phoenix, Arizona
*Transport of the Critically Ill
Obstetric Patient*
*Special Considerations for the
Patient with a Multifetal Gestation*
*Management of Complications
Associated with Administration of
Tocolytic Agents*

HARRIS J. FINBERG, MD
Assistant Professor of Radiology,
Mayo Medical School, Rochester,

Minnesota; Director, Diagnostic
Ultrasound, Phoenix Perinatal
Associates, Phoenix, Arizona
*Role of Sonography in the Obstetric
Intensive Care Setting*

MICHAEL R. FOLEY, MD
Director, Obstetric Intensive Care
and Associate Director, Maternal
Fetal Medicine, Good Samaritan
Regional Medical Center and
Phoenix Perinatal Associates,
Phoenix, Arizona; Clinical Associate
Professor, Department of OB/GYN,
University of Arizona, Tucson,
Arizona
Diabetic Ketoacidosis in Pregnancy

MICHAEL C. GORDON, MD
Chief of Labor and Delivery,
Director of Outpatient Services,
Obstetrics and Gynecology, Wilford
Hall Medical Center, United States
Air Force, San Antonio, Texas
Maternal Sepsis

ROBERT L. JOHNSON, MD
Good Samaritan Regional Medical
Center, Phoenix; Associate Director,
Maternal-Fetal Medicine, Phoenix
Perinatal Associates, Phoenix,
Arizona
*Thromboembolic Disease
Complicating Pregnancy*

MICHAEL F. KOSZALKA, Jr., MD
Associate Director, Marshfield
Clinic, Marshfield, Wisconsin
Cardiac Disease in Pregnancy

WILLIAM C. MABIE, MD
Professor of Obstetrics and
Gynecology, University of
Tennessee, Memphis, College of
Medicine, Memphis; Director of the
Obstetric Intensive Care Unit,
Regional Medical Center at
Memphis, Memphis, Tennessee

Basic Hemodynamic Monitoring for the Obstetric Care Provider

MICHAEL C. McQUEEN, MD

Director, Neonatal Intensive Care Unit, Phoenix Children's Hospital, Phoenix, Arizona

Fetal Considerations in the Obstetric Intensive Care Patient

DANIEL F. O'KEEFFE, MD

Medical Director, Maternal-Fetal Medicine, Good Samaritan Regional Medical Center, Phoenix; Partner, Phoenix Perinatal Associates, Phoenix, Arizona

Trauma in Pregnancy

ALVIN H. PERELMAN, MD

Clinical Associate Professor, University of Arizona College of Medicine, Tucson, Arizona; Director, Pediatric Endocrinology, Phoenix Children's Hospital, Phoenix, Arizona

Management of Hyperthyroidism and Thyroid Storm During Pregnancy

JORDAN H. PERLOW, MD

Associate Director, Maternal-Fetal Medicine, Good Samaritan Regional Medical Center, Phoenix; Partner, Phoenix Perinatal Associates, Phoenix, Arizona

Obesity in the Obstetric Intensive Care Patient

PHILIP SAMUELS, MD

Associate Professor of Obstetrics and Gynecology, Director, Fellowship Program in Maternal-Fetal Medicine, The Ohio State University Hospital, Columbus, Ohio

Acute Care of Thrombocytopenia and Disseminated Intravascular Coagulation Complicating Pregnancy

SHIRLEY K. SAWAI, MD

Associate Director, Maternal-Fetal Medicine, Good Samaritan Regional Medical Center, Phoenix; Partner, Phoenix Perinatal Associates, Phoenix, Arizona

Acute Fatty Liver of Pregnancy

HOWARD S. SMITH, MD

Assistant Professor, Department of Anesthesiology and Internal Medicine, Albany Medical College, Albany; Obstetric Anesthesiologist, Albany Medical Center Hospital, Albany, New York

Respiratory Emergencies During Pregnancy

Fluids and Electrolytes for the Obstetric Intensive Care Patient

THOMAS H. STRONG, JR., MD

Clinical Associate Professor of Obstetrics and Gynecology, University of Arizona College of Medicine, Tucson, Arizona; Clinical Assistant Professor of Obstetrics and Gynecology, University of California San Francisco, San Francisco, California; Director of Resident Research, Good Samaritan Regional Medical Center, Phoenix; Associate Director, Phoenix Perinatal Associates, Phoenix, Arizona

Transfusion of Blood Components and Derivatives in the Obstetric Intensive Care Patient

Obstetric Hemorrhage

HARRY S. TAMM, MD

Clinical Associate Professor of Neurology, University of Arizona College of Medicine, Tucson, Arizona; Vice Chair, Department of Medicine, Good Samaritan Regional Medical Center, Phoenix, Arizona

Neurologic Emergencies During Pregnancy

Foreword

In recent years, the focus on health care has shifted from intervention to prevention, a strategy that will hopefully improve the quality of life and reduce costs. Similarly, the emphasis on education for health care providers in obstetrics and gynecology has been in the area of primary care. The Residency Review Committee in Obstetrics and Gynecology has emphasized continuity of care and training for our house officers in internal medicine, family medicine, emergency medicine, and geriatrics. These changes may impair our ability to identify and care for critically ill women and their babies. For example, many of our residency programs have had to reduce the length of rotations in intensive care units or even eliminate them entirely, and pregnant women requiring intensive care are not commonly seen, even on a busy obstetrics service. Nevertheless, the critically ill obstetrics patient should be managed by individuals who have been trained to appreciate the impact of hemorrhage, sepsis, or other insults on the physiology of the pregnant woman and fetus. Caring for these cases demands an understanding of these issues and how they impact on the management of such complex problems.

How, then, can we meet this challenge? *Obstetric Intensive Care* by Drs. Michael R. Foley and Thomas H. Strong, Jr. will help with these difficult cases. I can think of no one better prepared than Dr. Foley to edit this textbook. As a resident in obstetrics and gynecology and a fellow in maternal-fetal medicine at The Ohio State University Medical Center, Mike helped organize our critical care program in obstetrics. He proved to be a skilled teacher in this area early in his career, preparing lectures on intensive care for our resident didactic lecture series. Mike had the ability to take a complex clinical situation and present it clearly and thoughtfully, using acronyms and flow diagrams to help his audience remember key points. Now, Mike has assembled a group of experts in obstetric intensive care. Their comprehensive discussions of virtually every important topic in this field are marked by the same clarity and practical approach that have been a hallmark of Dr. Foley's presentations. In other words, the book describes the important concepts of obstetric intensive care in a way that will be extremely valuable for primary care providers facing these challenges.

Steven G. Gabbe, MD
Professor and Chairman
Department of Obstetrics and Gynecology
University of Washington School of Medicine
Seattle, Washington

Foreword

Obstetric Intensive Care by Michael R. Foley, M.D., editor, and Thomas H. Strong, Jr., M.D., assistant editor, and published by W.B. Saunders, will find its place among easily available reference handbooks. Dr. Foley has assembled a group of authors that are not only distinguished but are also active practitioners of obstetrics and gynecology, especially high-risk obstetrics.

The goal of this book is to try to decrease the intimidating circumstances that a patient presents and to direct a hands-on "how-to-do-it." The editors and authors have used memory aids such as mnemonics and algorithms to help facilitate the thinking once a basic diagnosis is made of a precise condition. Management is concise and priority based and will be helpful to any obstetric care provider. The recommended reading list includes state-of-the-art papers, as well as American College of Obstetricians and Gynecologists Technical Bulletins.

This book began as an outgrowth of the activities of the Phoenix Perinatal Associates, the largest perinatal group in Arizona. It was apparent that many critically ill patients, when referred, could have been managed differently to facilitate health care. This handbook can be used as a reference for a specific condition in the high-risk obstetric patient and will facilitate either managing the patient in the local environment or sending the patient to a tertiary care center where more manpower is available.

Additionally, the explosion of technology in the past decade has made possible a book such as this, since specific monitoring for high-risk patients is now almost commonplace. The key to health care is to know when you can take care of the ill pregnant patient yourself, when you need to refer the patient, and if referred, is the patient really going to get better care than you can personally provide.

The handbook has 28 chapters and very adequate, practical reading lists. The topics are written by individuals who do hands-on medicine and have very special areas of interest, and all consider it a privilege to transmit their knowledge to you in this format.

My prediction is that this handbook will become well worn and that its use will become part of the obstetric physician's modus operandi for high-risk patients. It will also be found in many residents' white coats, as well as in the pockets of others who provide health care for pregnant women.

The list of authors not only embraces the maternal-fetal medicine specialists but also the pediatrician, the neonatologist, the radiologist and ultrasonographer, the internist, and the toxicologist.

It is inappropriate for me to comment on each of the 28 topics presented in this handbook. Even if I wanted to, why should I spoil the fun that each of you will have in acquiring the knowledge of these specialists in a specific area? Your joy will be to use the book on a day-to-day basis and to find out just how helpful and time-saving it can be in your evaluation of the critically ill pregnant patient. May you enjoy.

Frederick P. Zuspan, M.D.
Professor and Chairman Emeritus
Department of Obstetrics and Gynecology
Ohio State University College of Medicine
Columbus, Ohio

Preface

As an active educator in the field of Obstetrics and Maternal-Fetal Medicine, I have been enlightened to the fact that the subject of obstetric critical care medicine is viewed as extremely intimidating. However, the number of obstetric patients presenting with critical care diagnoses to less experienced centers is clearly on the rise. The purpose of this book, therefore, is to present the subject of obstetric intensive care medicine in a less intimidating fashion, allowing the obstetric care provider more simplified access to the specifics of "how to medicine" in preparation for "what appears to be" the inevitable presentation of critical care obstetric patients to their practice. This book is organized as a handy "peripheral brain" that provides a short review of pathophysiology, diagnostic methods, and priority based management techniques that prepare the resident, nurse, and practitioner in obstetrics to design a practical care plan while gaining a clear understanding of the "basics" of disease. As the "tide of medicine" appears to be shifting from the subspecialist toward the primary care provider, my hope is that this book will "bridge the gap" during this difficult transition. I am extremely indebted to Dr. Frederick Zuspan, Dr. Steven Gabbe, and the physicians and staff of Phoenix Perinatal Associates for their continued guidance over the years in preparation for "real life" practical obstetric care delivery. Many thanks as well to Dr. Thomas Strong, assistant editor, for his tireless dedication to the preparation of this book and the outstanding contributing authors for their excellent chapters.

"To know that you do not know is the best. To pretend to know when you do not know is disease."
—Lao Tzu

. . . as educators and caregivers, we should strive to capably manage and understand the true essence of "disease" . . .
—Michael R. Foley, MD

Michael R. Foley, MD

Acknowledgment

Drs. Foley and Strong would like to express their gratitude to Lois McConville for her invaluable editorial assistance.

Contents

xvii

WILLIAM C. MABIE

Basic Hemodynamic Monitoring for the Obstetric Care Provider

The pulmonary artery flotation catheter has given an identity to the practice of critical care medicine and has enabled functional application of the principles of cardiac catheterization at the bedside. The rather precise and continuous monitoring of fundamental cardiovascular parameters has allowed for more optimal decisions about therapy. In this chapter I discuss the pulmonary artery catheter, its indications, what it can measure, and how the hemodynamic concepts can be applied.

■ Indications for Invasive Hemodynamic Monitoring

The Swan-Ganz pulmonary artery catheter was introduced into clinical practice in 1970 for the evaluation of patients with cardiac disease. The first publication on its use in obstetrics appeared in 1980. Swan-Ganz monitoring needs to be considered for any critically ill patient as an adjunct to the clinical examination. The standards and criteria for invasive monitoring should be the same for pregnant and nonpregnant patients. Common indications for pulmonary artery catheterization in obstetric patients are listed in Table 1–1.

The Swan-Ganz catheter is useful for differentiating cardiogenic forms of pulmonary edema from noncardiogenic forms. The information gleaned with the catheter may also be used to guide diuretic therapy, preload and afterload manipulation, and inotropic therapy (Tables 1–2, 1–3). In patients with oliguria, the catheter may be used to assess volume status. Central venous pressure is not adequate for assessing volume status in pre-eclampsia. The changes in wedge pressure and cardiac output in response to a fluid challenge are important guides to intravascular volume. While invasive hemodynamic monitoring is not necessary for acute resuscitation from hemorrhagic shock, it is

Table 1–1

Indications for Pulmonary Artery Catheterization in Obstetrics

Refractory or unexplained pulmonary edema
Refractory or unexplained oliguria
Massive hemorrhage
Septic shock
Adult respiratory distress syndrome
New York Heart Association class 3 and 4 cardiac disease
Intraoperative or intrapartum cardiovascular decompensation
Respiratory distress of unknown cause

Table 1–2

Definitions of Hemodynamic Terms

Wedge Pressure

Also known as the pulmonary artery occlusion pressure—(PAOP), wedge pressure is a measure of left ventricular preload. The pulmonary artery wedge pressure is obtained with a balloon-tipped catheter advanced into a branch of the pulmonary artery until the vessel is occluded, forming a free communication through the pulmonary capillaries and veins to the left atrium. A true wedge position is in a lung zone where both pulmonary artery and pulmonary venous pressures exceed alveolar pressure.

Preload

Initial stretch of the myocardial fiber at end diastole. Clinically, the preload to the right and left ventricles (end-diastolic pressures) is assessed by the central venous pressure and wedge pressure, respectively.

Afterload

Reflected by both the wall tension of the ventricle during ejection and the resistance to forward flow in the form of vascular resistance (vasoconstriction). The pulmonary vascular resistance (PVR) and the systemic vascular resistance (SVR) are the primary afterloads for the right and left ventricles, respectively, in a normal heart.

Contractility

The inherent force and velocity of myocardial contraction when preload and afterload are held constant.

Table 1–3

Hemodynamic Therapy

Decreased Preload	Decreased Afterload	Contractility
Crystalloid	Volume	Dopamine
Colloid	Inotropic support	Dobutamine
Blood	Vasopressors	Epinephrine
	Norepinephrine	Calcium*
	Phenylephrine	Digitalis†
	Metaraminol	

Increased Preload	Increased Afterload	
Diuretics	Arterial dilators	
Furosemide	Hydralazine	
Ethacrynic acid	Diazoxide	
Mannitol	Mixed arterial-venous	
Venodilators	dilators	
Furosemide	Nitroprusside	
Nitroglycerin	Trimethaphan	
Morphine	Venous dilators	
	Nitroglycerin	

*May produce marked increase in systemic vascular resistance.

†Of questionable value and safety for acute management.

Adapted with permission from Rosenthal MH: Intrapartum intensive care management of the cardiac patient. Clin Obstet Gynecol 1981; 24:789.

useful in the subsequent 24 to 72 hours to guide fluid therapy in complex cases when it is not clear if internal bleeding is continuing or if oliguria, pulmonary edema, liver dysfunction, or severe coagulopathy is present. In septic shock, invasive hemodynamic monitoring allows for timely manipulation of cardiovascular parameters with fluid and inotropic therapy as well as assessment of response to therapy through such calculations as oxygen delivery and consumption. In persons with adult respiratory distress syndrome, the catheter is used to exclude cardiogenic pulmonary edema and to guide supportive therapy with mechanical ventilation, positive end-expiratory pressure, intravenous fluids, diuretics, and inotropic agents. New York Heart Association class 3 and 4 cardiac patients require invasive monitoring to guide fluid and drug therapy, as well as for anesthetic management during labor and delivery. The cause of sudden intraoperative or intrapartum cardiovascular decompensation may be clarified by obtaining pulmonary capillary wedge pressure and cardiac output. The final indication includes patients in whom the contribution to respiratory distress of cardiac or pulmonary disease is unclear by clinical examination. The pulmonary artery catheter can help to distinguish heart failure from pneumonia, pulmonary emboli, adult respiratory distress syndrome, and chronic pulmonary disorders.

■ Risks Versus Benefits of Catheter Insertion

The risks and benefits of bedside catheterization have been extensively reviewed by Matthay and Chatterjee. The authors considered four areas: complications, obtaining reliable data, clinical versus invasive assessment of hemodynamic status, and the effect of monitoring on outcome.

Complications associated with invasive hemodynamic monitoring include pneumothorax, ventricular arrhythmias, air embolism, pulmonary infarction, pulmonary artery rupture, sepsis, local vascular thrombosis, intracardiac knotting, and valve damage. Complications have decreased over the years, at least partially because of greater physician and nursing awareness. The prevalence of pneumothorax has decreased from 6 to 1% in the early literature to less than 0.1% now, that of pulmonary infarction from 7.2% in 1974 to 0 to 1.3% in recent studies, and that of pulmonary artery rupture from 0.1 to 0.2% to almost 0%. Local vascular thrombosis has decreased with the use of heparin-bonded catheters. Septicemia has decreased from 2 to 0.5%. Still, complications have not been eliminated.

The continuous generation of hemodynamic and oxygenation data can be mesmerizing, and this can be viewed as a complication. The obstetrician may spend excessive time calibrating, debugging, and collecting data while ignoring such equally important aspects as the fetal heart rate tracing and the progress of labor.

There are multiple causes for interpretive error in catheter readings, including improper calibration, air or blood in the lines, the use of digital readout rather than a hard paper printout, and failure to measure wedge pressure at end expiration, when pleural pressure is zero. Pulmonary capillary wedge pressure may not reflect left ventricular end-diastolic pressure in the setting of aortic insufficiency, mitral stenosis, or mitral insufficiency. In addition, the relation between left ventricular end-diastolic pressure and left ventricular end-diastolic volume may vary with changes in left ventricular compliance, as during myo-cardial ischemia.

Two studies have shown that the prediction of cardiac out-put and wedge pressure based on history, physical examination, and chest x-ray may be as high as 75% accurate in coronary care unit (CCU) patients. Three additional studies, however, have shown that clinical criteria accurately predicted wedge pressure and cardiac output in only 50% of a more heteroge-neous group of general intensive care unit (ICU) patients. Infor-mation from invasive monitoring also clearly made a difference in treatment (fluids, diuretics, vasopressors, or vasodilators) 50% of the time.

Does use of the Swan-Ganz catheter improve outcome? No data have been published that prove this, and a large, prospec-tive, randomized trial would be needed. It should be empha-sized that the Swan-Ganz catheter is only a diagnostic device. It improves outcome only if the diagnosis is for conditions for which treatment exists. For example, it may improve outcome in acute myocardial infarction with heart failure because afterload reduction, inotropic agents, and intra-aortic balloon counterpul-sation may be applied. By contrast, patients with septic shock are unlikely to benefit from the catheter because no new thera-peutic option exists for this condition. However, invasive moni-toring can make management of the hemodynamically unstable septic patient more rational.

■
Inserting the Swan-Ganz Catheter

The Swan-Ganz catheter is most often inserted through the internal jugular vein or the subclavian vein. It may also be inserted through the basilic vein in the arm or the femoral vein. Several commercial trays containing the necessary equipment are available for central venous cannulation using the Seldinger technique (i.e., over a guidewire). The procedure is performed under continuous electrocardiographic monitoring. The equip-ment needed for inserting the Swan-Ganz catheter is shown in Figure 1–1. The technique for venous cannulation and passing the catheter through the heart will not be described here. Unless the obstetrician performs at least 12 of these procedures per year, it may be safer for the patient to have this done by an anesthesiologist, internist, or cardiologist who has more experi-ence. Even though someone else inserts the catheter, the obste-trician is frequently called upon to troubleshoot or to manipulate

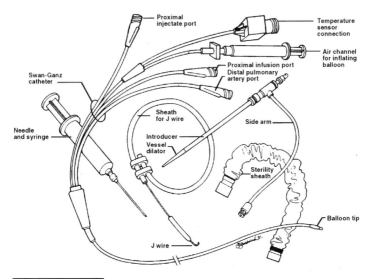

Figure 1-1

Equipment needed for inserting Swan-Ganz catheter. The use of each piece of equipment is described in detail in the text. (From Gabbe SG, Niebyl JR, Simpson JL (eds): Obstetrics: Normal and Problem Pregnancies, 2nd ed. New York, Churchill Livingstone, 1991.)

the catheter because it is not wedging, the waveform is damped, or the nurses do not trust the numbers. I will therefore discuss the waveforms seen as the catheter passes through the heart.

■ Hemodynamic Waveforms

The right atrial pressure tracing (Fig. 1–2A) consists of three distinct waves, a, c, and v. The a wave is a small wave due to atrial systole. The declining pressure that immediately follows the a wave is called the "x descent." The c wave may or may not appear as a distinct wave. It reflects the increase in right atrial pressure produced by closure of the tricuspid valve. The negative wave following the c wave is called the x^1 descent. The v wave is caused by right atrial filling and concomitant right ventricular systole, which causes the leaflets of the closed tricuspid valve to bulge back into the right atrium. The y descent immediately follows the v wave. The pressure changes produced by the a, c, and v waves are usually within 3 to 4 mm Hg of

Acknowledgements

I cannot imagine how I would have completed this book without the editing and encouragement of Carole-Lynn Saros, CPA. Her knowledge of the fine points of the English language combined with her uncanny ability to spot the errors, both of the typographical and just plain wrong category, have saved me many an embarrassment. Her encouragement in the, for me, painful time of cutting and editing have kept me sane and focused. Also, I owe a debt to her long suffering husband Greg who shouldered family responsibility as she took on the task of making me sound reasonably smooth and educated.

I also want to thank my son Jacob, our business manager, as well as his wife Sara. They, along with my talented and able staff members, Catherine Judd and Melissa Parker, have kept the Personal Wealth Coach® business running even as I have labored to create the book.

My gratitude has been earned too by Gary Curry, whose encouragement and support once the first draft was done has helped to keep me going when I thought the race should have been over.

My deepest thanks goes to all my clients who have been so faithful in giving me feedback on the scenarios in this book. It is you who have taught me over the years at least as much as I have taught you.

Finally, and certainly not least, I want to thank my wife and family who have tolerated seeing the back of my head and hearing my fingers hammering on the keyboard for these long months when they would have much preferred the attention I was devoting to this work.

Jeff McClure,
Salado, Texas
July 14, 2003

Forward – The Reason for this Book

The first question any person who is interested in the subject of investing needs to ask is: "Am I an investor or am I a speculator?" If you are an investor then both the question and the answer will be important to you. If you are a speculator, you probably won't be interested in the question anyway!

If you are a serious investor and you are serious about what you want your money to do for you after it is invested, then this book is written to you. If you are a person who is looking for a "hot tip" or a sure fire method to "beat the market" and find "wealth without risk," then don't waste your time here. After decades of experience in the world of investing, it is my sincerely held opinion that you will obtain the entertainment you are looking for, but it will be an extremely expensive process.

The question then is, "Are you serious about investing, or are you looking for a quick and exciting experience?" To the degree you have one, you probably won't have the other. Riding a roller coaster may be thrilling, but in the end you wind up back where you started minus the price of the ticket. Moving across the country to take a better job in order to lift the financial status of both yourself and your family is anything but quick or thrilling, but it is the stuff true change and growth comes from. It is your decision.

I have read many books on investing. Some were easy and entertaining, others were academic tomes of profound thought that, frankly, made me want to put them down and take a good nap after the first chapter! The more entertaining version almost universally offered a *method* of investing with the assurance that it was all quite simple. The promise was made or implied that by following the *method* espoused by the author, one would certainly be successful in some investment type or market. The problem with any *method* is that it will only work as long as nothing *assumed* by the method changes. One of the great difficulties with investing is that the vehicles through which we invest and even the underlying nature of the things we call "investments" are *constantly* changing. The method that seemed to be a sure-fire winner just a few years ago may be an almost certain disaster today. More on that later...

The heavy intellectual tomes produced by the academics and pseudo-scientists of the financial planning community are often just as unreliable, or worse. Even after plowing through the stilted wording of these monuments to intellectual egotism, the validity of the conclusions is commonly largely or completely unproven. On the rare occasion when the author of an acclaimed intellectual work is actually so convinced of his or her theoretical validity that a real investment fund is started based on the author's theories, it is almost inevitably a failure!

In 1998, the world financial system was placed in very real jeopardy by the faith some of the largest American financial institutions placed in a hedge fund called *Long Term Capital.* The operators of that fund were two professors who had recently received the Nobel Prize in economics for their brilliant explanation of the mechanics of the international bond markets. *Long Term Capital* was their attempt to capitalize on the practical application of that "brilliant" understanding. Unfortunately for them, their elegant mathematical proof of an unchanging principal did not shield them, or their investors, from a complete reversal of all they had "proven!" Were it not for the personal intervention of the chairman of the Federal Reserve, their folly could have generated a world wide economic crisis resulting in the financial default of major U.S. banks and whole countries! There is a valid argument that the necessity for the Federal Reserve to keep the money supply high following the collapse of *Long Term Capital* may be part of the cause of the stock market bubble that followed.

As recently as the early 1980s, there was a general belief among many professional and serious amateur investors that all one needed to do to have an outstanding return in stocks was to religiously follow The Value Line Investment Survey and make the purchases or sales as called for in that publication. A few years later, the best seller *The Bardstown Ladies Common Sense Investment Guide* was published. In that book, the claim was made that the Bardstown Ladies Investment Club had achieved a whopping 23.4% per year over an extended period of time. That impressive return was better than most professional investors and any of the popular indices! The "secret" of the Bardstown Ladies was their reliance on a combination of the *Value Line* publication and good "common sense." Only after record sales of the book as amazing as the investment return claimed on the cover of their book did someone take a serious look at the actual returns of the investment club. As it happens, the club treasurer included the money the members of the club had contributed each month as "gain" for the purposes of computing the return! If one discounted those contributions, the actual average annual *investment* return, *9.1%,* was somewhat below what the ladies could have gotten from a good certificate of deposit over the same period.

The question of how the Bardstown Ladies could have done so well should have raised alarms immediately, but professionals as astute as Peter Lynch, the famed manager of Fidelity Magellan Fund, endorsed the book without taking a look at the underlying assumptions. The Value Line Investment Survey still enjoys a wide following of true believers, despite the now rather clear evidence that there is little or no value in the Value Line Survey. Over the ten-year period ending on October 31, 2001, the average annual compound rate of return of the "no load" Value Line Mutual Fund, a near perfect reflection of the survey's recommendations, was 9.63%. That return was over 3% less than the Standard & Poor's 500 Stock Index and below the return of 62% of the mutual funds with similar objectives! The five-year return was even worse at 4.7% and 70% of similar funds had better returns! A year later in 2002, the Value Line Fund had achieved the unenviable record of being in the bottom quarter of similar funds for the trailing ten years with a total return of less than 6% per year. Not too surprisingly, one could have done as well or better in a good certificate of deposit over the same period. In other words, the Bardstown Ladies did about as well as the *method,* but the method didn't work as well as they thought.

Another prime example of how method investing works, or more accurately, doesn't work in the real world, is the Dogs of the Dow theory. That theory, published in a book called *Beating the Dow* by M. O'Higgins and J. Downes and made quite popular by *The Motley Fools* both in their books and on their website, proposes that an investor who purchases the ten stocks out of the Dow Jones 30 Industrials (the Dow) with the lowest ratio of price to earnings (P/E ratio), and then annually sells those that no longer are the lowest priced and replaces them with those that are, would substantially beat both the Dow and the broad market. Unfortunately for those who were convinced by the historic research that seemed to "prove" the validity of the theory, as soon as it became widely known and practiced, it disappeared and even *reversed!*

According to the semi-official Dogs of the Dow website http://www.dogsofthedow.com, the Dogs returned 1.8%, 7.7%, and 15% for the three, five and ten year periods ending December 31, 2001. Meanwhile, the Dow Jones Industrial Average returned 5.7%, 12%, and 15.5% for the same time periods. That does not deter the true believers who continue to publish the fiction that investing in the Dogs is a wonderful way to "beat the market." Then there is the little issue that the returns listed on the website do not include the transaction costs or the taxes due. The same website noted that by the end of 2002, the brilliant strategy still followed by the faithful had managed to under-perform its targeted Fidelity Magellan fund, and the Dow Jones Industrial Average for both the trailing five and ten years.

In their book *The Motley Fool Investment Guide,* David and Tom Gardner report that for two decades, from 1973 to 1993, the Foolish Four strategy returned an average annual return of 25% and that "it should grant its fans the same 25% annualized returns going forward as it has in the past." The Motley Fools dropped the strategy in 2002 after it became painfully apparent that rather than beating the general market, it trailed the indices, even after being tweaked ("evolved" according to the *Fools*) several times to improve its apparent past performance.

Perhaps the most glaring recent example of investment practices that do not work was seen in the dramatic run up in large growth stock prices in 1999 and the first quarter of 2000. With 20:20 hindsight, we can now look back and see the mania and resulting stock bubble that developed from a combination of "irrational exuberance" as it was so well coined by Chairman of the Federal Reserve, Alan Greenspan, and a mass movement into S&P 500 Index surrogates that distorted the index into a form of large company growth fund. One part of the mania was an almost exact replay of the railroad mania that gripped America's investors in the decade following the Civil War. The second cause was a pure market mania that repeated the behavior of every stock mania since at least 1720. As I have spoken with supposedly sophisticated investors, both professional and amateur, they have demonstrated an almost universal lack of knowledge that those historic events even occurred!

10

In all of these examples there is a common error—each is a methodology. Some of the more sophisticated methodologies utilize high levels of complex numerical analysis and are filled with statistical terms such as "reversion to the mean" and "standard deviation" but actually are little more useful than the method of simply picking the lowest P/E ratios in the Dow. Others were simplistic ideas based on concepts like "lower cost means higher return." and "stocks always go up after they split." The fact is that these methodologies seemed to work long enough to draw in millions or even billions of investor dollars only to suddenly fail without warning. The question that is missing is: "*Why did it work?*"

If we do not know *why* something works, and the *why* goes away, presuming there was a "*why*" to begin with, we won't know it is gone until long after any advantage we may have gained through some methodology has disappeared. The inverse failing, getting out of a position when it is down but is still a good investment is generated by the same assumption. If the underlying *why*, or reason for superior performance, is still there, it is clearly a bad idea to sell when the value is "down." On the other hand, if the *why* is gone, then getting out of the investment may be an excellent idea even if the price is "down," but was an even better idea when the price was "up."

In the example of the Dogs of the Dow, the reason for the historic behavior of the stock prices was that there was (and is) a tendency by investors to overreact to bad news. At any given moment several of the extremely well known stocks in the Dow would likely be under-priced because of that overreaction. The practical result of such an overreaction would be that there had been more selling of the stocks in question than was justified by the facts. As soon as a substantial number of investors discovered this inefficiency in pricing and made resulting purchases of the under-priced stocks, they ceased to be underpriced. Actually, from that point forward they began to be *overpriced* as many investors were now irrationally buying the stocks of companies often in some sort of trouble!

Other examples of "data mining" strategies like the S&P 500 indexing strategy are still in vogue and others appear each year. Data mining is the practice of sorting through past data and finding a pattern, then proclaiming it to be an irrefutable law of the universe. With the advent of the mind-boggling ability of computers to comb mountains of data, patterns in the past can be found. That those patterns exist cannot be challenged. That they represent anything but a random series of events that happen to line up is the foolish conclusion of their promoters. Because investment prices respond, at least in the short-term, to irrational inflows of cash, indeed each widely published theory does seem to work for a time. Like the *Ponzi scheme,* (which I will explain in some detail later) the gains are an illusion that more often than not leave the true believer bereft of cash and wondering how it could have gone so wrong.

In the example of the S&P 500 Indexing mania, the drumbeat of "low cost means high return." was based on a recent historical period when accelerating cash flows into the S&P 500 Index had already inflated the price of the larger capitalization stocks in that index. Further buying resulted in higher prices in a classic market mania that seemed to "prove" the validity of the theory. According to articles in the *Wall Street Journal,* the largest inflow into index funds was in the first quarter of the year 2000, and the largest outflow was in the summer and early fall of 2002, almost precisely at the top and bottom of the market cycle respectively.

An examination of the 100 largest mutual funds in the *Morningstar* data base, both bond and stock, shows the S&P 500 funds to have returned less in performance than about ¾ of the largest stock or bond funds for the past five years, and about half those funds for ten and fifteen years. Considering that ten and fifteen-year returns included *both bond and stock funds,* something is clearly wrong with the idea that the "low cost" index funds will "always" outperform the managed funds. If we eliminate the bond funds, then we discover about 62% of the largest equity funds outperformed the S&P 500 Index over the past fifteen years.

The premise that "low cost means high return" was a marketing idea that became, for a short time, a self-fulfilling prophecy. History has demonstrated that whenever a simple slogan describes a reason for buying any investment or class of investment, a mania and bubble in that asset is not far behind. The simple fact is that when the mass of investors began to purchase something based on a slogan rather than underlying value, then the "something" will soon be overpriced and the more overpriced it gets, the more dramatic will be the price decline that follows.

Of course that leads us to the issue of determining the definition of "overpriced" and "underpriced." One of the investment terms I hear commonly coming out of the mouths of professional investors is "priced at the market," meaning that a given stock is properly priced for the market on a given day, or simply neither over nor under priced. What does that mean? Why might it be different from one day to the next? Why is a share of a given corporation (a stock) worth a given amount at all? For that matter, why is it worth *anything?* Quite a number of companies, some of them the leading forces in our economy, have as corporate policy decided never to pay dividends. If you were to attend one of the major business schools in the country and earn a masters degree in business administration or finance, you would learn that the "proper" value of a stock is the present value of the future dividends. So, if the present value of a stock is the future dividends, why do we give any value at all to a stock that will never pay dividends? If we don't know the answer to that question, and it changes, we might just be left holding investments that we had assumed had some intrinsic value only to find that the "value" disappeared when we weren't looking.

Why is it that professional investors generally seem to make a substantial profit from investing and amateurs who try the same thing commonly do not? Just what do professionals do that amateurs do not do, and what do amateurs do that professionals do not? Is it as many of the popular finance magazines put it, that mutual fund companies gain their profit from overcharging investors for what the amateurs could be doing for themselves at much greater gain? As simple and rational as the magazine article makes it sound, survey after survey has shown that individual investors do poorly... and more poorly when they are on their own!

I have had the opportunity on a number of occasions to have serious discussions with some of the best investment managers in the United States. While their approaches to buying a stock, bond, or other investment were often radically different, most of them at one time or another mentioned the principal difference between a successful professional and an amateur investor. A professional buys a company, not something called a "stock." A professional looks at a publicly traded company from the point of view of becoming an owner of that company. The question that is asked by at least the better investment managers is whether they would want to own the entire company. If they

13

would, then owning a small part of it makes sense. If they would not want to own the entire company, then owning a small part of it makes no sense. What they do that is very different from the amateur, at least in their perspective, is know *why* they like the company and *why* they would want to own it all.

They also all seemed to agree that another one of the principal differences between amateurs and professionals is that the professionals know when to *sell*. Amateurs will buy a stock or bond because it "looks good" (speculation). Professionals will know the underlying *why* that caused it to look good and exactly what would cause it to no longer look so good. They will then translate that knowledge into an event or events that will trigger an automatic "sell" order. Knowing when to "buy" involves knowing *why* one is buying that investment. Knowing when to sell is to know when the *why* no longer exists.

Obviously, one of the major issues in investing then is the *why*. The first *why* refers to understanding the reason you are investing *before you invest*! Many, if not most, investors actually have little or no idea why they are using a particular investment. My experience indicates that most believe they are in an investment so that their "money" will "grow." That reasoning goes a long way toward explaining why it is so common to note massive liquidations of stocks by individual investors at or near the absolute bottom of a bear market. In other words, because they invested to see (speculation) their money "grow," as they watch the daily price of the investment decline in a bear market, the investment is simply not doing what they bought it to do! Using that logic, it is perfectly rational to then only buy investments that "are going up" (read: "have *seen* a price increase over an extended period of time") and sell investments that are "going down" (read: "have *seen* a price *decrease*"). Thus is revealed a pattern of logical, rational, *speculative* thought that leads directly to "buying high" and "selling low."

How then should we invest? That is what this book is about. There are no short cuts, rules of thumb, or simple methods here because they simply don't work. On the other hand, endless jostling of figures from financial statements and astute estimates of future earnings are not in the works either. We live in a wonderful time, in a wonderful country, and in a wonderful economy. You *can* be an effective investor without becoming a Chartered Financial Analyst or succumbing to the seductive lure of the speculative method peddlers. That is what this book is about. More, I believe it can be fun to learn exactly what you need to know to make it happen.

If you are ready to embark on that journey, turn the page!

Section I: The History and Foundation of Investing

Chapter 1 - A Definition of Investing

Investing as Part of Life

The world is changing; at least the part of it we call America is certainly changing, and *fast!* We entered the 20th century as a nation with over half our population working on the farm producing food for the other half. We exited that same century with just over 2% of us down on the farm. The other side of the equation is even more pressing. Less then 1% of Americans were involved in the ownership of corporations as a source of future wealth in 1900. By the year 2000, over half of all families in America had some form of ownership in corporations.

In less than two lifetimes, we transitioned from a nation of farmers to a nation of investors. Still, for most of us, the cliché is far too often true that "he doesn't know the difference between livestock and common stock." The Dalbar Corporation ran a study of mutual fund investors beginning in January 1984 and ending in December 1997. Over that period, while the S&P 500 Stock Index gained an average of 17.8% per year, the average equity investor gained about 6.4%. Bond fund investors did as poorly versus a government bond index. Anecdotal evidence indicates that investors in individual stocks did as poorly as or worse than the mutual fund investors. According to a story in the *Wall Street Journal,* the study was updated to bring it through the end of March 2002. While the overall historic market returns had declined to about 14%, the individual investors did *worse* with an average annual rate of return of just over 4%! The issue is not that index investing will lead to a larger return. It is that the individual investor who does not use a professional advisor does not have the discipline necessary for effective investing.

Books have been written and professionals have proclaimed over the airwaves that buying good investments and holding them for long periods of time is by far the most productive way of investing, but the Dalbar study revealed that the average equity investor holds his or her investments for an average of 3.4 years and that number is dropping as we move forward in time!

In my twenty plus years of advising aspiring investors, I have found that we don't know the history or the reason investing works in one place and not in another. Worse, what we think we know is not only wrong but also generally pretty much the reverse of reality!

The issue is not that we are incapable of understanding, or even don't want to understand what it is we are doing and how to do it better, but simply an abysmal lack of effective education. Perhaps I should say more accurately that most investor's education on the subject has come from popular periodicals like *Money Magazine* or some similar faddish publication. Those magazines are well known among professionals to have all the credibility of *The Globe* or *The National Enquirer* and about as much usefulness. It has been noted on several occasions that the announcement of a bull market or the picture of a bull on the cover of one of the popular newsweeklies is an almost sure sign that a major market downturn is imminent. The reverse is true as well, as soon as the popular press announces that equity investing is dead and the future holds only low single digit returns for investors, a major bull market seems to start up immediately! Why do these things happen? Is there a way to avoid the emotional exuberance and depression that seem to accompany the rise and fall of the market indices?

Most importantly, is there some basic knowledge that we can gain to allow us to move from the position of uninformed amateurs who always seem to come out on the tail end of the deal to become the informed investors we need to be to create the income we will need as we leave the workplace or send our children to college? I think there is such knowledge, and I think it can be fun to learn.

Investing is not depressing or dry, nor need it be a terrifying roller-coaster ride from the threat of imminent bankruptcy to the overconfidence of paper riches and back again. Investing can, and indeed should, be a part of our lives as routine as the regular purchase and maintenance decisions we make for an automobile.

First, though, we need some tools to allow us to understand the nature of investing as well as a little history of what successes and mistakes others have made before us. Then we will have the tools and knowledge to give ourselves the ability to use that strange thing we call "the market" to our advantage.

Words as Tools

Although I am going to spend much more time on this later in the book, contrast the meaning of *investment* with *speculation*. The root here is *specultis* as in to be a spectator, spectacle, or speculator, in other words, to "look at" or "watch" something. The financial definition of *"speculation"* is "to buy or sell at great risk, hoping that one will profit from price changes in the market."[1] Contrast that with the modern definition of *"invest"*: "to buy something", such as stocks or property that is expected to produce profit, income, or both."[2] Investing is done *in* something, while speculating is done *on* something. Investment suggests involvement while speculation involves something very much like gambling. The word that follows "invest" in many dictionaries has the same root and clearly indicates a difference between *investing* and *speculation*. It is "investigate."

The implication here is pretty obvious without researching the Latin roots. One should "investigate" before one "invests" or else the action will be "speculation." An investor in*vestig*ates beneath the outward appearance for the *"vesti*ge" or "surviving trace" of the thing in which he or she might "invest." The *speculator* does not investigate the essence of the *thing* he or she is buying, but purchases "at great risk" and then *watches* (speculates) for a rise or fall in *the market.*

Investing involves a change in the nature of the value of the thing invested. Invested money (or time) becomes *capital. Capital* means "the head" in Latin as well as English, but the meaning goes beyond the physical part of a body. On the negative side, we have "capital punishment." In every case, it is not *just* the head but life itself that is indicated by the word "capital." The seat of government, the *capitol*, is where the government "lives." Capital punishment takes away the life of a person. A person who is incapable of functioning in life is called "incapacitated." *Capital* is the financial representation of life itself in any civilization.

In other words, the act of investing is to turn your money or your time into *capital,* something that is "alive" and thereby has the opportunity to *grow.* It is very different from speculation where the objective is not to see the growth of the thing purchased, but only *to hope* for

19

profit from a transitory fluctuation in market price.

Another word that deserves some attention is "stock." The origin of that word is found in the more ancient word "stalk." The original meaning refers to the main part and the roots of a plant. If one, for example, wishes to purchase and plant a grape vine, the most effective way is normally to buy "root stock" rather than waiting the years necessary for a grape vine to grow from a seed to a productive plant. Stock is purchased for its potential to produce fruit, and thereby "value" in the form of a useful product. The stock can then "grow" into a profitable plant.

Contrast the word "stock" with "bond." The origin of that word is "bound" as in "obligated." Unfortunately for many people who do not understand the nature of a "bond," the binding goes both ways. The issuing entity is obligated to make the payments and return the money, but the purchaser (loaner) is obligated to leave the money with the borrower for the entire term of the bond. If you are bound, you will not grow.

The way out of this seemingly bottomless pit is to actually understand what investing *is,* and what creates the value in an investment.

Capital

The history of capital begins with the history of man. Our earliest ancestors were what we now call "hunter-gatherers." The time the most primitive of our forebears invested in creating tools was not available to hunt or gather food. The idea of actually spending valuable food-gathering time doing something else, like knocking chips off of a piece of flint, is what sets us apart from animals.

We humans are unique in that we do spend rather tremendous amounts of time developing and administering tools and methods to improve our quality of life. Over the uncounted years since that first flint chipping event, we have gradually changed from a species who spent the vast majority of our time trying to find food to spending our time mainly cultivating food and now to spending very nearly all our collective time manufacturing, managing, and creating the methods for increasing our comfort, and that most elusive of desires, happiness.

What has created these changes that seem to be accelerating faster with each passing decade? The answer has been slow in coming and much debated, but there is an emerging belief in the field of anthropology that the *tools* created us as much as we created the tools! In other words, we are, at our very core, a result of investment of time and resources by the many thousands of generations of our ancestors! Those investments have paid off over the long term in a standard of living in the "developed" world that is beyond the wildest imagination of any generation that preceded us. That cumulative investment has moved us from primitive hunter-gatherers with life expectancies of less than 40 years, and an infant mortality rate that allowed only two in ten children to reach adulthood, to a culture in which less than 5% of the population is involved in growing food and any death of a child is seen as a calamity!

The name we have for that cumulative, amazingly productive investment is *capital*. Investing creates capital. Capital, if properly used, increases wealth. Increased wealth creates a higher standard of living. That higher standard of living allows for more investing.

How then shall we invest? Just as our ancestors had to make decisions on where to invest their time to be the most productive, so we have to make the same decision with our money. Over the years and through many studies, certain principals have emerged that are consistently associated with effective investing. Let us then proceed to explore the origins of this wondrous thing called investing and move from there to understanding the principles that have been gleaned with so much effort by those who have traveled this way before us.

First though, we will take what may appear to be a detour, although, in fact, it is anything but a detour. It is the laying of an effective foundation. An analogy may be found in the recent history of automobile maintenance and repair. Many of us older guys (over 50 or so) well remember when it was sort of a rite of passage for a young man to learn to maintain the engine of his car. Some went on to rebuild engines and many of us could do a basic "tune-up." I was one of those bright young men who prided themselves on their knowledge of carburetors, points, distributors, and other such vital automobile engine trivia.

We recently bought a new vehicle, and I thought I would impress my 15-year-old daughter with my mechanical knowledge by pointing out the various engine parts and telling her what they did. After some serious searching, I consulted the vehicle manual and finally figured out how to open the engine compartment. What I saw under the hood baffled me. All that was there were several smooth, curved surfaces. I couldn't even locate the engine, much less expound on its functions. Had I been so rash as to make an attempt to "tune-up" that engine using the tools and knowledge that worked so well for me in the past, I probably would have rendered it either greatly reduced in value or nearly worthless!

As with the issue of user maintenance on a 21st century automobile engine, many of the things we think we know about how things work will soon be so obsolete as to be dangerous if used. That is particularly true of investing. But, if we understand the basic fundamentals, we can at least avoid doing what is wrong and damaging and ensure that the fundamentally right things are done. I may not understand the function of the various parts of that *turbo-charged, diesel injected, laterally-mounted transaxle-engine unit,* but I still know that the oil needs to be changed regularly (would you believe every *10,000* miles?), the tires need to be rotated and properly filled with air (different air pressure levels for front tires versus rear), the coolant needs to be checked regularly (but don't open the cap, just check the reservoir), and the right type of fuel needs to be used. I don't even have to depend on my rusty knowledge of automobile maintenance; all I have to do is read the owners' manual and follow the recommended steps. *Unfortunately, the purchase of an investment portfolio does not include an owner's manual!*

Many of us are sadly unaware of the depths of our ignorance. We use methods such as asking our fellow workers what they are using for *their* investments in the company retirement plan, reading one of the popular investing magazines, or following the advice of a television commentator or author of some popular book espousing the use of some investing methodology. In each case, the information we are relying on may be oversimplified popular misinformation.

Given the complexity of effective investing in the 21st century, you may well decide to use the services of a professional rather than try to do it yourself. Even so, choosing the right professionals to assist you requires an understanding of what investing is really all about and what works and does not work.

Chapter 2 - A short history of Capitalism

Value

Investing is about *value*. If investing is buying something with the reasonable intent of either generating income to live on or selling it later at a higher price, then the whole point in investing is to either buy something that you have reason to believe will be worth more in the future, or to buy something and then *make* it worth more in the future. Someone who starts a business is in that second category. The concept of entrepreneurial activity is a relatively recent innovation in our culture and is a large part of what has created the high standard of living and unprecedented wealth we enjoy today.

In the field of economics, value is referred to as "utility" meaning "useful" or "capable of being used." Once again, now that you have entered into the arcane world of Etymology, you probably can see the origin of the word. It appears to be a combination of "vale" and "use," thus "vale-use" becomes "value" and takes on the meaning of land that is productive or useful.

As soon as our cultural ancestors began to create tools, the verb "value-able" was added to our language. Something capable of creating production, something that could be used to improve our condition, was valuable. That something started as geography meaning a place where there was food and water and has now become descriptive of anything that can produce improvement in our lives or standard of living and is commonly measured in terms of money.

There are some other definitions important to grasp before we move on to the foundation on which our wealth is built. Those include *consumption* and *saving,* as well as our old friend *speculation,* all of which are very different from investing. To consume is composed of two terms, "con" meaning "to use" and "sume," meaning literally the "sum." To consume is then to use up the entirety of a thing.

Most of our money goes to consumption, as it should. Consumption is buying something that you will *use*. In most cases you will not only use the thing, you will indeed *use it up,* at least in part. Often I have heard people speak of "investing in a house" when what they are doing clearly falls under the heading of consumption. Houses, cars, stereos, furniture, and all the other things we buy to make our lives more enjoyable are things on which we expend wealth that will not come back to us enlarged.

I recognize that many who purchase a home think of it as an investment. But, with rare exception, the total value we expend on a home will exceed any price we could reasonably expect to recover when we sell it. Yes, I know that homes have rather long life expectancies and tend to rise in price with inflation, but after maintenance, taxes, interest, inflation, and fees, the only way a house can actually be sold for more than the owner paid, would be for the demand for homes in a given locale to increase dramatically and unexpectedly. Almost inevitably, after the sudden rise in demand and price, those who purchased the homes will find they are faced with an equally dramatic fall in price as the builders in the area catch up with, and commonly exceed the demand. New houses are just worth more than "used" houses.

Saving money is also quite different from investing. Saving is the avoidance of loss. The avoidance of short-term loss is an important factor in our lives, but will almost never lead to a gain. Savings and investments are almost diametrically opposed. "Saving" involves loaning money to an institution for its use as investment with the understanding that the institution will guarantee a small interest payment on the loaned money. In a free market system like ours, that interest rate should be just about enough to accommodate inflation and taxes. Over a very long time, one loses money in a savings position. For example after taxes and inflation, a savings position earning the same interest rate as a 90 day U.S. Treasury bill over the last 50 years would now have about seventy-two cents in buying power for every dollar saved a half century ago. If that same dollar had been deposited in a savings account, it and all the interest it had earned, minus taxes and inflation, would now be worth about thirty-four cents!

Speculation, on the other hand, is a form of gambling. Those who "play" the market or "make a bet" on a stock are not investing as much as gambling. The reason for the difference is the word *reasonable*. Consider that study after study has shown that the movement from day to day of the market or even a given stock is *random*. Buying into a random event is the classic definition of gambling. Although I have had the opportunity to review no small number of speculators' stock portfolios over the years, I have yet to find one that even came close to matching the return of the broad market. Not too surprisingly, almost without exception, the speculators who were attempting to "manage" their investment portfolio had no idea what return they had received on their investments over the years. One who had actually *lost* money during a bull market period was convinced that his portfolio was returning *35%* per year!

Another thing that is important to recognize is *change*. Our value system, our culture, is constantly changing, and at an accelerating rate. By understanding from whence we have come and why, where we are, and how we got here, we can come to understand something about where our values are *going*. If we know where our culture is going, we can invest in the values that will be important in the future and, hopefully, avoid those things that will be rendered valueless by change.

Thus, before we can discuss investing, it is critical to understand just exactly what it is. In order to have that understanding, it is vital to learn the system in which it takes place. Not all societies and cultures allow investing. In fact very few do. In much and perhaps most of the world, what we call the virtue of investing is seen as a serious *sin*. We live in a socioeconomic system, or *culture* unique in the history of civilization. It also happens to be the most effective system in history. Even as the Roman culture, or civilization, dominated the western world two thousand years ago, so ours is dominating the world today. There is a reason that other systems fail when confronted with ours. There is a reason why this system we are in works. Understanding those reasons is perhaps the most important key to effective investing.

Capitalism as a System

We swim in a sea of capitalism. Our lives are so wrapped up in the creation, transfer, and effects of invested capital that we are very nearly blind to them. Capitalism is to our society and economy as the ecosystem is to the physical world in which we live. Rarely do we consider that plants are generating the oxygen we assume to be in every breath as a natural by-product of their growth. Nor do we consider the fact that every drink of water we take has cycled through thousands or even millions of plants and animals, rivers, streams, and very likely, other water systems before reaching us. We only are aware of our ecosystem when it fails to operate smoothly, such as when we so load up an area with our waste products that the ecosystem breaks down and then takes a while to recover. From time to time we note that natural forces also seem to cause a failure of that same system, as when a volcano erupts and spews tremendous quantities of gasses not at all unlike those generated by an area of heavy industry. Left alone, assuming the source of the polluting gases ceases to vent, *nature*, as we call the ecosystem of this planet, will reassert itself rather surprisingly quickly.

Some of the great achievements of civilization have been the mechanisms we have created to blunt or even negate these natural events that have historically been great disasters to mankind. The ecosystem of our planet and the socioeconomic system we have created that we call *capitalism* are very much alike. Both are chaotic systems that seem to have variations that routinely occur but are often a greater surprise to the scientist trying to forecast them than to the people who are experiencing them. Both can be severely disrupted by large-scale artificial events. Both are amazingly self-stabilizing under most circumstances. Finally, and most importantly to the purpose of this book, both have sets of principles that can be understood and put to good use by those who are subject to the changes inherent in the systems.

Perhaps one of the best examples of the parallel natures of these two systems can be seen in the 20th century history of Russia. From the imposition of Soviet Communism in 1917 until the collapse of the Soviet Union in 1991, the leaders of the largest country in the world attempted to dictate the laws of economics and the laws of ecology by political orders! By the beginning of the last decade of the 20th Century, both the economic and ecological environments were devastated. One of the most common sayings in the old Soviet Union was "we pretend to work and they pretend to pay us." Factories churned out outdated farm implements according to quota that were missing critical parts because some other factory had been subject to an "emergency" diversion of the workers to hand harvest crops that would have otherwise rotted in the fields. At the same time, whole sections of the country were rendered nearly sterile by heavy metal pollution from those same factories, and the fish in the rivers and lakes where they still survived were so loaded with toxins that most of a generation who ate them will never function at any reasonable level of effectiveness in society. Through it all, the birth rate and the life expectancy of the average Soviet citizen fell steadily until. by the end, the life expectancy of the average resident in The Soviet Union was down to the level the area had experienced in the Middle Ages!

The Cold War was won not so much by military might, although that was an essential element, but by a superior socioeconomic system that simply *out produced* our foe. World War II was won in much the same way, although far more violently and quickly.

The same principal holds true for the American Civil War, World War I, and most certainly for the recent rather lopsided victories in the Middle East. The more effective socioeconomic system wins. The wonder of the Cold War was that we did not need to defeat the Soviets on the battlefield. We simply out-invented, out-researched, and out-produced them to such a degree that they never felt confident enough to attempt an attack.

So, what is this wondrous system we call capitalism, and if it is so amazingly effective, why is it that adopting it has seemed to cause such great economic pain in other parts of the world? More practically, what are the advantages of taking the time to understand this sea of capitalism in which we swim?

The reason capitalism works so well in America and not elsewhere is exactly the same reason farmers can be more effective in America. One of the principal reasons farming works so well in America is that the American farmer has access to great quantities of capital. Nearly every other farmer in the world is denied access to capital, even his own!

I am going to take the liberty of referring to the general socioeconomic system of the United States as simply the "American Culture". For our purposes, a *culture* is the totality of the social and economic systems a society has adapted to deal with its environment, relationships, and technology. A good point to remember is that the only reason a *culture* exists is to accommodate those three elements. In our world today, where the environment is rarely a threat to our existence, the most critical elements are *relationships* and *technology*. As we enter the third millennium it is rapidly changing *technology* that is even changing the nature of our relationships. Today, the primary purpose of *culture* is to accommodate *relationship* to *technology*. Without technology, there is no culture. Without an adequate culture, rapidly advancing technology will destroy both relationships and the environment and result in a socioeconomic collapse and depopulation.

I realize I just made a *huge* statement. Rather than spending several thousand words explaining and defending that last paragraph, if you really want to get into the subject, read *Structure and Change in Economic History* by Douglass North. He received a Nobel Prize in Economics in 1993 for that work. Unlike many Nobel Prize winning works in economics, it is actually readable (and I think useful) by someone who knows nothing of either economics or mathematics.

The Birth of a Culture

Most of what we know about the glorious civilizations of Rome and Greece comes from bits and pieces of documents that were overlooked in the destructive frenzies of the various looters and idealists that dominated this end of the globe for nearly a thousand years.

History is an inexact science. We know about a lot of things that happened at various times, but which of those things were causes and which were effects is mostly guesswork. Communication and transportation (which up until fairly recently were the same thing) were mind numbingly slow and difficult for almost all of human history. Most people not only didn't get more than a few miles from where they were born, but even if they had, would not have been able to understand the people they met.

When we read in the history books about some great event, whether it be the act of an Emperor of Rome or the Norman Invasion, we project our current level of literacy and communications on the people of that day. For all but a few at the very top of the ancient food chain, life did not change at all from one day to the next or even from one generation to the next. History is made by the literate people of any period. For nearly all of what we call history, that group of literate people has amounted to only a very, very tiny part of the populace. Thus, what we call "history" has been limited to the acts of the few.

An agricultural worker (read "field slave" in Roman times, "serf" in the Middle Ages, "peasant" in the renaissance, "crofter" until the last couple of centuries, or "sharecropper" in our recent past) lived out his or her life in pretty much the same fashion no matter when we look at history. Times were marginally better if the workers were on an economically successful estate during the more prosperous period of the Roman Empire. It was somewhat worse in the depths of the dark ages, but life for the field worker was short and miserable as a rule. Because the technology of agriculture was primitive to the extreme, slave labor in one of its various guises was the only effective way to grow enough food to survive.

Society was divided into two classes. Those who owned or held the land were in one class, the "gentle nobility" and those who worked it were in another, the "villain," "serf," or "peasant." The land-holding class was composed of the warriors and decision makers and the working class belonged to them, usually as chattel property.

There is a tendency to romanticize the hunter-gathers of pre-civilization as having a nobler lifestyle because they theoretically did not have the class divisions of civilization. Actually, the warriors of those societies lived relatively well and the rest of the tribe worked to support them. The bargain was that the warrior fended off the raiders, and often paid with his life, and in return, the others would work harder to feed him. After all, if they didn't keep him pretty well fed, the neighbors would come along and take all the food and make slaves out of the non-warriors anyway!

Once again, I may have offended some idealists here, but the evidence is pretty overwhelming that the simple, primitive people of the world "living in harmony with nature" were pretty much all slave holders and occasionally, slave eaters.

The Greeks, and later the Romans, increased the efficiency of the operation by incorporating an improved organization model on society. Fundamentally, they did two rather radical things. First they concluded that having more than one person in the decision process worked better than a single decision maker. Their form of democracy was what we would call an autocracy, or rule by the few, today. For all its shortcomings, it was a great improvement on the previous method of governance where the eldest son of the king or chief took over the role until he died or was assassinated. In addition to the concept of primitive democracy, the Greeks and Romans added the idea of writing down what worked and what did not work. By doing so, they were able to build on what worked in the last generation and avoid having to repeat all the mistakes of their forbears.

George Santayana's most famous quote is "those who do not remember history are condemned to repeat it." He saw history as what we remember. The more primitive a culture, the shorter is its collective memory. The longer the collective memory of a culture, the more effective that culture will be.

History is perhaps more like cosmology or quantum physics than any other discipline. In both of those fields, with each thing we know, comes a host of things we do not know so that our known ignorance seems to grow exponentially faster than our knowledge. It is also clear that the further in the past something occurred, the less we are capable of knowing about it. Still, assembling what we do know and filling in some of the blanks with things we surmise in light of the fairly constant elements of human nature can give us valuable insights into the critical "why" of the cultural elements on which we depend.

Three-Field Rotation and the Creation of Wealth
For the purpose of this book, the history of our culture begins at the end of what are commonly called the Dark Ages, a poorly defined period that encompasses the time between the collapse of Roman civilization and the re-emergence of a new civilization in Europe. Fairly recently, historians have defined that end as a specific time when a specific action took place, in this case the Battle of Hastings in 1066. There are more than a few historians who question that date and for good reason. Recently, I have seen references that put it between 1000 and 1500. Either way, it is a vague period of time between the fall of the Roman Empire and the beginning of the Renaissance.

Have you ever noticed, by the way, that the more poorly defined something is, the more likely it will be called a word in an archaic language? In my experience, when lawyers are asked a question about which they know little, they immediately lapse into Latin. Medical doctors seem to have the same habit. Stockbrokers and investment bankers lapse into French, which is not a dead language but is well on the way and will surely follow classic Latin if the stockbrokers don't cease to use it to confuse the issue. For example, when an investment banking company is packaging bonds to be purchased by the general public, it is not unusual for them to put those bonds in "*tranches*" (French for "slices.") Those *tranches* are graded on quality so that the ones likely to perform poorly can be identified and sold to the public while the same type of bond in high quality tranches is offered to the brokerage firms' better and larger customers. Actually, in my experience, as in the case of doctors and lawyers, when brokers talk about *tranches,* they generally haven't the foggiest notion on the subject, but it does sound sophisticated to use a secret word so the uninitiated will think they do know something.

As with most such things, the origin of the modern era in the Western World has a beginning that is unmarked. What we do know is that as the Roman Empire disintegrated there was a critical technology that did not exist. But, at the opening records of modern Western Civilization it was so entrenched in our socioeconomic system as to not be notable. In other words, the writers of the time around 1100 A.D. assumed that this technology had always been present. They were unaware of the very thing that had allowed their society to emerge.

This new technology to which I refer is an agricultural practice called *three-field rotation.*

As civilization emerged along the banks of the rivers in Mesopotamia and Egypt, perhaps the most important reason for it coming into existence was the annual flood. That flood renewed the fertility of the land once a year with a fresh layer of flood silt. Of course, if one did not schedule the annual planting to have the crops harvested before the flood, then the annual renewal would result in famine with the crops ruined by the water. It has been theorized that one of the beginnings of writing was to record the positions of the stars when planting was appropriate to avoid having the harvest washed out.

Because the crop yield in this annually fertilized ground was substantially better than had been experienced in the other places in the world, and there was no necessity to move on after a couple of years when the land "played out" and became infertile, people could afford to invest a greater amount of effort in dwellings and other structures. That also gave them enough extra food to allow some of them to take a serious look at the world around them. Noting that crops planted any other time than when certain patterns of stars were overhead in the middle of the night resulted in the destruction of those crops, it naturally followed that something in those patterns was causing the floods. After all, by this time, the local shamans had figured out that the Mediterranean (literally, the sea of middle earth) rose and fell in response to the location of the sun and the moon, so it made perfectly good sense that the Nile River would rise and fall in response to the position of the stars!

Whoever figured that out first had some very real power in his hands. The rains causing the annual floods were not observable in the desert where the civilization was being born so they seemed at first to come at random times. The invention of the calendar at about the same time by the Egyptians and the Mesopotamians was the key to abundance. Failure to heed the mystic scribblings of the Magi would cause failure and famine. From this we get the word "magic" or "of the Magi." We also get the idea of "casting spells" in that a "spell" is the same word we use when we "spell" a word. The Magi or magicians were those who could *read and write*! They could tell when the floods were going to come simply by observing the stars. Thus came astrology, *The Old Farmer's Almanac,* and the calendar.

The reason this was so important was the wonderful soil deposited by the flood each year. For quite a long time, civilization was stuck in only those places where the annual flood would provide sufficiently fertile soil to produce the extra food needed to have a *thinking* class that could do some serious Research and Development (R&D). To provide the priests (thinkers) with food (not to mention nice house and proper buildings to honor the deities that only the intellectuals seemed to be able to influence), there had to be a tax on the farmers and that required some method of keeping up with who had what, and thus accounting (and tax collecting) was born. Meanwhile, there was still the issue of providing for the warriors, particularly because this wondrously fertile ground and the abundant food it provided were greatly desired by the neighbors.

Later, the Indus civilization developed a ten character system of writing quite different from their spoken language, which we now call "numbers", to make the job of tax calculations even more effective. To this day, we maintain the tradition of writing our tax system in a different language than is spoken by the masses. If you question that little observation of mine, *you* just try to read the tax code and explain it in simple English. *Good luck!*

Sometime in the midst of this development of what we call civilization, someone either conducted an experiment or made a very accurate observation. Away from the flood plain, the land could be irrigated but would wear out rather quickly. But if it was farmed only every other year and allowed to lie fallow on the off years, it could be farmed again! Thus was born *two-field rotation* allowing civilization to expand beyond the flood plain (and by the way, doing some serious damage to the power of the priestly class).

Two-field rotation took civilization around the Mediterranean and provided the food to supply much of the Roman Empire. Actually, the Romans really took off once they captured Egypt and were able to grab the grain from the Nile Valley. Even the noble Romans were dependent on that old one-field rotation and the annual floods. Ultimately, the strength of the Roman Empire was based in agriculture. They had agriculture in the form of two-field rotation, and the relatively primitive tribes that surrounded them did not. The fact that Rome was dependent on grain from the Nile Valley was one of those odds and ends that actually moved economics along nicely. In order to pay for the grain, the Romans had to first standardize and then defend their money. I am not suggesting, by the way, that the Romans invented money, but they did standardize it and defend it. They also gave it the enduring name we use today. Roman money was initially all minted in the Temple on Mons Juno, thus it was *money*.

By the way, here in the early 21ˢᵗ century, it would be worth our time to note how and why the Romans transitioned from a minor city-state near the middle of the Italian peninsula to the greatest empire in the history of the western world. Prior to 390 B.C. the Romans, or more properly, Latins, had a middle-sized city-state that had become the leader of a league of cities to the south. Some had aligned themselves with Rome after military conquest and others voluntarily. Rome's principal occupation was in agriculture and trade. At the same time, as the leader of the alliance and a principal seaport, Rome had assumed a role not unlike that of New York City in the United States today. It had a substantial thinking class and was proud of its status as a republic governed by a senate of elected officials. The executive power was divided among tribunes, elected by both the senate and the common citizens.

As the year we now call 390 B.C. dawned, Rome was confident in its military strength, its wealth, its institutions, and most of all, its secure trade with the rest of Italy and across much of the Mediterranean. The world was a relatively peaceful and prosperous place following the recent war that had left Rome as the undisputed leader of the city-states of middle and Southern Italy. In that year, the Gauls, who had been gradually moving southward into the Italian peninsula, passed through the territory of the city-states to the north and attacked Rome.

The reason they had not attacked Rome before was that the terrain of ancient Italy was crossed with thick forests and often impassible streams and rivers. Moving across country in those heroic times was not only difficult but sometimes simply impossible. Then the Romans introduced a new technology to the Italian Peninsula, *roads*! The Romans were merchants by nature and learned to be quite wonderful engineers to support their mercantile tendencies. They quite brilliantly determined that if truly excellent roads were built up and down what is now Italy, goods would tend to move over those roads. They were not adverse to even building those roads in other people's territory. The hitch was that *all roads led to Rome*. If a merchant wanted to move his goods, he had the choice of using the dirt tracks and fording rivers with the constant risk of bandits or using the Roman roads and bridges. If he used the Roman roads he would wind up in Rome and be obliged to deal with Roman merchants and pay Roman taxes.

Using the new relatively high-speed Roman road technology, the Gauls were able to penetrate far deeper into the peninsula than ever before. Following those wonderful roads they, like the merchants, inevitably came to Rome. There they found a city-state that refused to pay them their accustomed bribes, so they did what barbarians and terrorists have done throughout history, they attacked. The Romans were able to drive them off, but not before they burned down three major Roman buildings. Whether the year is B.C. 390 or 2001, primitive barbarians tend to use the technology of the culture they wish to attack against that culture. Unfortunately for the Gauls, the Romans, like the Americans two millennia later, were a very healthy culture of merchants who had figured out how to wage war in a business-like fashion.

After the Gauls withdrew, the Romans first sent delegations to the city-states to the north requesting they form an alliance to defend against future attacks. The northern city-states rejected the request, pointing out that the incursions were a minor thing compared to the extensive trade they conducted with the barbarians.

The Senate debated and came to the conclusion that if the city-states to the north were not interested in cooperating with Rome in defeating the Gauls, then they would be treated as allies of the Gauls and attacked. In publishing that edict, the Roman Senate effectively declared the city-state no longer relevant and inadvertently invented the nation-state. The Romans expanded northward for the next several hundred years, but their drive was to expand the defense zone around

Rome. In order to fund this immense enterprise, they were driven to expand to the south and east to secure the resources to pay, feed, and equip their growing army.

Through it all, the Romans were part of a new element in human history. Other empires had been born grown and died, all with the purpose of taking their neighbor's wealth. The Romans were more interested in commerce than empire. Their system of laws and money standardized the ownership of property and provided the means for an orderly transfer of that property and the ability to book and retain a profit. They insisted on good, easily traveled roads and readily attacked either pirates or bandits that interfered with commerce. The Roman Empire was created in pursuit of a world free of threat to Rome and its commerce. It expanded initially out of a necessity to acquire even more trade to finance that quest.

Our quest for security in the dawning years of the 21st century began as a result of an attack on the Rome of the modern world, New York City. Following that attack, our President addressed the nation and, in effect, announced the end of the nation-state as a relevant political entity. He spoke for our Congress and our people that any nation that failed to cooperate with us in defeating the barbarians who had destroyed three of our buildings would either be ignored or replaced. Most Americans missed the parallel in history but many in Europe recognized the significance of that speech. What we are witnessing today in the world may well be as significant to the next two thousand years as were the events and pronouncements of Rome in the 4th century B.C.

Toward the end of the Roman's time as the preeminent civilization of the Western World, they were busily shipping grain northward from Egypt to Rome and then on to their garrisons in the colder climes. That grain had to go by boat mainly as the cost of feeding grain to horses was prohibitive. Oxen were available, but at best, they could pull a cart and then only for a limited period of time. Oxen can survive off almost any forage, but they are inefficient beasts of labor. They are slow, and they cannot pull the weight that a horse can. One horse can be a pretty effective puller of a plow although in heavy soil, two are preferable. The same soil takes as many as eight oxen. The further the Romans moved from the sea, the greater the cost of moving food to the frontier.

So, why did the Romans not have more horses? Simply put, it takes about ten field slaves in a two-crop rotation field to supply the fodder for one horse! If the horse is used to cultivate the field, a two-field rotation farm will not provide sufficient food to feed the horse and the slaves. In other words, a horse would consume more than it made. Horses then were like warriors, priests, and chiefs; nice to have to hold off the neighbors who want your food but not practical to have too many of. Only the very well off could afford to have a large enough holding to support a horse or two. Even as today's horse owners find that they are, in fact, horse supporters, with the possession of a horse quite an expensive proposition, so did the classic Romans.

Civilizations tend to be quite innovative as long as they are in serious competition with other civilizations. As long as the Romans had competition, they were not only innovative but also very much the Microsoft of the ancient world. It has often been noted that while the Romans didn't invent very much outside of the tactics of their military forces, they were masters of taking what others invented and mass producing the innovation all across the empire. There is a certain lesson here, by the way. The civilization with the better military gets all the inventions and innovations that the conquered civilization worked so hard to invent! That harks back to the primitive tribal cultures where, unless the warriors were well taken care of, everyone else lost everything to the first tribe to come along with more (or better fed) warriors.

This brings us to the thing the Romans didn't have, and that may well have been the major cause for the re-emergence of civilization in Europe around 1000 A.D.: *three-field rotation*. The Romans also didn't have steel, an efficient numerical system (although Roman numerals were a distinct improvement over using words and letters more or less at random to represent numbers), the horse collar, or the stirrup. What they did have was sewers, aqueducts, roads, ships, and most importantly, law and legions. That law was the glue that held everything together. The legions were the enforcers of the law. All of this was based on the very basic issue that the Romans could feed themselves better than could other cultures. Having more food allowed for time and energy to develop better soldiers and gave the commanders of those soldiers more time to think about how to best use those soldiers. It also gave the Romans the luxury of being able to support a relatively large *thinking* class who were in the business of having thoughts and then carefully capturing those thoughts in written words. In English, the deepest meaning of "spell" is to create a magic set of runes on a surface that captures a thought. The term "word" even comes from "weard" meaning "to capture and hold safely" as in "ward(en)" and in its magical sense, "weird."

The fall of the empire had a very real and unpleasant effect on the rest of Europe. The Roman legions had enforced a system of law and banished the destructive raiding and pillaging that has always plagued the uncivilized part of our world. In the chaos following the withdrawal or collapse of the legions, barbarism in its most primitive form reigned.

Where did this apparently sudden onslaught of barbarians come from? We know with certainty that Germanic tribes overran the Western Roman Empire. We also know that the thinking class had stopped doing much original thinking and certainly was not too interested in spending money on those nasty legions that were by now mainly made up of recruited barbarians anyway. Knowing that Roman "things" were by their nature quite superior to anything else in the world, the landed nobility of the empire spent their time seeking peace and pleasure. Weakened from within by an absence of perceived threat, by the 5th century A.D., they were ripe to be overrun not by another empire, but by barbarians who the Romans considered not even to be *human!* As far as they were concerned, the Germanic people were well suited as beasts of labor and perhaps as soldiers, but totally incapable of thinking. After all, they didn't even *speak* Latin, much less *write!*

We also know that those tribes were experiencing a population growth that created a food crisis that in turn led to the massive southward migration. The origin of the population growth was quite a mystery until relatively recent times. Ultimately, the cause of the Germanic invasion was the same technological innovation that drove the Romans into a continuing expansion, *agriculture.* Quite simply, the barbarians to the north had effectively copied the two-field rotation agricultural methods of their Romanized neighbors. With a more adequate food supply, the barbarians experienced a lowered death rate. That worked quite well until the burgeoning population outstripped the ability of the local farmland to produce food. The result was strikingly similar to what we see happening in Africa today.

The Germanic raiders from the north, who pillaged all they considered worthy of taking and destroyed what they could not take, prospered on the accumulated food and wealth of the Roman settlements for some time, but as has been the pattern following the fall of civilizations all over the world (including Africa in our own time), the pillagers and raiders finally ran out of things to take. Some would simply move on looking for more loot to take by force. Eventually though, what loot was left was held by tribes that were as well prepared to fight as the wandering raiders. At this point, the raiders discovered that if they are to survive they needed to settle down and start producing something.

Gradually, local warlords established themselves in fortified positions and set about the relatively unexciting task of setting up farms and more permanent shelter. The raiders, in other words, became potential targets of other raiders.

Just as things stabilized at what seemed, to the Europeans of the day, to be a comfortable level of misery and violence, a couple of inventions changed everything. Which came first and exactly when they were invented is completely unknown (although libraries could be filled with the speculative works on the subject). What we do know is that they were first seen in Europe around the time of Charlemagne, and they marked the beginning of the culture we know today as the Western or Anglo-American, or more recently (and simply) *American*.

Three-field rotation revolutionized the production of food, and at about the same time, the *stirrup* revolutionized warfare. My best guess is that it was the stirrup that came first. Some brilliant person came up with the idea of running a broad strap down from each side of the saddle and attaching an iron footing at the bottom that would allow the rider to place his weight on his feet rather than simply sitting on the horse while hanging on for dear life. Charlemagne is often credited with the introduction of the device, but early accounts and tapestries indicate that he didn't have one himself. Later in his rule, after defeating the Lombardis near Rome, stirrups suddenly appear in tapestries of the day.

The stirrup allowed the rider to hang onto the horse in much more violent maneuvers than ever before, and more importantly, let go of the horse with his hands so he could hold a weapon while mounted! The lance and the long-sword quickly followed to give the mounted warrior weapons that could reach sufficiently beyond the horse to impact other warriors without dismounting.

The stirrup and the need for a sword that had enough length to be used by a mounted soldier started the progress to modern steel. The Romans were quite adept at working iron and had extensive brick and ceramic furnaces to heat the iron and purify it. Following the thought of the Greek natural philosophers, the Romans believed that the more pure they made the iron the better it should be. The fact that the highly purified iron was actually weaker than iron with certain impurities in it was contrary to their beliefs and thereby could not be tolerated. The medieval blacksmith was far more primitive in his methods and that probably led to the improvement. In order to take a bar of iron and make it into a long sword, a new type of metallurgy would be needed. Simple iron as used by the Romans did not have the rigidity and strength to be used in a long sword. The rare long sword of the day was made from extremely rare meteor iron (which comes ready mixed with nickel) and was considered a sacred and magical relic.

Our medieval blacksmith, not having a handy meteor, was probably under some pressure from his local lord to make a better, longer sword to be used by his lord's warriors while mounted. Knowing that he would probably not be able to make the required longer blade and still have it not break when it was used to bang on some other soldier's shield, he still gave it his best try. Not having the wonderful brick ovens of the Romans, he was forced to lay the iron bar directly on the hardwood coals to heat and then to hammer over and over again on his anvil while one or more assistants worked bellows to keep the heat high. Unknown to him, he was also adding a new element to the iron of the bar, *carbon*! Carbon, when thoroughly mixed in small quantities with iron, produces a kind of *steel*. Thus was born a new technology that we still enjoy today.

The Roman cavalry were really mounted infantry who would ride quickly to a point on the battlefield and immediately dismount to fight. The combination of the inability to fight from the back of a horse and the rather extreme cost of maintaining horses caused the cavalry to be a less than decisive force in the ancient world until well after the fall of the Empire.

Solving problem one, the ability to fight from the back of the horse, leads us quickly to problem two, feeding the monsters! Because the imperative issue in a near chaotic dog-eat-dog society is the ability to wreak violence on one's neighbor before one's neighbor does one in, the invention of true mounted warfare had the potential to completely upset the order of things... and it *did*! The problem with this is that horses don't do well on plain grass. They must have grain to be healthy and oats are the ideal grain for them. Worse, they eat quite a lot more than an ox!

In my imagination, I can see a manorial lord of some level who, as most, didn't consider his peasants human beings at all but saw them very much as the southern planter in the Confederacy of America in the mid 19th Century: simple property owned by him to create production. His peasants, or serfs, were fairly skilled in the matter of two-field rotation. One year they grew food crops on a field and in the next, it was used as grazing land for the livestock. The productivity of the land wasn't as good as fresh land, but it didn't completely wear out either. This imaginary lord in my illustration decrees that fodder (probably oats) will be grown for his horses so he can stomp his neighbor before his neighbor stomps him. As it would be impractical to clear more ground given that his peasants are already fully employed, he has a brilliant idea! Why not simply grow fodder one year, then food the next and then let the land lie fallow for the third year!

It is critical to know that the idea of literacy and general education was not considered a virtue in a medieval man of the world. The study of such useless things was left to the clerics of the monastery or perhaps to some women. Our noble lord was far more focused on the important things of life, like how to more effectively chop up the neighboring lord and his soldiers. Just about everybody below the warrior and cleric classes were pretty seriously malnourished in those days of yore. For a woman to have ten babies was not unusual. For more than two of them to survive was. The most effective way to gain more security against the ever-present threat of famine was to reduce the local population. The most preferable means of accomplishing that end was to butcher the neighboring lord's army and family, thereby leaving the victorious lord with more peasants, land, and food!

Of course there is the issue of now having more food and more land, but about the same number of soldiers to defend it! As the victorious lord expanded his holdings, he became an ever-riper target for *his* neighbors, *and* had his area to defend go up accordingly. The mounted soldier was the obvious answer to the prayer of the innovative lord of the manor.

The reason the issue of education and numbers is so important to our story is that it probably never occurred to the manorial lord that the time the land was producing *food* had been cut from one half of the years to only one third! Even if it had crossed his mind, the local lord would have concluded that because three is bigger than two, he should wind up with more food. People still think that way, or else why would corporations and governmental agencies be convinced that by increasing the requirements while at the same time "downsizing" the work force it would increase output?

Anyway, our imaginary nobleman institutes three-field rotation, probably over the strong objections of the farm manager and the peasants. I doubt they complained too much. After all, the lord was the one with the swords and the soldiers, and probably by this time, the horses.

To the surprise of the peasants who *know* the boss is crazy and is going to take them straight into starvation, the food crop yield is *bigger* than before. The peasant may have been poor, miserable, and illiterate, but he did know his farming. I am quite confident he immediately grasped the danger inherent in changing the way things were done. It was probably about this time that the lord of the manor got a promotion in the eyes of the field hand. To this day uniquely in our culture, we refer to our God as the *Lord*. From the perspective of the laboring peasant, their manorial Lord had worked an honest-to-God miracle that stood right up there with multiplying the loaves and the fishes.

It was almost a thousand years later that the scientists caught up with the peasants and figured out that the fodder plants fixed nitrogen in the soil from the air and the additional manure and straw from the stables spread on the soil in the fallow year returned the vital minerals allowing the food raised every third year for the humans to actually increase in both volume and quality. The odd thing here is that our imaginary lord of the manor was actually *right* when he assumed that one third was bigger than one half!

Two more inventions popped up at about the same time. One was the *horse collar*. That high tech item allowed the horse to pull a plow. While the Romans had harnesses for their horses, the act of pulling a plow requires that horse to strain quite hard and with hard straining, the horse in a Roman harness would wind up choking. The amazing horse collar allowed the horse to strain quite hard without choking. Actually, the Romans didn't need a horse collar because horses were just too valuable to use plowing fields! With the advent of three-field rotation, there was plenty of feed for the horses over the winter. That allowed horses to be used to plow. Plowing with a horse using a horse collar allowed more fields to be plowed than with oxen. The combination of more ground under cultivation and higher production from that land produced an amazing result, an actual food surplus!

The other invention that came along was the steel shod plow and the horseshoe. Yet another problem with horses was that their hooves were prone to cracking and infection if they were used on wet ground. Again we have no idea who came up with the brilliant plan to actually *nail* a metal horseshoe onto the bottom of a horse's hoof, but it worked, and worked well.

In another undocumented development, the local blacksmith began making blades to go on the peasant's plow. A steel plowshare enabled the horse to have less resistance when plowing, again increasing the amount of ground under cultivation. Prior to the iron or steel plowshare, breaking new ground was an amazingly difficult project. With a combination of the horse collar, the metal horseshoe, and the plowshare, food suddenly was no longer the limitation on growth.

There is a critical lesson here. The Romans had all the elements they needed to make stirrups, horseshoes, horse collars and certainly three-field rotation for nearly eight hundred years. The fact that they didn't take advantage of these innovations was and is a testimony to the power of the top-down societal structure to stifle innovation. It was only in the chaotic, crazy world of the Middle Ages that the inventions began to pop up like mushrooms after a rain. The carefully orchestrated socioeconomic structures of socialism in the 20th century produced little or no innovation while the chaotic, unplanned, and discomforting society of American capitalist democracy created new ideas and inventions at a dizzying rate.

As the manors had more food, more children lived to adulthood and health was generally better all the way around. More peasants combined with more food allowed some of them to leave subsistence farming and begin to learn new skills. As they learned new skills and began to make more implements, furniture, etc. than they needed, the opportunity for trade with other manors presented itself.

During the Middle Ages, most of Europe was not settled. There were great swaths of forest covering most of the ground. In those forests were bandits, wolves, bears, and who knows what else! Travel from one manor to another was a major project. The roads were in less than optimal condition, and one had to take along a sizable armed escort lest the bandits feel the danger to them was less than the potential reward that came with taking all that you were carrying. With the advent of mounted soldiers, sufficient horses to pull wagons, and items to trade with the rest of the world, the lords began to clear the roads and eliminate the bandits. After some years of this, the roads became by and large relatively safe to travel on.

The combination of the availability of horses to facilitate the transport of goods, enough food to create goods for sale, and improved safety on the roads, the society of the Middle Ages was doomed. The exchange of goods began to create *wealth* for those who were not manorial nobility. The merchant class emerged as a factor in society. As wealth accumulated around the markets where goods were exchanged, those manorial lords and ladies moved into the towns and cities to participate in the opportunities and enjoy the new luxuries that were only available in those cities.

Thus began the second great migration in human history. The first migration was toward the *frontier*. That migration had, at its foundation, a quite accurate assumption that the basis of freedom and improvement in one's life depended on having access and the use of sufficient land. Land produced food and food was the critical element. For most of history and probably all of prehistory, starvation was the most critical threat to any person. When the food shortages came, those who controlled the means or source of production not only had a tendency to live through the event but also quite commonly came out of it possessing those who did not have the means of food production. The second migration only began when food production raised to a point that its perennial shortage was no longer the defining factor. From that point to the present, the migration has been accelerating away from the farm and farming community and to the city.

With the dramatic increase in commerce, a need arose to be able to transport the value earned from the sale of goods. In the medieval fairs, commonly held annually, the exchanges tended to be "in kind" or barter. Pigs could be traded for cows, and a complex system of understanding allowed for conversion of almost anything found in a community for something else. The concept of *money* as we know it today was almost unknown. Gold and silver were in use, but they carried a value of their own as either the raw material or the finished goods of jewelry.

In order to create *wealth* another item was needed, *money*. Money was certainly not a new invention, but in times of near starvation such as were experienced by much of Europe in the Middle Ages, the possession of a disk of silver with a dead Roman's head impressed into it was not of much value. As the effects of three-field rotation began to be felt, one of the first and most pressing shortages was that of money. Gold and silver began to have a greater and greater value as the need emerged for something that could be used for exchange and was lighter and more stable than a cow or pig. As the rather amazing expansion and prosperity of the late medieval period spread across Europe, the issue of money became not only one of the limiting factors but ultimately, one of the causes of its end.

At the same time, the improved transportation created a much improved communication capability. Soon, goods were not only flowing to the cities from the manorial communities, but peddlers, minstrels, and merchants were visiting the manors. Each of these brought news of the outside world. As the information flow increased and the cost of information dropped, the serfs of the local manor began to become aware that the entire world was not like their experience.

Throughout this increase in wealth and population, the life of the peasant was not materially changed. There was more food and thereby, improved health and less infant mortality, but the status as a nonperson, literally as a possession of his master, left the serf or peasant still living in the dirt floored house with probably the family cow in residence during winter months. Still, when the father of the family died, it was the practice for the lord to get the cow! The custom, or fee, was to compensate the lord for the loss of his servant. From that practice we get the concept of the *estate* or *death* tax.

Thus, the system or culture of the age became unstable. As long as the peasant needed the lord of the manor and his soldiers for defense against the roving bandits and raiders that were endemic to the countryside of the dark ages, and the manorial lord needed food produced by the serf, the social contract held firm. When the lord improved his position by utilizing the technological innovations of the stirrup, horse collar, three-field rotation, and improved weaponry, he also generally abandoned the drafty castle for the comforts of urban life. In town, he became less and less dependent on the food produced by his peasants as he became involved in trade and government.

The peasant, meanwhile, could theoretically buy his freedom but rarely was allowed to get ahead far enough to do so. More often than not, the absence of serious threat on the frontier, peace generated by the growing trade profits and the desire of kings to limit their losses from banditry, enabled the peasant to simply leave the estate and strike out into the wilds of uncivilized areas. It helped that the 13th century (1200s) was a period of particularly mild weather.

By the end of the 13th century, small farms had sprung up beyond the previously settled area all across Europe. Unfortunately, many of the farmers still did not have either ownership of the land on which they lived or status as persons under the custom or law of the day.

As the year 1300 dawned, the wealth of the wealthy had been magnified beyond even that of the ancient Romans. Cathedrals unmatched since then were built in all the cities of Europe. At the same time, the population had increased. As such things have a tendency to do, the number of people began to outrun the ability of the new agricultural and transportation technology to feed. Farming was going on in marginal areas that were not again cultivated for three hundred years.

The glue that held the manorial society together was the social contract between the peasant and the local lord or *mayor of the manor*. When that bond was dissolved by changes in technology, it was just a matter of time until a crisis would occur. That crisis came in 1337. For two or three years the harvest was nearly non-existent as rain and cold weather continued through the summers. Then England and France clashed over ownership of what now is a significant part of France, initiating the Hundred Years War. Within 40 years, Germany was shattered into small fiefdoms and the population of Europe had been reduced by half. With marauding bands of raiders again endemic, the people of the countryside were forced inside the walls of towns where, with poor to non-extent sanitation and malnutrition the norm, plague devastated almost every area of the western world. Even when the normal summer weather returned, the collapse of government and order meant that crops could not be grown with any degree of reliability.

By the 1400s, prosperity again began to return. A new institution was now the centerpiece of society in Europe, the Church. Prince-Bishops established their rule over Germany and Europe, and by the end of the century, it was divided into nation-states that would be recognized today. It was near the beginning of the 15th century that a series of events occurred that would bring forth the form of economic life we today call *capitalism*.

The stage had been set with the fall of the Roman Empire and the chaos that followed. The props were in place as the tools needed for a single family to produce enough food to both feed them and have extra to sell had been invented. One last element was needed to create the productivity and human potential explosion that was to change the world. That element would have been even harder to comprehend for the rulers of the day than any that preceded it.

Chapter 3 - Henry V, Agincourt and the Birth of Modern Capitalism

History, the Uncertain Science

In the year 1415, Henry V of England had assumed the throne following the death of his father Henry IV. Henry V, or *Harry* as he called himself to the dismay of his courtiers, was a bit of a rogue. While his father was still ruling, he was known for going out among the commoners and would frequent the pubs of London. He was most unusual among the Norman nobility of early 15th century England in that he actually spoke the *English* of the common Saxons. Shakespeare celebrated this most unusual prince in his play Henry IV, to the great pleasure of the now universally English-speaking people of Elizabethan London.

Any story of what happened in the year 1415 must be composed of a few things we know with some reasonably high probability, a number of things that we are fairly sure happened and quite a large amount of educated guessing. We can never be completely sure of what really happened. History is just that way.

We do know that English life and culture changed after Henry V made his adventure into France. His choice to speak English as a first language marked the beginning of a very slow end for the two class system whereby the French speaking Normans who had conquered England in 1066 ruled, and the Saxons, Welch, and other earlier cultures of Britain provided little more than slave labor as conquered peoples. That accomplishment alone would have earned him at least a nice little footnote in history as English has proven to be the most effective, if sometimes irrational, language in the world. Its propensity to absorb terms from other languages combined with the rather chaotic nature of the language structure, has allowed it to become the language of choice to communicate the accelerating technological changes that have come to dominate our existence.

His major contribution to the future of civilization was far more profound than even his part in establishing English as the language that has come to be as vital to 21st century civilization as Latin was to the Roman Empire and Renaissance. Henry had a claim to the throne of France dating back several hundred years to William the Bastard, or as we know him in the English speaking world, *William the Conqueror*. Through his mother, William was entitled to be the King of France. Unfortunately for him, the powers that were in charge of such things all seemed to agree that the Kingship of France could only be passed through male lineage. That certainly did not deter William from claiming it, nor did it discourage his descendants. The result of the contest was a rather lengthy event now known as *The Hundred Years War*. Actually, it might be better called the Several Hundred Years War as it continued in fits and spurts as long as William's descendents continued to rule England. Elizabeth I, the patron of William Shakespeare as the ruling monarch of England and a woman, probably enjoyed the Bard's depiction of the defeat of the forces of France on the battlefield of Agincourt as much as the commoners, albeit for a very different reason.

A Royal Adventure

On October 25, 1415, Henry V found himself faced with a grand opportunity. Upon taking the throne, he asserted the more or less pro-forma claim to the throne of France, as had his ancestors for 350 years. In this case though, the person who would next occupy the French throne really was in question. The King of France *Charles VI (The Mad)*, had gradually slipped into insanity and was widely believed to be near death. At the time of Henry's ascension to the Throne of England, Charles was reported to believe he was made of glass and was in danger of breaking! The heir apparent, or Dauphine, was quite sensitive about his claim to be the next king. He not only had the claim of Henry to consider, but no less than two other claimants from the French speaking nobility had put forth an argument that they should be the rightful king. Those claims gathered weight with the evidence that the Dauphine was already suffering from the early stages of his father's insanity. Then, his mother, Queen Isabeau, declared him to be illegitimate. The claimants had all appealed to the Pope for a verdict from the mouth of God's spokesman on earth. Unfortunately, there were at this point no less than four claimants to the Papal throne.

As in much of the world today, the European nobility took the view that when such an issue was in question, a contest of arms would establish God's will. After all, God was on the side of the righteous, and no one could stand against an army (or a knight) with God on his side. That whole concept is rather hard for us to reconcile today, but a rather impressive tome of theology had sprung up around the issue that the victor in battle was the one chosen by God. An obvious exception occurred when the victor was an infidel. That, clearly, was an exception sent by God to teach the losers a lesson.

With the reopening of the question on whom should be rightfully King of France and following a series of calculated insults from the Dauphin, Henry saw an opportunity to press his claim. Taking advantage of the division in the nobility and the insanity of the king, he was determined to possess a sufficient part of France to place him in the lead position. Known for his innovative approach to things (another way of stating that most of his peers thought him either foolish or crazy), Henry devised an ingenious method of obtaining victory. The battles of the early 15th century were still often formal affairs. The concept of single combat dominated the military engagement. While armies did meet in mass on the field of battle, such slaughter was considered to normally be a last resort. Vastly preferred was the noble contest of arms between gentlemen. In that case, the challenger would offer the same number of knights as the defender had available, and the end of the battle was when quarter was asked and given.

That noble system had never been quite as noble as the legends have it, but it worked quite well anyway. The issue was to not slaughter the peasants and ruin the crops and shelter. Only about 100 years earlier, most of Europe had suffered horrible famine, largely from the depredations of unregulated war. After a while, it occurred to the local warlords that there was not much gain from conquering one's neighbor if in the process the crops were destroyed, the buildings burned and the local workers slaughtered! Even as today when we send knights into the sky in jet fighters to settle things, so then they found that ritual war worked just as well as general war to settle which king would rule over what manors and was far better for everyone concerned.

Henry assembled a dream team of knights from all over England, the best of the realm. To that esteemed group, he added a host of his personal Yeomen, or English longbow archers. His force is reported to have totaled about 20,000 as he set sail. Of those, about 5,000 were knights and the rest largely Yeomen. He crossed over to France in early autumn, after harvest time. That was the traditional time to do such things, as the crops would not be unduly affected by the trampling of horses and men, and the farmers were free to go along to support the knights. As he ventured from holding to holding, the local lord would trot out his best men at arms who would be rather promptly tromped by Henry's professional knights.

All went according to plan until Henry arrived at the port city of Harfleur. The mayor of Harfleur determined that he would not send his local constabulary out to be defeated by Henry's knights. Instead he opted for the second method of warfare in those good old days, siege! Knowing he was commanding an important port city, important to the survival of the existing King, he fully expected he would receive relief from Paris and a great reward for holding off Henry.

Unfortunately for him, the French throne was in chaos. The king was quite mad, but not yet dead, and no one was willing to step forward in leadership until such time as he was. Even then, the French were far more interested in fighting each other at this point than in fighting Henry. Henry accepted the decision of the mayor not to yield or meet on the field of battle and did indeed lay siege to Harfleur. It was a long hard siege, ending only when Henry's siege engines opened a breach in the city wall, and the English troops and knights successfully fought their way into Harfleur. During the siege, Henry's men contracted dysentery, a not unusual disease of the day given the extremely unsanitary conditions that prevailed both in the camps and in the city itself. Disease, battle injuries, deaths, and the need to garrison the captured castles, towns, and Harfleur itself had reduced the English army by over half before its departure for a return to England.

Henry's schedule was now well behind what he had envisioned. The weather was turning bad and he was critically short on food. Still, in order to lay proper claim to the throne of France, he had to physically set foot on quite a lot of territory before returning to London. His exhausted, sick, and hungry army, now down to less than 2,000 knights and about 7,000 Yeomen struck out in the rain for a tour-de-France.

In order to touch all the bases, he was forced to initially head away from Calais, where the boats waited to return him and the remnant of his army to jolly old England. As he made his way around in a great half circle, word reached him that the Dauphine had managed to get the Marshal of France, Jean Bouciquaut II, and Constable Charles d'Albret to issue a call to arms in the name of the dying King. Although such a call had not been issued in many decades, each gentleman of France was obligated to answer such a call from the king and to provide forty days of service to the throne along with sufficient supplies and servants to make war at the king's pleasure.

In this case, the king's (or more accurately the marshal's) pleasure was to cut off Henry's passage to Calais. The reason the "call to arms" existed at all was to engage either Moors or barbarians invading the realm but never before had it been used against fellow gentlemen. To the French the world was fundamentally divided into to two realms, gentle folk and those who did not speak French (barbarians). Anyone who has visited a French speaking area will readily recognize that attitude has not changed greatly in the ensuing 600 years. In this case though, the *real* French had an opportunity to defeat the used-to-be French Normans who were now branded as "English."

Before we go any further, it is critical to understand that the French-speaking knights were "gentle" and thereby human beings, while the English-speaking Yeomen were effectively "property" and thereby "villains." Yeomen were very valuable property in that they were rather expensive to maintain and train. The English longbow was one of the most sophisticated and effective weapons of the age. A Yeoman spent his entire life learning the skill of using that weapon, and then in his old age (over 40), teaching it to the next generation. A well-trained Yeoman could put twelve cloth-yard arrows into the air per minute out to a maximum effective range of as much as 400 yards. Several thousand Yeomen could create a storm of high-speed projectiles descending from the heavens that would strip the retainers and infantry from an advancing force of armored knights.[3]

Note though that Yeomen did *not* fire directly at gentlemen or their horses. The armor of the 15th century was carefully designed to deflect the falling arrows, and it was unlikely that too many knights would be lost to Yeomen. Even the horses were outfitted with armor on top to protect them from the deadly rain. No significant protection was worn or even considered against the *direct fire* of those arrows. Yeomen simply did not fire at gentlemen! Property was absolutely forbidden in the common law of France and England from assaulting humans! Admittedly, the falling arrows might indeed injure or even kill the odd knight, but *that* was an "act of God" and not the intent of any archer. Longfellow, drawing on the memories of his childhood in England, may indeed have retrieved that ancient English tradition of common law when he penned the opening line of *The Arrow and the Song*, "I shot an arrow into the air. It fell to earth I know not where."

The Battle of Agincourt
Henry found a series of river crossings held against him by the growing French army. Recognizing that his now greatly reduced and weakened force was in no shape to fight a serious battle, he plunged deeper into France seeking a crossing and a way around the forces blocking his escape. His only hope was to move directly to the coast and return to England.

The critical moment arrived on October 24, 1415, when after a forced march of three days and nights with little or no food for his soldiers, Henry found his way forward blocked by an army of French knights. The marshal sent an emissary to Henry offering him the opportunity to yield. He advised Henry that the forces opposing him were fully six times his in number and were in the great majority gentlemen-at-arms, or as we know them, knights. Military historians have estimated the French force to be between 35,000 and 60,000 strong. In fact, because gentlemen and their retainers were showing up continuously, even during the battle, and there was in reality no commander of the force, the actual number was and probably always will be unknown. What was clear, however, was that the relatively small, exhausted, starved, and sick force Henry commanded stood no reasonable chance against such overwhelming odds.

A persistent tradition exists that a second message was delivered directly to the Yeomen. They were to be granted passage through the French and to England if they would abandon their king and leave France immediately. Alternatively, should they be captured having fought against the overwhelming French army, they would have the thumb and first two fingers of their right hands removed before being released.

The importance of this second message, presuming it existed, cannot be overemphasized. It revealed the fear and loathing the mainland French had for the English Yeomen. The knight had reigned supreme for the several hundred years since the invention of the stirrup, the long sword, and the lance. The very nature of society at that time was focused on the principle that "might makes right," and the knight was the might that made that right. The gentleman-at-arms was the only member of society authorized to bear a sword, own property, to participate in any form of government, and to be treated civilly. It was by "might" or force of arms, that such rights were established and enforced. The relatively recent innovation of allowing common Saxons and Welshmen to be trained as Yeomen and wield a weapon every knight well knew could penetrate his armor, was one of the prime reasons the French had so readily assembled to fight Henry. It too was the reason the chivalrous gentlemen of France felt justified in opposing Henry's small force with such overwhelming numbers. It was finally the right time to put this upstart king in his place who, it was rumored, even called himself *Harry*, an Anglo-Saxon version of the properly French name *Henri*.

The concept of allowing commoners, those who had not been specifically authorized to bear arms in the defense of the state, to own and use weapons was and is a controversial issue. The upper class of the 15th century recognized, as have most others in history, that the commoners outnumbered them and could overthrow them any time they were able to effectively take up arms and get organized. Perhaps the worst offense though in the eyes of the French nobility was the news that Henry had actually been encouraging the Yeomen and their families to become *literate*!

The standard procedure until that point in England and over the rest of Europe was to have letters written and records maintained by clerics, who were assigned to the service of the nobility by the Church. Kings knew that one Pope or the other was also reading what they wrote to other kings. Henry may well have been the first monarch to order troops loyal solely to him to be trained in the art of letters in an attempt to become independent of what was, in effect, a foreign intelligence service.

The Yeomen on their part were facing quite a quandary. They had great loyalty to their "Prince Harry" as they still called him. A king who spoke their language and even took a name as if he were one of them was a cherished dream of all the non-Norman English. On the other hand, the issue of claiming the throne of France was none of their business. Even if they won the battle and Henry went on to become king of France as well as England, the lot of the Yeoman and his family would be unchanged. They would still be the property of the king or some lord and no better off. If they lost, they stood to lose their means of living and quite probably their lives. A Yeoman was valuable as long as he could "pluck yew" or "shoot the bird" (referring to the feathers on the arrow), as the act of using the English long bow was known at the time. The valuable Yeoman could "give the shaft," as the English, cloth yard arrow was known, to his master's enemies at great ranges, but only if those critical fingers remained on his right hand.

Henry's Offer to the Yeomen

On the morning of October 25, 1415, King Henry once again rejected an offer of quarter from the French. While in that era before camcorders and near universal literacy, no scribe took notes; the rendering of Shakespeare nearly two centuries later rang true to the nation that had been shaped by that speech and serves us today as well or better. While there is certainly no way we can know today what Henry actually said to his Yeomen on that day, whatever it was he said inspired those exhausted, sick, and hungry men to accomplish what was clearly impossible, and in doing so laid the foundation for our world today. If Henry was not as eloquent as Shakespeare, he was certainly as effective as if he had been.

KING HENRY V, Act 4, Scene 3 Excerpt, By William Shakespeare:

Enter the KING

WESTMORELAND. O that we now had here
  But one ten thousand of those men in England
  That do no work to-day!

KING. What's he that wishes so?
  My cousin Westmoreland? No, my fair cousin;
  If we are mark'd to die, we are enow
  To do our country loss; and if to live,
  The fewer men, the greater share of honour.
  God's will! I pray thee, wish not one man more.
  By Jove, I am not covetous for gold,
  Nor care I who doth feed upon my cost;
  It yearns me not if men my garments wear;
  Such outward things dwell not in my desires.
  But if it be a sin to covet honour,
  I am the most offending soul alive.
  No, faith, my coz, wish not a man from England.
  God's peace! I would not lose so great an honour
  As one man more methinks would share from me
  For the best hope I have. O, do not wish one more!
  Rather *proclaim it, Westmoreland, through my host,*
  That he which hath no stomach to this fight,
  Let him depart; his passport shall be made,
  And crowns for convoy put into his purse;
  We would not die in that man's company
  That fears his fellowship to die with us.
  This day is call'd the feast of Crispian.
  He that outlives this day, and comes safe home,
  Will stand a tip-toe when this day is nam'd,
  And rouse him at the name of Crispian.
  He that shall live this day, and see old age,
  Will yearly on the vigil feast his neighbours,
  And say 'To-morrow is Saint Crispian.'
  Then will he strip his sleeve and show his scars,

And say 'These wounds I had on Crispian's day.'
Old men forget; yet all shall be forgot,
But he'll remember, with advantages,
What feats he did that day. Then shall our names,
Familiar in his mouth as household words-
Harry the King, Bedford and Exeter,
Warwick and Talbot, Salisbury and Gloucester-
Be in their flowing cups freshly rememb'red.
This story shall the good man teach his son;
And Crispin Crispian shall ne'er go by,
From this day to the ending of the world,
But we in it shall be remembered-
We few, we happy few, we band of brothers;
For he to-day that sheds his blood with me
Shall be my brother; be he ne'er so vile,
This day shall gentle his condition;
And gentlemen in England now-a-bed
Shall think themselves accurs'd they were not here,
And hold their manhoods cheap whiles any speaks
That fought with us upon Saint Crispin's day.

Note that in that speech he offers first "passport" and then "crowns" (money) for a passage home to any who would not desire to die with him on that battlefield. This refers to the offer by the Marshal of France to allow passage to Calais for any Yeoman who would desert his King. Then, he makes the most effective offer ever made by any leader before any campaign. He proclaims that "...*we band of brothers*" (to be brother to the king was to be a human being, a peer of the realm) "*For he to-day that sheds his blood with me/Shall be my brother; be he ne'er* (ever) *so vile,* (common, villain, of a village, literally a possession of another) *This day shall gentle* (make noble, create gentility of) *his condition;* (status, state within society)."

This was not just a grand motivational speech, although it certainly qualifies as one of the best in history, but an offer of personhood to the commoners standing before him. Should they by some grand act of God win this unwinnable battle, the Yeomen, who were at that moment in effect the chattel property of Henry V, would be free men. They full well knew the common law of 15th century England that obligated the king to give land, traditionally forty acres, money in some form, a horse, and a sword to any man he "gentled." It was long known that penniless gentlemen were an embarrassment to the ruling class. To protect the landed class from having too many "dependents," the obviously quite easy act of creating a man from a slave had restrictions. The nobleman "gentling" the peasant was obligated to provide him enough land to support him, his family, and to pay a portion of his produce to his lord. A common method of accomplishing this act of manumitting was actually to adopt the servant into the lord's family. Obviously, if one were related to a gentleman, one was in turn a gentleman as well.

It was then up to the manumitted "gentleman" to "improve" the land and pay taxes to his "liege lord." Barring some criminal act, the only way the newly designated gentleman could lose his freedom was to fail to pay his taxes. Should he so fail, the lord would seize the land, and the freeman would be either confined or sold back into servitude.

Of an equally great significance to the freeman was the status of his sons. They too would be free if he were granted freedom and was able to sustain that grant. His daughters would no longer be subject to his lord's direction as to marriage, and he would have as his right the ability to rise or fall according to his own effort and action rather than the whim of some Norman's desire.

Henry was a well educated man and by all accounts exceptionally brilliant. There is little doubt he studied Latin and the history of Rome. He may well have been offering what he knew the Romans had offered to their great gain. One of the elements that allowed Rome to rise to greatness and maintain that supremacy for eight centuries was that it uniquely allowed commoners to rise to the status of citizens through military service. A Roman legionnaire could retire after twenty years of service, disqualifying injury, or exceptional valor in battle. His retirement was in the form of a grant of Roman citizenship and land in one of the colonies, although the land itself was technically the property of Rome and not the soldier. Thus, Rome not only provided for the upward mobility of its subjects of any ethnic group but also ensured a reserve of loyal, militarily trained citizens across its vast domain.

The Rules of Battle
Battle was extremely formalized in the 15th century and, in some

ways, was more like a sports event than the warfare we know today. The commanders would commonly agree in advance where the battle would take place and even how many knights would be present on each side. The end of most battles was not mass slaughter but quarter given and accepted. After all, the purpose of war was the ownership of land and resources, even as it had been shortly after the introduction of the stirrup, long sword, and lance.

Occasionally, though, the rules would be broken. Ultimately, it was a matter of winning or losing. If the stakes were small or even trivial, both sides would abide by the rules knowing that a violation by one side would give cause for a violation by the other. Even in the 20th century as we fought the Axis powers, the Nazi's never resorted to the use of what we now call "weapons of mass destruction." They had poison gas and both sides had used it freely in World War I, but they never brought it to use knowing that we too had the same weapon and could strike their homeland with it, while they could not strike ours.

After the defeat of Germany, one of the critical issues was the "un-civilized" treatment of American prisoners and the mass slaughter of populations in occupied countries by the Imperial Japanese Forces. That, combined with the "illegal" attack on Pearl Harbor led to the decision to use nuclear weapons against Japan. Here again, the issue was the conventions of war, an often unwritten but understood set of rules about the conduct of warfare in a "civilized" manner.

Henry had used the rules quite well in his own favor, but his victories had now reached the point where obeying the rules no longer had any advantage for the French. If they obeyed the rules, Henry might well defeat an equal number of knights and take the throne of France. Thus, when the Marshall of France called for every able bodied gentle-man-at-arms in France to stand forth against the remnant of Henry's force, he knew he was violating the rules of chivalry but depended on the victory to be so great that his offense would be buried by the glory of having saved the throne of France from an English speaking barbar-ian.

Henry chose to risk all on his perception of what his Yeomen would do if given the opportunity to be free landowners. He had chosen to stay within the rules of battle but to exploit those rules to the fullest. Prior to that day, there is no record of the English Yeomen actually firing *directly* at an approaching knight. With his proclamation that they were officially "gentle" as soon as the battle began, he depended on their determination to win and thereby lay claim to that freedom to turn certain defeat into possible victory.

The Battle Joined
[1]Henry's lines were set up between two heavily forested areas where the open terrain narrowed. Each Yeoman carried an iron tipped wooden stake that was driven into the ground with the point angled toward the enemy. Theoretically, the pointed stake would dissuade the horses of a mounted cavalry charge from overrunning the Yeoman position. The French were quite aware of this tactic and had equipped their cavalry with long lances that would reach well into the stakes. Additionally, the soft mud of the recently plowed field exposed to three days of rain did a poor job of holding the stake at the required angle.

As the morning fog lifted, Henry's force stood ready to engage the vastly superior French force. By ten o'clock the sun was well out and beating down fiercely on the soldiers, but there was no sign of movement from the French camp.

During the preceding night the French forces had celebrated their upcoming victory quite thoroughly. As there was no formal French commander with the King terminally insane and the Dauphine too fearful to be seen on the battlefield, there was no one to discipline the huge force of gentlemen. The drinking, singing, and gambling had continued far into the early hours of the morning. As a result, the cream of French nobility faced St. Crispin's day with little sleep and either still intoxicated or in full possession of a severe hangover.

Henry realized that his forces were growing weaker with each passing minute of inaction. He again made a bold move by ordering the raising of the stakes and a slow movement forward in formation. (Incidentally, this may be where we get the term "raising the stakes" when someone increases the investment in a given outcome.) His weakened

---

[1]The most complete account of the Battle of Agincourt comes from Jehan de Wavrin, A French Knight's Account of Agincourt, Chronicles, 1399-1422 translated by Sir W. Hardy and E. Hardy, 1887, and published in John Keegan's *The Book of War, 25 Centuries of Great War Writing*. Although I have summarized the description here, de Wavrin's first hand account takes precedent over all others.

force crossed an open area where an assault by the French would have been able to outflank them with ease and continued their careful advance until the English forces were again bounded on either side by thick woods. Once more, he had the archers set their stakes and prepare for battle. This time though they were a mere 250 yards from the gaily decorated French tents with literally thousands of banners displaying the symbols of nearly every noble family in the realm.

Around noon, as soon as his forces were again properly assembled, Henry ordered his Yeomen to begin to fire volleys into the French encampment. Amazingly, the French still had not noticed that Henry's army had approached so close to their camp. I am confident that as the arrows began to drop through the tent roofs, the screams of those who were unfortunate enough to be in the path of said arrows soon alerted the warriors of France that the battle had begun whether or not they were ready.

For the next half hour or longer the arrows continued their slow, steady shower as the confused and befuddled French knights fought to arm and armor themselves and, in the case of the cavalry, mount and organize for action. The horses and heavy cavalry had been sited to the rear of the camp and, as such, were relatively unscathed by the bombardment. The battle plan, worked out the previous day, was to have two forces of cavalry attack the archers on Henry's flanks as the main force started forward on foot to engage the English knights.

As each knight was ready for battle, he moved to the front of the camp and joined a mob of other gentlemen-at-arms. Because of the still falling arrows and the absence of the king's standard on which to rally, the force had more than a little trouble assembling in any form of battle order. Finally, in frustration, some of the knights started forward down a slight slope through the mud of the freshly plowed field.

Thus, the force that started down hill toward Henry's assembled knights far more resembled an uncertain mob than a coherent fighting force. Even those in the front ranks of the mob were not certain they should be there and probably in some fear of the wrath of the more senior lords who were supposed to be leading.

As the main force began to move without orders, the cavalry recognized their cue to begin the assault. On either side of the packed stream of armored French nobility, the huge warhorses of the heavy cavalry started forward in the mud. Normally the cavalry would then have accelerated to a gallop, but the thickness of the mud combined with the short distance to the English archers never allowed them to reach that stage.

As the mounted knights, each bearing a long lance extending well in front of his horse, closed on the Yeoman an unexpected event occurred on the battlefield. The archers broke off their indirect fire, as was expected, but rather than scattering in front of the mass of horseflesh and armored knights rushing toward them, they stood their ground. As the horses came closer, they lowered their bows, and for the first time in history, the English long bow was used in direct fire against mounted knights.

Although the long bow could penetrate a knight's armor at short range, the main damage was not done to the knights themselves but to their horses. One of the most cherished rules of medieval warfare was that one simply did not go about intentionally injuring a knight's horse! As you might guess, the Welsh and Saxon archers did not hold such niceties in high esteem. Because the knight was largely behind the horse's head and neck from their perspective and as the horse had no armor over its neck and chest, the pragmatic Yeomen fired on the target of opportunity.

As the arrows slammed into their necks and chests, the horses collapsed forward—screaming in agony. The knights, only a moment before riding confidently on the back of what had until then been an unassailable weapon of war, found themselves thrown forward over the heads of their wounded horses into the mud of the battlefield.

Many of the horses struggled back to their feet, flailing wildly at the barbs that continued to pierce their flesh. As the horses regained their footing, they charged back up the slope—directly away from the archer's positions.

Meanwhile, the knights of the main force continued to pour from the encampment and funnel together down the hill toward the center of the English position where they could see the banners of Henry and his lords. According to de Wavrin, the French were so packed together as they struggled down that muddy field that they could not even raise their arms.

The terrified warhorses of the heavy cavalry slammed into this packed mass of armored humanity. John Keegan notes that there are examples of police horses hitting packed crowds that have been filmed from above. When the horse hits the mob, a visible compression wave spreads across the mass of people, knocking them down, almost as if a bowling ball had hit pins packed together. The maddened warhorses must have temporarily disabled a large number of the advancing knights. Many of those who fell would have been hit hard enough to stun them and would have been pressed down into the mud by the weight of the other knights falling on them.

Meanwhile, the Yeomen were continuing to behave in a most unexpected manner. Not only were archers expected to scatter at the approach of heavy cavalry, they were never expected to advance into hand-to-hand melee. Henry's grand experiment with the force of freedom had produced a new element on the battlefield that would doom his successor George III to failure in the American Revolution 350 years later.

The Yeomen dropped their bows and swarmed forward to attack the fallen cavalrymen. As they approached the fallen knights, who were probably having quite a difficult time rising to their feet after being plunged into the mud at some significant velocity, they put their mallets, axes, and knives to a use that would have been profoundly illegal only a few moments before. As *property* they were universally forbidden to attack a gentleman in any way. Now though, having been "gentled" by the blood they themselves had just caused to be shed on the battlefield, they were free to express their rage against the nobility who had been their overlords for the past 350 years.

A fallen knight need not worry about another knight using such tactics, as no gentleman would attack another who had fallen. This new breed of gentleman, however, had not been so schooled and quickly dispatched the fallen knights who had been sent against them.

While the cavalry were being eliminated from the field and the main force quite effectively attacked from the flanks by the lightly armed and totally unarmored Yeomen, Henry's other surprise tactic was put into effect. Rather than line his knights up side by side to allow for the one-on-one-warfare that was the tradition of the day, he had arrayed them several layers deep. The front row held shields and swords, while the rows behind extended pikes and lances forward of the front row. The effect was a hedgehog of sharp objects sticking forward from the English position and backed by multiple ranks of rather large strong men leaning forward. Not waiting for the first of the packed

French force to hit his lines, Henry commanded a sudden advance as they closed. The sudden and quite unexpected shock of this mass of armor, preceded by solidly anchored weapons, threw the front rank of French knights backward into those that followed.

Once again, the very mass of numbers that the French had depended on to give them certain victory turned against them. As those knights in the lead ranks of the French force attempted to turn back and away from the sudden hedgehog of English weapons, they were prevented from doing so by the combined momentum of tens of thousands of advancing French warriors. It may be surmised that a shockwave rippled backward through the advancing mob, but it is almost certain that many, if not most, of the leading ranks went down into the mud, felled not so much by the English as by the mass of their own advancing force.

In their probably befuddled alcoholic daze, the French only knew that they needed to press forward if they were to have any part in the glorious victory they believed they had already won. Unfortunately for them, as they arrived at the point of battle, the ground was obscured by layers of fallen knights. The armored warriors behind them continued to press forward as the lead knights lost their footing on the armored bodies of those who had fallen before them.

The battle continued well into the afternoon. Henry's knights began to move forward just to get past the mound of dead and injured French that had accumulated in front of their position. According to at least one French survivor, the mound of dead men and horses across the front of the English positions was higher than the top of a man's head. Another account claimed that in the center, the mound of dead was twenty feet high.

By the time the exhausted English knights were able to struggle over the fallen French, the battlefield had turned into chaos. The Yeomen were stripping the French injured and dead of anything of value and were so weighed down they could barely walk. Upon finding a fallen, but not dead Frenchman of high rank, the Yeoman as well as the knights would take him prisoner to hold for ransom.

Henry was hard pressed to reorganize his forces but was finally able to cause them to regroup near the original positions. His concern was that he could still see impressive numbers of French assembling on the other side of the field. His men were universally at the end point of fatigue, and his archers had expended their arrows. He was then shocked to hear that a contingent of French had attacked his baggage trains. He hastened back to see what damage had been done and found that the young pages that had been left in the supply trains for safety had been slaughtered. Once again, the French had broken the rules of war. Baggage, or supply trains were routinely left undefended, and it was a clear understanding that gentlemen did not attack undefended servants or for that matter, children! Among the dead was the king's page, a boy he had personally pledged to defend.

Returning to the front, he could see that the French had managed to rally their surviving forces, and those had been substantially increased in number by new arrivals straggling in during the day. He knew that he could now be easily overwhelmed, and his concern was heightened by the news that the number of prisoners greatly exceeded the number of surviving English who had captured them! Fearing that the French might attack at any time and the prisoners would then join in that attack, he ordered all prisoners executed at once. A number of his nobility refused the order and stubbornly defended their right to hold the prisoners and demand ransom. Henry assembled a company of his Yeoman and ordered them to kill any prisoners whose captors would not do so. The Yeomen unflinchingly obeyed the king.

The Battle Won

At the end of the day estimates of the number of French men-at-arms dead on the battlefield that would be called *Agincourt* after a nearby castle, varied from 13,000 to 35,000. The estimates of English dead vary from two low estimates (by the English) of 25 and 125 to a high (by the French) of 1,600.

Henry ordered that any armor or weaponry that could not be properly worn was to be either destroyed or abandoned. While that too met with some resistance, particularly by the Yeomen for whom quality armor meant wealth beyond their dreams, it was done. During the night the English dead were boiled to remove the flesh from their bones for return to England and burial.

As King Henry set out for England the next morning, the French forces, still assembled in their camp, made no effort to stop him. As they passed by the French encampment, undocumented tradition holds that the Yeomen held up the first two fingers and thumb of their right hands, with the back of the hand toward the French, and called out, "I can still pluck yew!" which degenerated rapidly into a chant of "Pluck yew! Pluck yew!"

The Results

Henry was declared heir to the throne of France and became the regent for the insane King Charles after being given Princess Catherine of France as his bride as part of the Treaty of Troyes signed in 1420. An interesting side note is that upon assuming the Regency of France, Henry had Charles brought back to the palace from the prison where the Dauphin had locked him away. Henry directed that he be well cared for as long as he lived. Sadly, Henry died within a few years placing his infant son Henry VI on the throne when Charles VI (The Mad) finally died. France was able to reclaim its throne during the ensuing years of a near leaderless England as Joan of Arc effectively handed Charles VII the throne. Thus, the immediate political effect of this amazing battle was negligible. On the other hand, the long-term economic and political effect of that battle could not have been more significant.[2]

Upon return to England, the Yeomen, who had departed as royal property were now accorded the status of gentlemen. Unfortunately, as with many other events in the 15th century, the documentation is missing for what transpired as a result of that history-shaping act. From the custom of the day and the very clear change in the status of the Yeomen from that point onward, we can surmise what happened.

---

[2] As an odd footnote to this critical battle, the hereditary disease *porphyria* that probably caused the madness of Charles VI, leading to the weakness and confusion of France and ultimately to the Battle of Agincourt, appears to have entered the royal line of England through his daughter Catherine when she was given in marriage to Henry. Their son, Henry VI appears to have been a victim of that same disease causing the English to lose the French throne. More significantly, the line of Henry VI led to George III of England whose madness, probably from the same affliction, resulted in the loss of the American colonies. Thus, this one battle led to the establishment of the economic system of the United States and to the independence that allowed it to take root. (*Purple secret (Genes, 'Madness' and the Royal Houses of Europe)* by J.C.G. Röhl, J.C.G., M. Warren, and D. Hunt)

Each of the approximately 7,000-8,000 Yeomen who had participated in the battle of Agincourt would have been granted the traditional land, gold, horse, and sword. Henry had made great gains in France and was more than willing to part with sections of crown holdings in England. Based on later holdings and tradition, the land was probably allocated to the Yeomen by company of royal archers and designated in sections of one-mile squares with each Yeoman receiving forty acres.

Just as important to the changes that would be wrought by these Yeomen was the fact that literacy was a prized skill of theirs. That they had both skills useful in battle and the ability to account for holdings and keep records enabled them to have a clear competitive advantage. Their ability to benefit from their labor and their skills in a manner unique in most of Europe at that time propelled their economic status forward.

As the Yeomen took possession of the land, it became clear rather quickly that by *sharing* ownership of the larger sections, rather than each family retaining their assigned forty acres, they could more effectively grow crops where the soil was appropriate for that and graze their animals where crops were not the optimal use of the land. In order to account for the division of produce as well as responsibility, each Yeoman was issued *shares,* both in the land itself and in the *common (live) stock* of the *company.* Thus, the holding in common of livestock by a military company became the term we use for the holding of interests in a commercial company, or corporation, today.

As the years and generations came and went, the sons of the Yeomen did not all stay on the farm. Some chose to sell their shares to the others and take the resulting money to begin businesses elsewhere. To facilitate these transactions, markets were declared for the buying and selling of shares of the various companies, often in conjunction with the buying and selling of livestock. While the origin of the terms "bull" and "bear" market are lost to us now, it is not a great leap to guess that during periods of prosperity, there were more bulls to be sold at such markets while in times of relative hardship, captured bears, or more likely bear skins, were more the stock in trade. The ability to raise money for a venture or even for improvements in the company's property by selling of shares was the beginning of modern capitalism. People had a means of converting capital into money and later, money into capital for further investment.

By the 17th century, the Yeoman had become legendary as hard workers and were much sought after as record keepers and scribes. In 1610, once again a socioeconomic collapse would devastate Europe, but England would be spared the worst of the effects, largely because of the highly effective food production of the Yeomen as well as their determination to remain on the land they owned. Across the rest of Europe, the peasants once again abandoned their master's holdings as war, famine, pestilence, death, and destruction became the norm for over forty years.

Chapter 4 - *Individualism, Ownership, and Capital:*
The Foundation for Wealth

Ownership

Land ownership by the Yeoman farmer was unique in 15th century Europe. As time went by, many of the lesser nobility also managed to maneuver themselves into the position of being the actual owners of land. What followed was a tradition that once a person (note that one has to be a person for this to work) owned property, his right to that property was sacrosanct, or not subject to sanction by the king or anyone else as long as the appropriate taxes were paid.

This put the Yeoman returning home from France in a position unique in not only Europe but as far as I can determine, the world. First, he was in the position of being a direct holder of property as a free man, something that did happen from time to time in Europe, but as an Englishman, he was not only the holder of the property but was entitled to "have" the land as well.

As the Yeoman took possession of his land, he effectively was established as a new class of person. The Yeoman is often referred to in history tomes as a "minor gentleman," but he was far more than a lesser version of a Norman lord. He was the beginning of a new class of person that would unleash the potential of each individual in society and create a level of wealth and a standard of living that would allow the followers in the tradition he established to become the dominate class of person in the world.

It is very difficult today to understand that in virtually all the societies of the world that recognized any division of land, or property, the king or state owned all the land. The world was, and for that matter still is, divided into those who believed that property could be owned, albeit by a king, and those who believed that property was held in common. The second position was and is the primitive position of the hunter-gatherer.

Hunter-gatherer societies do not recognize the ownership of property other than by the extended family. This makes a great deal of sense if no one is investing any time or effort in improving the property. On the other hand, the weapons, tools, and shelter of the individual in the hunter-gatherer society are considered to be sacred personal property. Each item is considered to be an extension of the person, embodied with the actual essence of the *man* who invested in them. Note by the way that women normally are forbidden to even so much as touch the weapons and tools of the man in such societies.

The first position of ownership I mentioned above was the type of ownership that the Europeans of the Middle Ages and renaissance considered normal. Agriculture requires that the owner of the property invest a great deal of time and energy into improving the land so that it will yield a produce that is far more beneficial to humans than "unimproved" property. In order to be willing to put the investment into that property to achieve the levels of production associated with agriculture, the person doing so must be convinced that someone else will not come along and take it from him. The only effective way of doing that is to reach an agreement with the other agriculturists that they will respect his *ownership* of the land he has improved *and* join with him in defending that land against the hunter-gatherer *barbarians* who still consider land and all it produces to be common property.

Initially, that ownership involved relatively powerful warlords who had sufficient warriors following their lead to defend the agricultural land from depredations by either the barbarians or the other warlords. The medieval system was a prime example of that type of society. The principal warlord, or king, was the actual owner of the land under cultivation and allocated certain areas to his "clients" who enjoyed the produce minus a certain portion that was given to the king. In return, the king and the other vassals would come to the defense of any of the lords who were attacked by outsiders.

The battle of Agincourt is an example of the kind of defense that was the glue holding medieval society together. The King of France (or at least his representative) noted that Henry V, an outsider, was taking the agriculture property of his vassals, issued a call to arms to defend the realm against that taking. The force that Harry unleashed against the status quo of the age when he made the Yeomen into persons, was destined to not only allow him to take France for his own, but ultimately destroy the "divine right of kings" to own their kingdom and hold all in that kingdom as vassals.

As the Yeoman took possession of his land, he was able to *fully* possess that land. They, in effect, were the "lords" of their own land, but unlike the other lords of the day, they worked their own property and directly invested their time and very lives within the boundaries of the real property they were given.

This new class, named appropriately *Yeomen,* was neither serf nor lord. The nobility despised them and the peasants resented them. Karl Marx renamed them the "petty bourgeois" and declared them the enemy of the working class. Today we call them entrepreneurs, meaning literally "a new entry" or "one who goes before." The evolution from a royal archer given the ability to own land to the closest thing we have to nobility in America involved a complex set of changes that we take for granted today.

At the risk of being unnecessarily repetitive, the idea that a person could both own property and work on that same property was revolutionary. There has been some speculation that somehow the English Yeoman was always a farmer and had retained the supposedly Saxon tradition of land ownership prior to the Norman invasion. First, there is no record of such a thing, and second, the dramatic decline of trained Yeoman archers in the next couple of centuries indicates they were doing something they had not been doing before.

Property Rights, the Rule of Law

While ownership of land by the person actually tilling the earth was revolutionary, it still did not qualify to create the economic revolution that followed. England had a system of land transfer and ownership law quite unlike the rest of the world. Again, the Magna Carta was the cause of that body of law. As long as the king technically owned all the land, as was the norm in Spain and France, the transfer of property was quite simple. Whomever the king said could use a portion of land could use it. The ability to transfer it to another was non-existent, other than by petition to the king. While this certainly went a long way toward elimination of the ruinous warfare that devastated Europe in the 14th century, it also effectively froze forward progress.

There is no doubt that having a king who determined who used what property was a great improvement over the "might is right" idea of the Middle Ages, but the user of the property still was very much like a renter today. Renters do not have any incentive to improve property.

To be a member of the Roman ruling class one must have had an income almost solely from rents (normally in the form of a set portion of the gross production), and the rental property must be overseen and managed by someone else. In other words, the rulers of Rome considered it one of the highest virtues to be among what we would call today "the idle rich." That concept seems to be almost universal in the "classic" societies from the Inca and Maya to the dynastic rulers of China and Japan.

That particular virtue was one of the crucial factors in the fall of the Roman Empire. A virtue made of not working will tend to put the ruling class very much out of touch with what is going on at the grass root level. It has been noted that when the barbarians arrived at the gates of Rome, the citizens of that esteemed city were shocked even though they had been drawing closer for two centuries.

Henry V unwittingly created the instrument that would both ensure the destruction of the medieval feudal system and at the same time prevent the collapse of England in the 1600s. The Yeoman, and later entrepreneurial class, would ultimately not only save England but also create a whole new type of society that could provide a standard of living to its members that improves with each generation. Even five hundred years later Hitler referred derisively to the English as a 'nation of shopkeepers'.

A nation of small farm and shop owners must have a code of law that provides substantial protection to the relatively small property owner. It must also provide a means for the orderly transfer of property. That functional protection combined with an effective market creates both value and liquidity. The combination of value and liquidity allows something to occur that has changed the world in a way that was unimaginable in the past.

I recently visited the island of Skye just off the western coast of Scotland. It is a picturesque place, in many ways unchanged in 200 years. It is also the home of the Clan MacLeod, headquartered at Castle Dunvegan. The principal reason it is so beautifully "unspoiled" is that very few people live there. According to the Clan MacLeod Society, there are several times more MacLeods living in Texas than on Skye. With the beauty of Skye one would wonder why a Scotsman would leave such a place for the heat, dust, and humidity of Texas.

The answer is to be found in the issue of property ownership. John

MacLeod, the hereditary chief, or laird, of the Clan, owns about half of the island of Skye. Unfortunately for him, he may own, or have, the property, but he does not hold most of the property he owns. Crofters, or as we call them in America, sharecroppers, occupy much of the land. They pay rent to the titled "owner" of the land, in this cast, MacLeod, but Parliament froze the rents in the late 1800s. Parliament at the same time created a right to the "crofting" that prevents the titled owner from evicting the Crofter other than for nonpayment of rent. The end result is similar to that produced by the "rent control" ordinances of New York City. The titled owner has lost control of his or her property and the renters have gained a right to minimal rent payments as well as the legal authority to transfer that rental right to another!

A Crofter may pay as little as £48 per year for a substantial piece of farmland. Worse, the local Crofters have the ability to prevent Laird MacLeod from using the property he does hold! It seems he made plans to build a hotel and resort in the Cuillin Mountains, his unfettered property. The local citizens, not wanting more tourists, tour buses, and the like on the island, petitioned their local representative on the Highland Council to block the construction. He was able to effectively prohibit any development of the mountain area, despite the fact that John MacLeod actually owns the land and had met every legal and environmental requirement.

The reverse problem strikes at those same Crofters. While they do not own the land, they do own the improvements on the land. Unfortunately, when they make improvements, they cannot borrow money to do so. Banks recognize that they will not be able to extract any value from improvements that sit on someone else's land and, as a result, will not lend money to the Crofters for such things. The inability to get a mortgage effectively locks out the children of the Crofter from staying on the land. The right of the Crofters to prevent use of the land on the island for development denies the same right to themselves.

While the Highlands of Scotland have a delightful beauty, the cost has been staggering. The children of the Scots still leave to find a place where they can have a hope of a higher standard of living. We visited glen after glen with names familiar to us as the surnames of people in America. No one lived there any more. The weather in those glens was certainly no worse than in many places in the United States, but the people whose name was taken from the glen chose to live in America where they could have full ownership of their land, and to a larger extent, their future.

In most of the rest of the world, the concept of a simple, untitled individual actually having complete, or fee simple, ownership of land is as alien as it would be for a person to claim ownership of a piece of the sky. As I write this book, even the supposedly now free market system of Russia forbids the private ownership of real estate.

In Mexico, just across the border, a Mexican cannot technically "own" property, and in the final analysis, the government can take the land from the "holder" without due process and without compensation. According to Douglass North in his book *Structure and Change in Economic History*, the principal reason Mexico's economy is routinely in a state of crisis while just across the border to the north, the same population groups have created relative prosperity in the United States is just that issue. In the United States, a previous occupant of Mexico can obtain fee simple ownership of land and thereby is willing to make significant improvements on that land.

A few years ago, I was escorted by a guide to a site in a mountainous region of Mexico where prehistoric pictographs were to be found. We entered a large ranch, and rode down a long and extremely rough dirt road. At the end of the road was the "ranch house," a long, low adobe structure with a thatched roof looking very much as if it had been built by primitive people hundreds of years ago. The "ranchers" were sitting under a shelter made from sticks, out of the mid-day sun. They, too, looked as if they were from a tableau made in the 17th century. After about half an hour of hiking, we stopped by a pool of water to rest and have our lunch. As I explored the granite outcroppings around the pool, I saw quartz veins that looked as if they were quite rich with gold. I mentioned this to our guide, a college-educated man from Mexico City.

He looked shocked, even frightened. "Señor," he implored, "please do not tell anyone that you have seen gold here. We know that there is much gold in the rocks of these mountains, but if the government finds that this ranch has gold under it, the ranchers will be evicted and the government will take their ranch!" He went on to explain that the family living on this ranch had been there for several generations and as the government had sole right to any mineral wealth found in the country, they would take the land from the family and leave them nothing.

After seeing the prehistoric paintings, we headed back out using the same route by which we had entered. On the way out, I again saw the family living in abject poverty. They were attempting to herd several cows that looked like they had seen far better days. It struck me that here they were barely surviving on a desert ranch while around them probably lay tremendous wealth that they could not even acknowledge for fear of losing *their* land.

The concept that a piece of paper can create ownership and wealth and give the owner the ability to sell not only the whole property, but even to sell interests in that property or borrow money based on the value of the property is perhaps one of the most significant developments in human history. It is a development found uniformly in developed countries where wealth is being multiplied and almost totally absent from the countries where poverty is endemic.

The Origin of Wealth

In those counties where there is the greatest divide between the very rich and the very poor, the rich hold land by virtue of their connection to the "state" or government, and the poor occupy land at the pleasure of the wealthy landholder or the state. In countries where the wealth is widely spread across the population, as in the United States, Canada, and Western Europe, fee simple ownership of property is the norm. Does this one thing explain the origin of wealth, or is there more to the issue?

At the base, it does explain the much higher median standard of living as well as the fact that the wealth of countries that respect and protect individual property rights tends to be found more in the middle class than in any form of upper class. In the United States and to a lesser degree in Canada and Western Europe, a large majority of the total income received by the nation is concentrated in the middle-income groups. In the United States, a majority of families own the home in which they live. In countries without a core code of law protecting the property rights of the individual, the absolute majority of the income received in the nation goes to a very small percentage of the population at the top of the social or government structure.

Thomas Stanley, in his book *The Millionaire Next Door,* points out that the number of millionaires in the U.S. is increasing faster than in the rest of the world combined. The small business entrepreneur who sells his or her business and retires or the twenty year employee with the million dollar 401(k) are examples of classes of people who are generating the great wealth and income of America. In those countries where property rights are not protected, very nearly the only way to rise from poverty to wealth is outside the system. Given that there are many people in such stratified societies around the world who have a growing desire to live a better life, it should come as no surprise that organized crime is considered a normal part of life in those countries, and that millions immigrate every year to America where advancement from "rags to riches" is part of our self image.

The origin of the wealth of those American millionaires provides a significant clue to why those of us fortunate enough to be born in what have come to be known as the "western democracies" have arrived at a general level of wealth previously unknown in history or in the rest of early 21st century contemporary world.

The first example from Dr. Stanley's book, the small business owner, was first able to start and run a business without ruinous fees, taxes, and bribes. After he or she developed the business into a profitable supplier of something others were willing to consistently purchase, then he or she was able to sell the business. The sale proceeds were then placed in another position where interest, dividends, and probably some degree of capital gain could provide income to support the now retired business owner.

In the second example, the employee of a company through participation in either his or her employer's stock or through investing in diversified equity accounts accumulated enough ownership in corporations to allow the proceeds of the sale of that ownership to be placed in a position to generate the income needed to be financially independent.

Both of those examples are indeed fairly common events in America, but outside of the developed world, they are as alien as living on the moon. In the first example, a great compendium of law as well as a powerful cultural set of values protects the small business from undue interference while providing a totality of ownership to the owner or owners. That "business" is recognized as an entity that had an existence and certain rights that accrued to its owner. The owner then has the right to transfer that ownership to another person or business in exchange for value received. Both of those elements are critical to the operation of a capitalist society. Both of them are things we assume to be universal and, as so many things in our society, are so ubiquitous that we soon no longer even think about them.

In other societies, a business may be operated by the supposed owner, and the owner may even be credited with possession of the "improvements," but if the state or some other person owns the land on which the business is built, the "ownership" is solely at the pleasure of the landlord. Coincident with the absence of land ownership by the majority of the population, inevitably there comes a disregard for contractual obligations toward those who do not own land. In the great majority of our world, land ownership is either the exclusive right of the state or of a privileged few. In those societies, land ownership denotes full citizenship and rights under the law. Absent land ownership, the lower ranking member of society has a distinctly reduced set of "rights," and even those fail when in conflict with a landowner.

If the ownership of the business is in question, then the business owner cannot effectively get a loan to expand or increase the business. It also becomes difficult, if not impossible, to offer ownership, either in part or in whole, to another person. Finally, the ownership of a business, home, car, or any other item of significant value, is conferred by some piece of paper. If the actual ownership of the underlying asset is in question, the value assigned a certificate indicating ownership is either non-extant or greatly reduced.

This ability to transfer the ownership of an item of physical or intangible property to another by a standard of words placed on a piece of paper is one of those things we, in the United States, take for granted. If I purchase a car in Texas and later wish to sell it in Maine, I simply assume that the *title* I received in Texas will be accepted in Maine as proof that I own the car. I further assume that by filling out and signing another piece of paper in Maine I can convert my automobile back into cash, albeit at perhaps a different dollar amount than my purchase price in Texas. The same is true of a publicly traded stock share purchased at one brokerage house and sold at another.

When I purchase a house or a piece of land, again I make an assumption. I assume that by the time the title company is done with its research and agrees to transfer the title for me that the person in fact owned the land from whom I am purchasing it *and* that all the previous owners of the land were the proper owners. With the piece of land or home normally comes *title insurance* just in case something does come up that brings into question whether some previous owner of the real estate had the proper authorization to sell it.

Not only does the system that we so take for granted allow us to own a piece of property and have confidence that it is indeed an actual private possession, but it allows us to actually create liquidity while still having possession of the piece of earth. The concept of having a mortgage requires that the land ownership be clearly defined and protected. In fact, the greatest producer of liquidity, or money, throughout most of our national history has been land. Liquidity created from an imaginary division of geography creates the concept that one could do the same with another imaginary division that we refer to as a "corporation."

The concept of a person who is in possession of property actually *owning* the property is so common in the United States that we assume it is the "natural" state of affairs. In fact, as I have outlined above, it is both a very new and very unusual system. To further assume that each owner of property is specifically protected against "unreasonable search and seizure" by the highest law in the land is a most unusual situation in the history of the world. We, in the United States, have taken it even further and have extended the rights of full citizenship to every adult. Those that own property are not only secure in that ownership, but those who do not own property are specifically granted the right to be the sovereign owner of property whenever they wish to do so.

Now think about a system where you purchase a home or a piece of land and there is no clear system for determining whether all of the previous owners have properly sold the land. Suppose you know of several people who have bought land that someone has sold them, paid cash for the land, and then discovers that a court has placed a lien on the property to recover a debt owed by some previous owner. Worse, you then hear that the lien holder has taken the property and the home and your friend has lost all he has paid. Suppose further that you accept this as the norm! You simply understand that if one purchases land from a stranger chances are that something like that will happen.

What effect would such a system have on the value of a house or a business? The market you might have if you were to sell your house or business or any other item of value with a long life would be limited to those who had a great deal of trust in your honesty and your attention to detail. No matter how honest you may be, if you had not been very diligent when *you* purchased the property, you might have overlooked some detail that would cause the new owner to lose it. If you were not completely and absolutely honest, it might be that you had discovered that there was what is known as an "encumbrance" on the property and simply wanted to get rid of the property before you had it taken from you! Now throw in the fact that in such systems, the only way to have any degree of security as to your purchase being in fact yours was to have more sway in the local government and the court system than your opponent. If that system were to exist, the very wealthy and po-litically well-positioned could purchase land, businesses, and homes at a bargain basement prices, while those with lesser wealth would be forced to sell at that low price *and* would effectively be locked out of the ability to purchase property other than from close friends and family.

In every society on earth today, the creation of wealth hinges on the ability to enjoy the rights of property ownership. As a result, those who are able to buy and sell property as well as receive any income from that ownership are likely to end up very wealthy. Everyone else ends up in lower classes that are dependent on the land owning class.

That, in fact, was the situation in 15th century England until the Yeomen began to establish their own system for the orderly transfer of property. They discovered that the key to property ownership once the king declared them eligible for such things was first that the person buying and the person selling the property must be clearly identified as a person with the right to do so. That meant that some type of record of exactly who a person was and who his parents were must be maintained by some unbiased organization. Next, the property itself must be carefully identified both as to its exact location and bound-aries and its lineage of ownership. Of course, each previous transaction must have also been subject to those same standards, no matter how long ago the transaction took place!

At various times in history, the Yeomen's records were challenged by the more wealthy and powerful who wished to reestablish the rule of the upper class in a small way, but as the Yeomen had carefully nurtured literacy, and had, as a class, established themselves as the clerks for the royal court and many of the nobility, the system they had created came to be the guarantor of *everyone's* right to property. The royal courts recognized that to unseat the property rights recorded by the Yeomen was to destroy the property rights of everyone.

Sadly, that same development did not occur everywhere. Today, at the beginning of the 21st century the difference between an economy where land ownership is protected by custom and law and one where it is not can be seen quite clearly along the southern border of the United States. By traveling just south of Texas across the Rio Grande, one is immediately struck by the amazing difference in the general cleanliness of the towns and more so by the poorly maintained and semi-finished buildings that seem to be scattered helter-skelter across the terrain. By traveling outside of town though, one can find beautiful villas with large holdings of well-cultivated land. With a little investigation, one discovers that there are relatively few, very wealthy people in that society and a staggering number of very poor. While the middle class exists, it is a small minority. At the same time, the entrepreneurial spirit of the citizens is evident almost everywhere. On both sides of the border, the worker is known for being energetic and willing to do a great deal of hard labor for a relatively small wage.

The essence of investing is found in *ownership*. Without the assurance that the full might of the law and the culture will protect the time and money one invests, investment will not be a common event. The privileged few of the upper class will do some investing, but even they will limit their commitment to their enterprise for fear of confiscation. It seems almost a ritual of the passage of government in cultures where ownership is restricted to have the "shocking" revelation that high placed government officials have secreted large amounts of wealth in some country where ownership is protected. Even those who have the greatest power in the countries where the government itself is the final owner recognize that they cannot really own anything of value, so they take the wealth they accumulate by being in power and move it as quickly as possible to another country where the culture protects that wealth. This regular and almost expected stripping of wealth magnifies the poverty that is already endemic in countries where private ownership is not culturally and legally protected.

In the United States, a high cultural value has been placed on developing a system that will lead to the inclusion of nearly everyone as an owner. It is almost unfair for a culture that excludes the vast majority of its population from the right to own or invest to compete with a culture like that of the United States where we have use of the time and money of over half of our citizens to use as capital. The many countries and cultures around the world that limit the right to join in the battle and share in the wealth to only the elite few are as poorly prepared to fight on the economic battlefield as were the French knights at Agincourt.

The Industrial Revolution

The history of capitalism would certainly be incomplete without the inclusion of the painful transition set in place by the self-reliant lifestyle established by those Yeomen. Very simply, there is a distinct limit on how much land can be placed under profitable cultivation. As we have seen in the 20th century, the increased efficiency of food production in the developed countries tends to provide literally *too much* food.

The improved survival rate of the Germanic tribes brought on by the introduction of agriculture was an important factor in the fall of the Roman Empire. Also, the increased efficiency of the Yeoman farmer created a reduction in the cost, and the profitability, of farming. That reduction in the cost of food condemned the medieval manor with its landowning "lord" and semi-enslaved "crofter" to extinction.

Another factor in the population explosion of the 16th and later, the 18th centuries was the introduction of a much higher nutrition series of crops as they were imported from the new world. The potato was much easier to grow and a much higher calorie food than the barley that was previously the main staple. Corn, or maize, rapidly became the staple high-energy crop for livestock, which in turn made meat available to a far larger segment of the population. The increased nutrition in turn made people far less susceptible to disease and increased the infant survival rate dramatically.

The high infant survival rate resulted in more people to work the land than the land itself could reasonably support. That, ironically, combined with the simple fact that there was a gradual improvement in agricultural practices, caused many of those who did not own their own farmland to be in a near starvation condition. At about the same time the gentry who actually owned the land concluded that, at least in the northern half of Great Britain, sheep were going to be far more profitable than crofters.

This seemingly contradictory situation where an increase in the quality and a reduction in price of food resulted in poverty and near starvation for a large segment of the population came from a major economic shift. The Yeomen were prospering, not only as they improved the land they farmed but were actively learning methods to make it more productive. The discovery that by keeping cows in barns and covering the floors of the barns with straw, then cleaning out that straw regularly and burying it for a year before using it as fertilizer was revolutionary. The cows were fed the grain but much of the nutrition from the grain passed through the cow unused. In the process, the digestive process fixed nitrogen in the manure, which, after a year of soil composting, would actually return more nutrients to the soil than the grain was removing! In other words, the Yeoman's soil was growing richer. The Yeoman sold his excess produce for a tidy profit and received in return, money.

On the other extreme was the crofter, who had no capital and almost certainly no barn. He simply used up the soil, year by year. He had no incentive to improve the land, as the soil he improved was not his anyway. The landlord too had no incentive to make improvements as long as he had sufficient money to enjoy his "townhouse" and conduct his recreational hunts. The actual operation of the estate was in the hands of a servant who, like the crofter, could not benefit from any improvement in the soil.

With the introduction of the potato, crofters throughout Britain begin extensively using this new and wondrous tuber. While it improved their caloric intake, it also resulted in more of their children surviving, placing an even greater strain upon the poorly managed soil. The small amount of money they might receive for sale of a small part of their produce went to pay the rent to the landlord. Food was cheap for those who had money, but for those who did not, the reduction in food prices meant they were often unable to do more than feed themselves meagerly and maintain their rent.

As the crofter's productivity fell, the value of wool rose with the newly available wool mills. It soon became apparent that sheep were more valuable to the land owner than crofters and it was not long before the absentee land-lords ordered the final breach in the social contract as the descendents of the medieval serfs were forced off the land.

Adam Smith in his seminal work *The Wealth of Nations*, published in 1775 observes that if the people in a society are left free to pursue improvements in their own personal wealth and well-being however each define it, insofar as they do not unduly interfere in the well being of others, then the welfare and wealth of all in that society shall be raised as if by an invisible hand. He also noted that the often-absentee landlords had no incentive to improve their land, as they were more than satisfied with the status quo.

Karl Marx's writings of a hundred years later as he witnessed the ruthless exploitation of the masses of people who had been forced off their crofts raised a profound objection to that philosophy. His premise was that the ambition and personal desire for wealth of the individual was the principal source of the evil he saw in the society around him. In *Das Kapital* he postulated that the welfare of a society would be best served by a creating a society in which the ownership of all property, or *capital*, would be by the *state*. His underlying philosophy for his utopian society was summed up in the statement, *"From each according to their ability; to each according to their need."*

Adam Smith envisioned an ideal society in which the highest level of individual economic and personal freedom would be defended by the popularly elected government. Karl Marx envisioned a society where an elite, highly educated few would dictate the roles of all people and be entrusted with the ownership of all property. Adam Smith's ideas and philosophy were both new and revolutionary. Karl Marx was attempting to impose the ideal republic envisioned by Socrates, right down to the benign dictatorship!

The Wealth of Nations had become the written justification for all that we now call the Victorian era. Marx was not the only commentator of his day to find ill in the effects of unbridled capitalism. Charles Dickens, without building any theoretical basis for a different society wrote profound novels that expressed the misery of the dispossessed agriculture masses as they moved into the sweatshops of the emerging industrial society of England.

In the end it was Dickens who prevailed. Capitalism did not

disappear from the society of England or much of anywhere else in Western Europe and North America. As the more privileged classes became aware of the depredations of the lower class they began a movement that ultimately resulted in a dramatically improved standard of living for the "working class." Meanwhile, millions of those "wretched masses yearning to be free" immigrated to the United States where they became the foundation on which the United States would grow to become the dominant power of the 20th century.

Marxism was imposed on the Russian Empire in the early years of that same 20th century. China followed in the 1940s, and the Marxist doctrine was exported to Eastern Europe at gunpoint at about the same time. The competition began almost immediately, but it was not until after World War II, with yet another experiment in economics and militant National Socialism finally consigned to the trash heap of history, that the competition began in earnest.

Despite the occasional eruption into "hot" war in places like Korea and Viet Nam, the experiment was principally one of economics. The United States had developed a form of capitalism following the collapse of the 1930s that actually incorporated some of Marx's theory. We had a graduated income tax and a system for providing a minimum standard of living to the most poor among us. Indeed our system did, and still does, take from the people with the highest ability and gives to the people with the greatest need, but it was not Marx we followed, but Dickens.

The grand experiment that was the Soviet Union lasted for about seventy-three years before collapsing into ruin. Initially, it was a serious attempt at the utopian society that Marx envisioned, albeit with a police state to run it and clean out those who were "reactionaries." As time progressed, it gradually became far more like the medieval society from which Marx believed capitalism had evolved. Those who were part of the Communist Party elite were in effect the possessors of all property, and those who were not so privileged were the serfs and peasants. In a clear repudiation of Marx, the children of the Communist Party elite were given special educations and promoted to high levels in the ruling class.

Meanwhile, the life expectancy of the average Soviet worker shortened to around what had been experienced in the middle ages. As I have mentioned elsewhere, the damage to the economic growth of

Russia was paralleled by the devastation of the ecology. Around the world, communism was hailed as a way the cultural system of relatively primitive, pre-agricultural societies could be brought into the industrial age while retaining their communal values. In practice, it became an example of the worst of the medieval barony with life greatly enriched for the few and greatly devalued for the many.

Ultimately, Marx's theory was revealed as a futile attempt to return to the simple communal society of pre-civilized humanity. His theory was already doomed on October 15, 1415, at the battle of Agincourt. Those who owned and worked their own means of production were simply going to out-produce those who did not. In a strange sort of back handed compliment to Marx, the practice of the Yeomen in owning "shares" in the common stock of their company has become a method of raising capital that has resulted in American families today owning interests in the corporations that make up the vast majority of our economy. It is indeed "the people" who have taken the collective ownership of capitalism into their own hands.

As we move into the 21st century, the debate is no longer between collective ownership enforced by an army on one side and unbridled capitalism on the other, but only what amount of money should be collected to provide a minimum safety net for those unable to find work in a capitalist society. Even China, still supposedly communist, has adopted a largely free enterprise, capitalist economy in order to survive. It is also clear now that the imposition of communism on countries has led to a lowered standard of living and a delayed entry into the culture of benevolent capitalism we expect as our birthright.

The version of capitalism we have here in the United States is winning. Even though it is harshly criticized abroad, and even here, we see it as having failures that both frighten and frustrate us, we remain the most desirable and effective culture on earth.

The Continuing Conflict

Whenever a new cultural system emerges in the world that competes more effectively than the existing cultures, the stage is set for violence. The mere continued existence of the more effective cultural system will ultimately be fatal for the systems that preceded it.

We now know well that there was another sub-species of humans that existed in Europe and in other parts of the world before the people we now call humans existed. The *Neanderthals* were a generally larger and more robust people with a larger brain on average than we have today. From the record of their tools and their bones, we have been able to determine that they pretty much had the upper hand in Europe for at least many thousands and perhaps as many as 100,000 years. We also know that they are now extinct.

The critical issue here is that the Neanderthal culture was unable to either adapt to or compete effectively with the *culture* developed by our Cro-Magnon ancestors. The Neanderthal was larger, stronger, had equivalent tools, and was there first, but the Cro-Magnon, our ancestors, ultimately defeated them and they no longer exist.

The modern humans still were certainly using tools made from stone and bone, but as they arrived in Europe about 30,000-40,000 years ago, they brought with them the ability to use different kinds of stone for different tools, and more importantly, some of their stone tools seem to have been designed to be wielded on the end of a piece of wood. Some were what we would call *axes* today while others are clearly specialized tools for making holes in skins or creating strips of skin to be used for tying and fastening.

One of the critical differences between the artifacts found in a Neanderthal site and one occupied by our ancestors was the presence of *trading blanks!* Trading blanks are pieces of flint chipped from a larger stone that can be later shaped into individual tools, or in some cases, multiple tools. Around the encampments of humans, fragments of trading blanks and the occasional broken trading blank are common. They are made of rock types that are sometimes found hundreds, or, in some cases, over a thousand miles away. Each group of Cro-Magnon had a distinct style used in making tools that archeologists use to identify and track those groups. We now know that bands of Cro-Magnon had tools, trading blanks, and stone types that came from areas where their people had never been but which had been shaped in their own unique way locally. In other words, they were involved in *commerce!* They were applying their own unique manufacturing skills to raw materials that had to have been produced by a very distant tribe with which they may have never had contact.

The commerce can be seen not only in the materials themselves, but when some innovation in weapon or tool design appears in one part of Europe, within a very short time it is found in varied forms across the continent. Such complex changes do not appear to have come from the transfer of the tool or weapon but from passing of *information*. They could *talk,* and they could transmit new ideas about things they had never seen! At the same time, not coincidently, what anthropologists call "non-utilitarian" items make a showing. Stones and bones shaped to look like animals complete with a drilled hole to allow for them to be worn around the neck suddenly appear. These new folks, these humans, have invented *art!* They have grasped the idea of the *concept.* They have begun to create symbols to represent ideas.

Just as the ability to make any kind of tool, and probably the ability to have some rudimentary form of communication, had set the pre-human people apart from the animals, the ability to make those complex tools set the being we now call *human* apart from his larger, stronger neighbor. Considering that Neanderthals had lived in Europe and across Asia for about 100,000 years and had made little or no advances in tool technology, the rapid technological development of these new arrivals was astonishing. Within the relatively short time of a few thousand years, bone harpoons that are recognized as works of art even today graced the end of spears specifically designed to lodge in a fish's body. Those harpoon points even contain a hole for the attachment of a line so that the fish could be retrieved.

Shortly after they entered Europe, humans invented a completely new concept that we take for granted today. This amazing concept was a leap into the future that is part of the key to who we are today. Homo sapiens invented the *idea* that tools could be made for the sole purpose of creating other tools. That quantum leap in conceptualization was as great as the concept of making tools itself. Antlers were shaped, using chipped flint knives, into pressure tools for delicate flint chipping (or knapping as it is properly called). The production of the pressure tools enabled humans to create small flint points sharpened on two sides and structured to be effectively tied to the end of a shaft.

Within a relatively short time, these new inhabitants of Europe demonstrated this new conceptual ability as they began painting images of what they saw. They created murals in caves that inspire awe in all who see them even today. Some were even cleverly designed to create the illusion of movement in a painted herd of animals when seen in the flickering light of a torch or campfire.

The mere existence of a culture that could communicate faster, better, and with a depth unimaginable was a death sentence (note the pun) to the Neanderthal. The only way the Neanderthal could have continued to exist was for this new culture to either overlook them in a harsh and remote area or to have mercy on them and confine them to a reservation. Considering that it is quite clear that Neanderthals were very much into the value standard that *might is right* and being defeated meant being eaten, they were probably not going to sit still and let the humans live in peace.

The relationship between the Neanderthal and the modern humans who moved into Europe is probably not much different from the relationship of the Europeans when they moved into North America to the Indian tribes who were already there. The Europeans had a dramatic advantage over the so-called "native-Americans." *They could read and write!* The innovations started in the uncertain climate of Northern Europe combined with the ability to pass the information across time and distance gave the Europeans an advantage over the American Indian that was unstoppable. That idea, along with the concept that an individual could and should own land, and defend it, spelled the doom of the native culture. The mere existence of Western European culture in North America placed the indigenous hunter-gatherers in a losing struggle for their cultural existence.

As time and culture progressed, it was the people who learned to write that dominated those who did not. As recently as the 19th century in the United States, it was illegal in many states to teach a slave how to read and write. One of the most offensive things that Henry V did in the eyes of his fellow French-speaking overlords was to teach the Yeomen to write. Spelling and the casting of spells (sending written messages) has been the exclusive power of the elite masters in every society of civilization until the very recent times, and only then in countries where the value of the individual is recognized and the right of ownership has begun to take root.

It is notable that the free exchange of information in a literate society, a value that we cherish in the western world, is one of the first that is suppressed and even criminalized in every totalitarian regime. Our culture insists on this value and is strengthened by the intellectual contribution of everyone who has the capability to do so. Any culture that unduly restricts information flow or the education necessary to use it is doomed as surely as the Neanderthal was doomed by the arrival of Cro-Magnon.

On September 11, 2001, we once again became aware that our culture, our very freedom, is a vital threat to the cultural existence of other people. It is anything but coincidental that the buildings attacked were The World Trade Center. The attack on the Pentagon occurred at the same time but certainly did not hit us with the impact that we felt emotionally as we watched the Twin Towers burn and collapse.

For at least thirty millennia, we humans in this culture have identified ourselves, sustained ourselves, and progressed based on *trade.* Just as the first humans in Europe were smaller, weaker, and less numerous than the Neanderthal, yet drove their larger neighbors out of existence, once again, we fight a culture that is larger and has resources we depend on for survival.

It was yet again the high-speed passage of information and the development of innovative tools through that free exchange of information that allowed us to destroy the primary government that supported those who attacked us. Our existence as a culture based on the concept that all men *and women* are created equal and endowed by their creator with certain inalienable rights, among them life, liberty, and the pursuit of happiness, is deadly to any culture opposed to those values. Islamic fundamentalists would argue that by allowing the information about our culture to spread—by allowing Pizza Hut and M-TV to come into their culture—we have attacked them at the heart of their identity. Their argument would continue to reason that because we have Pizza Hut, McDonalds, and Kentucky Fried Chicken in the Islamic Arabic world, they are justified in destroying the World Trade Center. We do not agree with that reasoning and now we are engaged in a great struggle to determine whether they or we will continue on the earth. From their point of view there is no middle ground; our existence as a people and as a culture will be fatal to theirs. They must destroy us or cease to exist as who they are.

In the long term, they offer little or no threat. The ability to innovate, to invent, and to create better ways of doing anything is allowed only to a small number of *men and men alone* in their culture. Our values let us include our whole population in the ability to innovate. Just as it was the *idea* of trade and communication that ensured the weak, small, humans would triumph over the numerous, strong

Neanderthals, so it is again. Meanwhile, the very value we put on every human life will be used against us to goad us and hurt us. No matter how unconscionable the attack they make on us, it will not deter us but increase our determination to eliminate the threat to our peace and well being. That is our nature and has been for thirty millennia.

The Source of Our Strength

Tactics and valor once won wars, but that was long ago. Tactics can lose a war—not win one. It is the side with the superior supplies and supply chain that will prevail, given that the will to actually win the war is there. As Carl Von Clausewitz put it in his seminal book, *On War*, "The sole legitimate reason for war is to eliminate the enemy's ability to make war."

The armed forces with the greater production and transportation resources will win the war if that is the purpose of the war. In the American Civil War, the South had the generals and the tactics; the North had the production capability and effective economy. In World War I, it certainly can be argued that the German soldier and officer was every bit as good as the allied troops, but a superior production capability in the United States determined the outcome. In World War II, it was our economy, not our tactics, which won the war. In that war too, the individualism of the American solder was a decisive factor.

As we fight in Afghanistan, Iraq, and wherever this new war takes us, the observations of Taliban war leaders will remain valid. An Army lieutenant colonel I have known for years recently shared with me some translated excerpts from Afghan diaries captured in isolated caves after the death or departure of their owners:

> "Americans are not like the Russians. With the Russians if you kill the officer, the whole unit simply stops and waits for orders, and we are able to destroy them as they mill about. If you shoot the American leader, someone else always immediately takes charge. It may even be a private who begins giving orders, and the rest of the unit responds like a team. The more an American unit is divided into small sections, the more effective it becomes. Even a single soldier will continue fighting and is able to make intelligent decisions."

Now it is up to us. When Al Qaeda attacked us, Osama bin Laden expected us to collapse like a deflated balloon. He did indeed choose the target that would make the most impact, but like the Japanese before him, he has underestimated our resolve to remove the threat to our safety. He simply does not understand our culture. It is beyond his comprehension (presuming he still lives) that women could command units and fly fighter jets. He simply is incapable of comprehending these new beings he has encountered who know that freedom backed by trade and commerce is the source of who we are.

World War II was won in 1934 when, with the broad stock market valuation down over 80%, we did not abandon our system. Enough of our wealth remained invested that we did not collapse but rebuilt our system into a production machine that would destroy the Axis powers. The Cold War was won in 1974 when we once again did not abandon hope but remained invested in our economy. Our economy did recover and created a level of economic wealth that literally drove the Soviet Union to bankruptcy trying to match our military innovation, while we enjoyed a steadily rising standard of living.

Once again, we have placed our well being on the line for our country. Other than the professionals in our armed forces, we citizens of America cannot travel to the places on earth where our enemies hide in order to fight them. Their hope is that we will be worn down and leave them again to organize an attack on our cities. What we can do is keep our money not only invested but in the hands of those who reward good management and punish the bad. It is our economic and cultural strength that our enemies fear and that powers our war machine as we pursue them.

Investing is not just about making money. It is an act of patriotism that has the potential to produce wealth. It is as Adam Smith said in *The Wealth of Nations*, "If all [people] are left free to [invest] as they will, insofar as it does not unduly impinge upon the welfare of another, then the welfare of that entire society will be lifted as if by an invisible hand." It is up to us to continue to provide the wisely invested capital that creates the wealth that we shall use to eliminate the threat to our existence and that we shall go on from there to improve the well being of those we defeat. That is our way.

Chapter 5 - Markets, Market Behavior, and the Nature of the Universe

Markets

The first kind of market is the kind of market we create when we have a garage sale. It is probably the most ancient kind of market, and although it is pretty much a one-time event, there is a certain linkage to the other garage sales at other times. Most folks who decide to have a garage or yard sale do not go out to garage sales around the town and determine appropriate prices for all of the items they plan to offer. Rather, they make a rough estimate of the value they believe they would assign to an item if *they* were going to buy it at someone else's sale. It is also generally understood at such an event that the prices marked on items are not fixed but quite negotiable. It is the *buyer* at that type of market who provides the connectivity and who tends to set the price. It is, in effect, a buyer's market.

Another example of a market is the local farmer's market where produce growers meet to offer their fruits and vegetables to the public. Here again there is room for negotiating, but the rules are more formal and a certain predictability of price enters into the equation. At certain times of the year there will be an abundance of a given product, such as apples. During that time the price of apples will decline because the apple seller is quite interested in getting rid of his abundance of apples before they spoil, and the buyer has an abundance of sellers to choose from, not to mention that the buyer may be getting tired of eating apples! Generally, the seller is the professional here and the buyer is the amateur resulting in a "seller's market."

The real estate market for residential homes is yet another example of a low volume market, but this time with a professional "market maker." While there are many homes bought and sold each year, nationally or even locally, the market value of a given home at any moment is unknown. It is common to have extensive negotiation with a number of buyers before the home is sold. Here too, seasonality comes into play. In most communities, the spring and summer are the times when there are the most willing buyers. That rotates around the school year and the desire by families with children in school to not interrupt the school year. Other seasonal issues come into play in a less obvious way. In times of good weather, people will commonly pay more for a home than during uncomfortable weather. Because borrowed money plays such a large role in home purchases and sales, prices on houses will often move inversely to interest rates as well. This comes from a fact almost unique to the modern developed free enterprise democracy. Homes are bought not on the basis of the property price but on the amount of the payment on the loan!

All these markets have several things in common. First, each item offered on the market is different. The difference may be small, as in apples, or quite large, as in flea markets, yard sales, or homes, but each item is unique. Second, the transactions either for the buyer or seller are sufficiently spaced as to cause the value at any given moment to be in question. Third, the difference between the offering price and the purchase price is settled either by direct or indirect negotiation.

This infrequent, negotiated price, unique item market is called an "inefficient" market. It is inefficient in that it is not at all uncommon for either the buyer or the seller to give or receive value quite out of proportion to the intrinsic value of the item. An extreme case would be the possibly mythological tale of a Gutenberg Bible bought at a flea market for $10. No small numbers of people in the United States either make or supplement a living by knowing the intrinsic value of antiques on one market and then searching for the valued items in the garage and yard sale market. This practice of buying on one market in order to sell on another market is called *market arbitrage.*

Obviously there are other markets. Perhaps the best-known market is the New York Stock Exchange (NYSE). That venerable institution is traditionally held to have started under a tree on the edge of town where the local holders of shares from joint stock companies would gather to exchange and sell their commercial interests. That practice was a clear descendant of the "faire" markets of old England where the Yeomen and their descendants would do the same.

As time progressed and the volume of shares or cattle that were to be sold increased and the means of transportation improved, the markets came to be held more and more often. Ultimately, in the case of the NYSE and other securities markets, the market was expected to be open each day for exchange. As the volume continued to increase, the expectation further came to be that one could readily purchase or sell any of a number of "listed" shares—shares of those companies with a sufficient number of shares in the hands of enough people that there was a steady business in trading that issue. Such a market rapidly became both "efficient" in that the current "market price" was *readily* available (could be *read* on the "big board"), and *liquid*, in that the *flow* of shares to money and money to shares was consistent and reliable.

Once again, we have created something in our culture that has defined the future. By the standards of history and the rest of the world a residential real estate transaction in the United States is a simple and speedy task. By the standards of our society, it is a slow and unpleasant experience. The conversion of money into capital in the form of corporate shares and the conversion to money of those corporate shares was once a slow, cumbersome, and unusual event. In the 21st century we simply assume the nearly instantaneous transaction from capital to coin and from coin to capital. This concept of *liquidity* in a capital market is one of the factors that create the high standard of living, or wealth, that we have come to take for granted.

Another artifact that remains in our language is the concept of "fair market value." That devolves from the word "fair" which harks back to the Old English *faeger* meaning, "pure and free from moral stain" and the Latin *f-ria* from which we get "feast."

At the "faire," items were sold in an *auction market,* as is the New York Stock Exchange today. In other words, when the farmer bought or sold at the "faire" or "fair", he would receive or pay a price for his livestock or his common stock that was based on the value assigned to the item by the highest bidder. If his purchase was not a necessity, he could be sure that he would not pay more than he planned for the item, and if he were selling, he could be confident he was getting the best price. That best price was then "fair," as it was pure and unspoiled by virtue of not only being from an auction, or negotiated, market but was on a "feast" or holy day, at a holy site, where the warring and conflict of the clans was set aside in the interest of "fairness."

Fairs were such important economic events that a significant body of law emerged concerning behavior at the *faire market.* When we who live in the United States approach the issue of either purchasing or selling something, we do so with certain assumptions. Just as the concept of actually having the *right* to own personal property is assumed in our society as a norm, so is the framework that supports that right. Over at least the past 600 years, a body of law and custom has emerged that is so well established in our culture that it has become invisible until it is violated. From all of this historical cultural investment, we have the concept of "fair market value" rendered from an efficient and liquid market and have come to consider it our birthright.

Perhaps one of the most fascinating assumptions in our society today is the assumption of "full (whole, holy) and fair disclosure." At the beginning of the 20th century, a person making a purchase of *anything* in the United States was subject to the standards that still prevail in most of the world. That standard was embodied in the law as it had been since the very establishment of law. It is best stated in the Latin that indicates only a small part of the age of the assumption: *Caveat Emptor. Buyer beware* was the warning of the wise when entering the markets of Rome and for the millenniums to follow.

Here in the United States, and to a lesser extent in Western Europe and Japan, this new standard called *full and fair disclosure* has emerged as the standard of conduct. The principal difficulties arise when the purchaser assumes the second standard when only the first applies. The most obvious recent example of *caveat emptor* was the dramatic growth of the Enron Corporation and its sale of shares to the public that, as it turns out, were quite a different issue from what they were purported to be. Despite numerous laws, the purchase of a used car is still no small risk, but we make the assumption that the purchase of a used share of stock or a house that has had several owners is a "no-surprise" transaction. Assumptions in any area are dangerous. When we take on debt worth a year or more of income, as in a home purchase using a mortgage or stake our financial future on a purchase or series of purchases of securities, they can be more than just dangerous.

Investing without understanding the underlying assumptions is probably the most expensive thing a person will ever do. It has led to the financial ruin of the well-connected and sophisticated as often as the common and naïve. I have developed a meaning for the word "assume" that I use in my firm and might well be a good one for any investor. *Assume* means (to me) *A(h), su(e) me.* As a professional, any assumptions I make are an invitation to be sued. As a purchaser of goods and services, assumptions are an invitation to go through the rather intense negative event of having to file suit against the seller. As an investor, and thereby an owner of an interest in something, bad assumptions might cause *you* not only to suffer the loss of your investment, but, in some cases, even place you in the position of being legally responsible for whatever it was you invested in!

Fortunately, in the United States there are laws in place that allow us to avoid many of the risks that are inherent in investing. Once again though, we have come to take these laws for granted. Many investors have suffered from the very hard lessons learned when we stray away from the safety of those laws and rules very carefully established three quarters of a century ago.

The Corn-Hog Cycle

One of the sayings that have remained with us from the days of the mainly agricultural fair market is a warning against buying a "pig in a poke." While most of us will readily understand the meaning of "pig" the term "poke" is not so clear. A poke is simply a sack. Normally, the person buying a pig for the production of meat or even other pigs would examine a pig very carefully before purchase. Of course that required some knowledge of pigs and what to look for in order to avoid purchasing one that was not well. Those who really didn't know what they were looking for in the first place would purchase the pig in the poke, or sack, and not examine the animal until after they returned home, if at all.

Today we make the assumption that the pigs, and the pork, have a certain minimum standard enforced by the United States Department of Agriculture. That assumption was only valid in the latter half of the 20th century. Prior to that time *caveat emptor* applied. The assumption before the USDA seal of approval was that you were sufficiently familiar with swine or that your local butcher was careful about selecting the right pigs to butcher and inspected the meat himself.

In the first case, there was also the issue that you, as a person who routinely bought pigs, not only knew quite a lot about the issue but could rely on the fact that the farmer from whom you were purchasing pigs had an interest in making you happy. Buying a pig from a stranger was generally considered a bad idea. In the second case, your local butcher bought the pigs and qualified as a knowledgeable pig buyer, and had a substantial interest in seeing that you did not get sick from eating pork he sold you.

Market Behavior

In order to understand modern markets let's take an imaginary trip back in time to the medieval period and view one of the early free markets that developed as the modern era began. In this case the market we explore is one of the most studied in history, the market for swine, or hogs. Even hundreds of years ago the swine market was noted to have "cycles" that moved as mysteriously as the floods of the Nile must have seemed to do before the invention of the calendar. Today we understand that the annual monsoon rains in the African highlands were the source of the Nile floods, so too we now understand that market cycles have a cause and effect relationship. In both cases the cause is often quite invisible to the person most directly affected by the change in level.

From the end of the medieval period until the mid 20th century, during periods of high hog prices it was not uncommon for newcomers to enter the "pork" market. Seeing the high price of hogs (swine) on the livestock market and noting the price they were paying for pork at the butcher's, people would consider the potential profit in raising a few hogs for the market as a worthy expenditure of their hard earned cash.

Remember that this was a time when refrigerators had yet to be invented, and it was not at all uncommon for even city dwellers to have a few chickens or even pigs. A higher percentage of the population owned livestock then than own common stock now. In other words, there were quite a large number of folks who were reasonably convinced that they could improve on their financial status by buying and selling stock. The fact that it was livestock and not common stock actually made little difference.

We generally don't notice markets or the prices at which things sell on a market until we either have a desire to effect a transaction in that market or hear someone report that they have either made a great profit or loss. Pigs and stock have a lot in common. Actually, as pigs are livestock then they both are pretty much the same thing. In both cases, the objective is to achieve growth that will allow the owner to sell the stock at a higher price in the future.

A person with the resources to raise pigs into hogs to be sold on the market, and who may have done so on a small scale for his own family's consumption, might well notice one year at the fair market that the price of hogs had gone up. He might have even heard a neighbor rejoicing in the profit he made from the sale of his hogs at that same market. With a little investigation he might notice that the price of the grain used to feed hogs was quite low. After his day at the fair as he visited the local pub or beer tent at the fair, he might sit down to have some refreshments and be pleasantly surprised to find the price of beer was quite reasonable when compared with last year. In his discussions with the other small farmers that had gathered for the fair and celebration afterward, it was quite clear that they too were thinking about buying a few pigs to raise. With all the facts lined up and his logic confirmed by the consensus of his peers, it would only be reasonable to consider that if he bought a few pigs (which he noted were also unusually high in price) and fed them until they grew into hogs, he too might profit from the increased price of swine.

While he is raising those pigs he might feel very certain that his decision was correct as the price of grain continued to be low, and the pigs could even be fed the vegetable scraps and plant stalks from his family garden to further lower the cost. As the pigs reached maturity, he had to make the decision about whether to sell them or breed them. Noting that the price of hogs had increased even more since he bought the pigs, he might well just keep the hogs and breed them to multiply his wealth. With the knowledge that was once common to most of our ancestors, he knew that he should time the birth of the pigs to occur in the spring so that more of the young pigs would make it to adulthood, and they would grow to marketable age by the fall fair market.

When that first litter reached adulthood, odds were he would sell only a few, still retaining pigs to breed in light of the still high price of hogs. At about this point, he would note that the price of feed was rising dramatically. "One more year," he might think, "and then I will sell them all and have enough money to…." All during that year though he would notice the price of feed was continuing to go up faster and faster. There was no doubt now that he would need to sell those hogs before the expense of keeping them was so high he could no longer afford to do so.

As the fall approached and it became apparent that he was no longer going to be able to afford the upkeep of his herd of hogs, our nascent pig farmer looked forward eagerly to his upcoming reward at the fall fair market. Getting the hogs to the market was quite a chore, but he was so enthused about the wealth he knew he was soon to enjoy that he suffered it more than willingly. As he approached the market, he was surprised but reassured to see that there were quite a few other farmers herding their hogs in the same direction. He even might think at this point that with so many others doing the same thing, the market must be really good for hogs.

As he attempted to use the pens at the fair, he was surprised to find that he would have to watch his pigs in the field because the pens were already full. Then, when it came time to actually put his pigs up for sale, he would have to wait in line behind several other farmers. Rumors begin circulating that the price of hogs was lower than he had thought, but he shrugged it off with the thought that even if he got only most of what he had hoped for, he would be better off than he had ever been.

Sadly, when he finally reached the auction, he found that not only was the price down for the hogs that had been sold before his, but he was only able to sell half his hogs, and at a price well below what he had paid for the original pigs. Through great effort, he managed to get rid of most of the rest of his hogs in trade for things he might be able to use, but ultimately, he brought home many more pigs than he had figured on keeping. His family was at least able to have more salt pork that winter, but he was convinced that the gods had conspired to take the opportunity for wealth away from him.

Our farmer had as much clue as to what was going on as the investor in the grip of the dot-com mania. What the farmer didn't understand was the same thing that happened to the "high tech" investor hundreds of years later.

The reason the price of hogs was high in the first place was there was a shortage of hogs. If there is a demand for something and it is less available than it was in the past, either because of increased demand or reduced supply, the relative value of the thing increases. People are then willing to spend more of the money they have available on it and the price rises. Agriculture is a relatively easy area to understand, as the amount of food we eat does not normally vary greatly once we have enough that we are no longer in danger of starving. Basic food source items vary in price mainly from variations in supply, not demand. For whatever it is worth, economists refer to this phenomenon as "*inelasticity of demand.*"

Our supposed farmer noted the high price of hogs and did a quick calculation based on that price and what he estimated it would cost to raise hogs. In that calculation he included the observation that the price of the type of grain used to feed hogs was low. Thus, he made a rational observation that he could raise hogs for far less than the price for which hogs were then selling. With the price of pigs being normally quite a lot lower than hogs, he figured that he could buy pigs, feed them, and then sell them at the market for a considerable profit.

Of course with our clear hindsight, we now know that he was only partly right. What he did was probably the most common error of investors. He failed to ask a series of critical questions, all beginning with "Why." Why was the price of hogs high? Why was the price of grain low? The high price of hogs was a direct result of a shortage of hogs available for sale in the market. That shortage came from the same reaction our farmer had after his failure to achieve the profit he anticipated. Not only was he disappointed about profit, he may well have spent more on the pigs and feed than he received back in money, trade, or even meat. Such an experience is commonly followed by a period of investor disgust. In other words, the same kind of common sense that told him that getting into the hog business was a near certain route to wealth was now telling him that there was some kind of conspiracy against him that would prevent him from ever profiting from raising hogs.

What actually happened was a natural cycle based in several time periods. Agriculture economists have even given it a name, *"the corn-hog cycle."* Over the centuries since its discovery, the length of the cycle has varied from five to seven years when measured by different economists in different areas of the world, but it does seem to have a great deal of persistence and reality.

If we begin the cycle at the bottom of the hog element, we can see what happened to our farmer. The oversupply of hogs where we end our story has dropped the market price of swine below the production price. Farmers then turn away from swine production, as it has become, in their minds, a losing proposition. That rising price of feed that has helped generate the loss to the hog farmer was a result of the fact that many more hogs were being bred and fed. The grain farmer cannot immediately react to the increased demand that emerged each spring as the hog farmers began to order feed for their new litters of pigs. The grain farmer has to determine what will go in each field in the fall or at latest, the end of winter, thus was always at least year behind the demand. With demand higher than supply, the hog farmers had to outbid each other to obtain the grain. The resulting high price would pay for transportation of grain from outside of the area, but it would also convince the grain farmer that he should plant more acreage next year in grain for hogs.

Meanwhile, the hog farmers, noting the high and rising price of grain, decide to reduce the size of their herds by selling more on the market. Because all of them are affected by the same grain price, a sell-off in hogs will come in the fall when the hogs mature and the market is held. That sell-off depressed prices so that fewer hogs are raised in the next year. The collapse of hog breeding and feeding leaves the grain farmer with not only a surplus of grain but perhaps even far too much land planted in hog feed for the following year! In the days when the prime hog feed was barley, at least the farmer could sell it to the breweries as it is the primary ingredient in the making of beer.

You can guess what happens next. The price of beer goes down and the resulting dearth of hogs results in a dramatic increase in the price of hogs at the next fall fair while the price of grain drops below the cost of production. This, of course, causes new entries in the hog market to conclude that raising a few hogs seems like a pretty good idea, and the cycle starts again.

Everything that happened to the hog farmer is common to the equity investor in the late 20th and early 21st century. While common stock does not have to be fed, as more and more people choose to buy into the stock market, it is not unusual for interest rates to rise on bank loans and on short-term bonds. The money the investor has invested in stocks could be earning a higher and higher annual interest rate in short-term positions. It is not unusual then for the investor to make the decision that he has gained as much from his stock holding as he desired and to shift his money to the now attractive interest bearing positions. During the time he had the money in stocks, he may very well be computing the cost of the interest "lost" by not earning the short-term rates. That, in effect, is the cost of "feed" for the stock investor.

The energy crisis in California resulted from the same cycle. As California deregulated the production and sale of electricity, the legislature forbade the local power companies from entering into long term contracts with their suppliers, fearing the power companies would be able to purchase power cheaply and then raise the price charged to consumers if their was a shortage. Further, to ensure the "greedy" capitalists did not profit from deregulation, the state government also fixed the consumer price for electricity. The end result was that when oil prices rose and demand for power rose as well, the power companies had not been able to build plants to keep up with the demand, nor did they have long term contracts for purchase of power. They were forced to buy power on the "spot" market at ultra-high prices but were unable to pass that charge on to the user. Rolling blackouts, bankruptcies, and a state in a fiscal crisis resulted from this classic failure to understand market forces.

The Business Cycle

There is another cycle that occurs in our economy that tends to drive the prices of companies represented by those stocks as well as most of the items we buy and sell in that economy. That cycle has been around as long or longer as the *corn-hog cycle*. In fact, the corn-hog cycle is part of this larger cycle. Most commonly, it is referred to as the business cycle.

As in our farmer's case, the business cycle is supposed to be primarily caused by the lag between a supplier sensing a change in demand, as in the example of the grain farmer, and the ability to change production to meet that demand. An otherwise inexplicable rise and fall in grain prices thus can be understood when one notes the rise and fall of demand from the hog farmers. The important thing here is that these cycles feed off of each other and, in turn, affect other commodities.

In the developed world, the largest demand is not for food or even fuel, historically the big movers of the economy, but in consumer items. Prior to the 20th century, if a family had sufficient food, shelter, and fuel to cook the food and warm them in the winter, that pretty much summarized their needs in life. With the nobility composing less than 1% of the population, the desire for the "finer" things in life was a very small element in the whole economy.

Perhaps the greatest economic change in history since the fall of the Roman Empire occurred in the 20th century in America, Western

Europe, and to a lesser extent, around the eastern rim of Asia. Most of the population attained the living standards and expectations of nobility. It is hard for us, living as we are in that society, to understand the profound implications of that change. For all of the history of the world and even today for the vast majority of the world, what we refer to as extreme poverty is and was the absolutely normal status. Having enough to eat to avoid starvation and having freedom from the fear of imminent death from the natural events of the world was beyond rare, it was imaginable only in heaven. We live today in a society and economy that very closely resemble the description of heaven in most of the religions of the world.

Just as within the rather oversimplified agricultural economy described above, the hog farmer drove the cycle, so the consumer, the nobility of the 21st century, is the principal driver of the business cycle. Unlike the hog farmer, the consumer is not looking for something to purchase to increase his or her wealth, or more often to fend off the threat of starvation. The consumer looks for things to buy to increase his or her *happiness.*

A major shift occurred when the transportation technology known as "the railroad" changed the market for meat. If a family decided to have beef for a meal instead of pork, the demand for pork dropped and so, ultimately, did the price. Meanwhile, the cattle being shipped needed feeding if they were to remain healthy to provide that beef. Grazing such large numbers of cattle was very impractical, so they were off loaded at intervals in their journey and fed grain. Because they arrived at their final destination in trainloads, with the next train load of cattle to arrive days or even weeks in the future, they again needed feeding in the slaughterhouse pens. The grain that was fed to the cattle was the same grain used to fatten up a hog for market. Thus, the price of grain rose even as the price of pork fell.

This is an important issue. The price changes that our medieval farmer noted were *cyclical* changes. They happened over and over because of our tendency to not remember history. An astute speculator or investor might note the cyclical nature of the changes and elect to purchase hogs or even pigs at the point where the farmers were dumping them on the market at below-production prices. By then holding (and feeding) the hogs for a year or so, the speculator might be able to sell the hogs at a much higher price without ever getting into the actual hog raising business. If the speculator were particularly astute, he might even hire one of the desperate farmers to feed his hogs for the necessary year.

This speculator is called a *stabilizing speculator*. He provides a buyer at the low point of the market, thereby keeping it from plunging to zero. He again provides a seller when the market price is abnormally high and limits the upper end of the price range. Just as importantly, the farmers who observe the activity of the stabilizing speculator may just learn from it and plan their hog breeding, feeding, and sale activities to take advantage of times when hog prices are higher. This is a wonderful attribute of the free enterprise system. It ultimately often results in a relatively smooth price variation and a fairly steady supply of things like pork.

It would seem like the speculator has it made. All he has to do is step back and "read the play" as they say in football. He would seem to have no more risk than the farmer and yet, has far less involvement and investment in the product than does the producer of the product. In fact, the stabilizing speculator is a critically valuable element in a market. If the speculator is left free to buy and sell, he will ultimately smooth out both the issue of having someone to buy the product from the producer and provide product to the consumer in and out of season.

The speculator is also at great risk for loss. If the cycle of pork and corn prices changes because of weather, disease, or some other outside event, he stands to lose the money he has invested in the product. The other side of the issue is that the speculator has to have a great deal of money compared with the farmer, and he probably has little or no use for the product if he cannot sell it. The stabilizing speculator thus becomes a "market maker" providing a market to buy or sell at times when the natural market is either non-existent or is distorted by production cycle times.

This wonderful mechanism breaks down though as soon as a new technology is introduced and put into use. In the cyclical market we assumed that nothing of any consequence was changing. Nature can certainly throw an element of uncertainty in the market cycle, but once the weather stabilizes, the cycle has a strong tendency to reassert itself. As soon as we change one of the elements in that market permanently though, all the assumptions we relied on before may disappear or even reverse!

The introduction of the railroad dramatically changed the market for hogs. Before this, we had some very simple elements in our equation: the hogs, hog farmers, grain, grain farmers, and speculators. Added to make things interesting was a wild card—the weather. Now, though, as the railroad comes to town, we need to factor in the cattle rancher, the trail drive, the extension of the railroad, and last and ultimately most important, the new ability to make a choice between beef and pork.

A speculator watching the pork market or participating in some aspect of pork production would see the price of grain start to rise and the price of hogs start to fall. Historically that would be a signal that too many hogs are being produced, and the opportunity to buy speculative hogs was approaching. It might well happen that with the sudden introduction of beef into the local meat markets, the slaughter houses might have a sale on beef to get people more used to eating it. This would cause the price of hogs to fall even further and might even result in an early collapse in hog prices. The speculator, confident in the repetitiveness of the corn-hog cycle, might well make a substantive purchase of hogs at what he presumed to be a low point in the cycle.

Soon the speculator would be in for a very unpleasant surprise. The price of hogs was indeed dropping and probably would continue dropping further than he had seen before. The real shock would be when the price of hogs did not recover to the highs seen previously. Instead, the hog prices might well stay in a range near the traditional bottom of cyclical prices! Hog farmers will be very slow to change to anything else as they have been doing the same thing for many generations through good times and bad. They will unconsciously assume that this is just another temporary downturn in the price of hogs. Success was achieved in the past by weathering the downturns and being there with hogs when the price went up. Their continued production of hogs at the pre-beef rate will ensure that the price of hogs will stay low.

Meanwhile, many of the traditional speculators and most of the newer speculators in the hog market will be eliminated, which is a nice way of saying bankrupted or financially ruined. One of the reasons the railroads, the slaughterhouses, and the cattle ranchers decided to spend the rather substantial amounts of capital to introduce beef to the market was the rising urban population. Breeding and raising hogs is a smelly proposition. People who are well off enough to live in town generally don't enjoy that smell. The hog farms, as a result, were being forced farther and farther from an increasing demand for pork. These elements caused the price of pork in the city to steadily rise over a period of time. Ultimately, the price became high enough that the high cost of transporting cows to market became profitable.

The same thing happened in the world oil market the in the early 1970s. As the world economy industrialized after World War II, the price of oil slowly and steadily rose. At the same time the dollar was inflating as America attempted to fight a war on poverty, a war in Viet Nam, and the cold war without raising taxes. From the perspective of the producers in Southwest Asia, the oil companies were steadily lowering the cost of oil they were buying from them while raising the retail price in the developed world. Using the 1967 Arab-Israeli War as a pretext, the Organization of Oil Producing Countries (OPEC) nationalized the oil fields, shut off the supply of oil and then raised the price fourfold.

The dramatic increase in the price of what had been a cheap commodity shocked the world into a global recession. Using a well-organized discipline, OPEC manipulated the amount of oil being sold from their fields to keep the price of petroleum high. The price of oil rose in the years that followed from $7 per barrel to as high as $40. In America, gasoline went from thirty-five cents to one dollar per gallon in the space of a few months and on to nearly two dollars in some areas over the years that followed, before declining to the levels we see today. With a known finite supply of oil discovered in the world and the consumption rate rising, pundits made the assumption that the world would effectively run out of easy to pump and deliver oil by the year 2000.

Oil and gas exploration along with exploitation of existing fields in the United States hit a fever pitch. Hundreds of billions of dollars were poured into oil and gas partnerships to take advantage of the coming high price of oil. Some of the most respected writers on such subjects suggested that the price per barrel of oil would soon hit $100 where it would either remain if we practiced good conservation or rise to unknown heights if we did not.

Thirty years later, the price per barrel of oil was around $20 and even that $20 was the equivalent of only about $7 after adjusting for

Jeff McClure

inflation over the three-decade period. In other words, the price of oil at the end of the 20th century was not the expected \$100 to \$200 per barrel predicted by those who assumed technology would not reduce the cost of oil production, but was almost exactly the same level it was before the Arab oil embargo.

This was not the first time the price of oil had gone through a dramatic increase. The impression that the price was on the way up again as it had done a half-century earlier was based on the assumption that no new technology would emerge to change things. In reality, the rising price of oil and the potential profits associated with it enabled research and development to proceed in the one culture in the world that associates change with virtue. Today, oil is being extracted profitably from under the North Sea off the east coast of Scotland, from the shores of the Arctic Ocean in Alaska, and from the tar in Venezuela that once was considered good only as an ingredient in road surfacing material. According to published reports in the major news magazines and newspapers, the quantity of oil discovered or reclassified as profitably recoverable in the last two years dramatically exceeds the volume of all the known oil on earth in the year 1975.

Important for the future is the fact that the change in refining and transportation technology now will allow oil to be extracted and delivered profitably from these "new" fields and sources at a price of \$12 per barrel or, in 1975 dollars, \$4 per barrel. Meanwhile, the threat of an oil embargo combined with the threat of high oil prices has changed the way our economy works so that our consumption of oil per dollar of gross domestic product (national business production) has been cut by 75% over the last 30 years.

The change in the price of oil that started in the early 1970s with the Arab oil embargo was not a cyclical change any more than was the change in the price of hogs and grain that occurred in the late 19th century. Those permanent, structural changes are referred to as *secular changes*. The resulting economic displacement in the market, which is a nice way of saying that a lot of people lost a lot of money and a few made a lot of money, is called a *secular bear*.

With almost clock-like precision, the United States economy had business cycle swings every ten years in the last half of the 19th century. This high level of volatility was brought on by the dramatic drop in the cost of transportation generated by the continent-wide expansion of the railroads. The expanded markets and sources of materials and products that resulted from that expansion introduced new elements into the economy at a rate never before seen. At the same time, the cost of information dropped nearly as fast as newspapers and books were printed in faster and more economical presses and the telegraph and Teletype revolutionized information flow.

Even as all that was happening, the extension of the railroad to more and more towns in the West made getting cattle to market less expensive. The explosive growth in the number of family farms, particularly near the railroad towns, reduced the cost of food across the country as a combination of inexpensive transportation and large number of individual farms increased the supply.

Ultimately, by the first few decades of the 20th century, the price of agricultural commodities had once again fallen below the cost of production for farmers in marginal growing areas. The food price decline that began after the American Civil War was anything but cyclical. Within that steadily falling price, the same fluctuations continued to appear every five to seven years in the price of hogs, but were nowhere near as severe and each recovery in price seemed to be lower than the last one.

The images of the socioeconomic crisis of the 1930s are familiar to anyone who has studied that time in history. That event marked the beginning of a great migration from agriculture. Because people tend to remain doing whatever worked for them before, the transition was long and painful. It was not until the threat represented by the potentially negative outcome of World War II that the American population began to leave the farm in mass. By the end of the 20th century, the individual family farm had become an oddity of almost museum-like qualities as agribusiness corporations assumed the role of food providers. The continued existence of the family farm in the 21st century United States, Europe, and Japan is largely if not completely a result of government subsidies in the form of substantial tax abatements and direct payments to farmers. The family farm is the basis of the nation state and all that we are today. It is hard for a people to let go of an institution of such cultural significance, so we agree to pay people to continue to act out that which we value culturally.

The whole process is a story of a *market*. This specific market was, and is, a hog market, but markets are what have enabled us to transform our living standards and our lives to actually bring into reality the intangible concept, "pursuit of happiness."

Participating in that market or any market is part of the generation of this wondrous economy. The question is whether you participate in that market as a gambler, an investor, or are just one of those who add value to the market for others to use. In some form, you will participate in the markets that make up our society just as you participate in the food market when you purchase food. If you have a retirement account, an insurance policy, an annuity, or a mortgage, your money is "in the market."

The whole underlying economy is a *market* as much as the fair where the farmer brought his pigs or the New York Stock Exchange. If you are working for an employer who pays you either by the hour or by the year, you are still selling on the market just as you are buying on the market as you stop by the local convenience store to pick up some milk and bread. Along the way you may unconsciously shop the price of gasoline as you select the station where you will fill up your tank.

Our very nature as human beings conspires against us as we attempt to invest. As a species we have survived the physical dangers encountered by our ancestors by practicing certain behaviors that are not only counter productive for an investor but also seem almost planned to lead to failure. Our ancestors had to deal with a world that changed mysteriously, but the changes were largely or completely caused by *outside forces of nature.* As they dealt with those changes and the danger they represented, they developed a complete methodology that worked very well.

As we charge into the 21st century we are dealing with another set of changes, but these are not generated by *outside* forces but rather by us, the ones who are affected by them! If your ancestors noted that the number of game animals, edible roots, berries, and other plants were steadily decreasing in the valley where they had been living, they got out. If they decided to hang on a bit longer to see what happened, they probably didn't get the chance to become your ancestors. As the visible produce of that valley became less valuable, to stick around was to starve.

The process they used to decide whether or not to move is still in wide use today. It works well for fishing, hunting, or gold prospecting, but it is a sure way to disaster for investing. Our model for ineffective investing, the speculative medieval hog farmer, used the ancient decision making model to shape his decision that ultimately led to a perhaps ruinous loss in the hog breeding business. What he encountered was amplified in the South Sea bubble of 1720 and clearly duplicated in the dot-com bubble and collapse of Enron (discussed in chapter 6).

Our hunter-gatherer and even our early agricultural ancestors, who formed the words and culture we use today to deal with the world, learned rather quickly the importance of depending on their fellow tribe members to help them make decisions. In that time of very limited changes from generation to generation, the wisdom of the elders was a valuable commodity. Not only had the elders been around quite a while to see the errors and successes of quite a few folks, they also were the repository of the wisdom of those who had lived before. Along with the wisdom of the elders, any decisions of consequence were left to consensus.

Today that same decision process can lead to ruin. If we wait to "get in the market" until we have abundant "confirmation" of the profits that are available, there is a very high probability we will join with our start up hog farmer for an exciting ride up and a very unpleasant decline in the *market value* of our investments. Confirmation that either "the market" or the ownership of the stock in a given company is profitable either means that people have seen a substantial paper gain in the value of their investment or they are actually realizing that profit as they sell. Either way, "getting in" at that time is by definition "buying high" and a sure fire way to see the market value of your "hogs" drop substantially.

If we listen to the wisdom of our elders, odds are they won't have a lot. They perhaps learned valuable lessons in an economy where the typewriter was high-tech and staying loyal to a corporation for one's entire working lifetime was the norm. Today, hanging on to the "tried and true" generally means being left behind, and loyalty to a corporation is a nearly sure fire way to wind up being "laid-off" in middle age. Montgomery Ward, the Amazon.com of the 19th century lasted for over a hundred years, and that represented stability to our forebears. Yet, if you had remained a loyal worker or investor in that venerable institution as the last decade of the 20th century dawned, today you would have lost any time, money, or loyalty you had expended on a now bankrupt company. The same applies to a host of other institutions and corporations.

Today, lay-offs in time of economic uncertainty are a way of life. Workers are not given the opportunity to buy the stock of a company as often as they are given the option to purchase the stock at today's price at some point in the future. The time of the company-funded, defined benefit retirement plan has passed, and we are reliant on a 401(k) or some similar device. In the recent past, companies that had been around most or all of the 20th century were considered to be as stable as could be. A man could depend on the company and the company could depend on the man. That has gone the way of the company town and the company store. Today, we jump from company to company in seek of better opportunities, pay, and benefits. The company has about as much loyalty as the worker, if the bottom line can be improved by laying off workers, it will happen. If switching companies can improve our bottom line, it will happen.

Just as our relationship with the corporations that employ us has changed beyond recognition, so has the issue of investing. As the loyal employees of Enron or Arthur Anderson recently found, having a substantial amount of your financial worth tied up in your employer can be hazardous to your financial health! Sure the possibility of hitting the ball out of the park by focusing your future on a single issue may be there, but it is wise to remember that Babe Ruth, once the home run king, now only holds one major league record—*strikeouts!*

In our rapidly changing economic and social universe, the consensus will most often be reached just as things change. Because of the value shift that has occurred from one generation to the next, following "dear-old-dad's" wisdom may just destroy your chances to ever have a comfortable retirement.

A couple of years ago, a couple came to see me for assistance in planning their financial future. One of their greatest fears was arriving at retirement age and not having enough money coming in to allow them to live a comfortable life. They were uncertain about the future of social security but thought that the husband's military retirement was pretty much a sure thing.

I reviewed their actual holdings. About 90% of their portfolio was in a single issue. The wife had told me that her father was making gifts to her and her husband every year of stock from the company in which he was an executive. It became quickly apparent that the hope they had for early financial independence was principally coming from these gifts.

In my recommendations, I strongly encouraged them to sell the stock her father had given them and diversify into a series of professionally managed accounts. I pointed out the danger of "having all your eggs in one basket" and, acknowledging the possibility that her father's employer might hit a home run, also pointed out that it might strike out. Further, I noted that because she had said her parents' wealth was almost entirely tied up in this one company, if there were a catastrophic failure of the company, they just might have to wind up helping their parents in their elder years.

Only the husband returned to the next meeting, and that was only to tell me that his wife's father had "erupted" at the thought of their selling the stock he had given them. He was completely confident that "his" company was going to do great things and that I was only trying to line my own pockets in advising them to sell the stock. He returned the documents I had provided and terminated the relationship.

The name of the company could have been Montgomery Ward, K-Mart, TWA, Pan Am, MCI, or a host of others. The father, in this case, had been an employee of Enron before it was a new-age company and had tremendous loyalty to his employer.

Asset Allocation: A Defense Against the Cycles

Is there a defense against these cycles? Because we know that the cycles in market prices of various commodities such as hogs, grain, and beer are generated by the overexpansion of capacity by first one sector of the economy and then another, it would seem to make sense that we could take on the role of the stabilizing speculator fairly easily by just stepping back from the fray and making strategic purchases and sales.

As you may have guessed, it isn't that easy. First, the cycles in just the corn-hog relationship vary quite a lot in both length and depth, and that is before we throw in beef and changes in transportation technology. Add in today's environmental laws and the cycle becomes even more varied and unpredictable. There is little question that the business cycle is driven by supply and demand and that a major factor in the cycle is the lag between the actuality of change in one or the other and the time the producer senses it. Beyond that, there are so many apparently random factors that influence the length and depth of the cycle that the cycle itself becomes questioned by the mathematicians. Several prominent economists have denied that there even *is* a business cycle.

If we presume that ups and downs occur in various industries and that those ups and downs come in cycles of apparently random length and depth, then there is a need to protect ourselves and, more specifically, our capital, from the effects if we can. If we consider the pig farmer, the grain farmer, and the beer brewer alone, a solution emerges that could smooth the ride out nicely. First, we have to fast-forward to the 21st century and an economy that has hundreds or thousands of each of those individual producers. Next, the producers must have incorporated so that we have the ability to purchase an interest in their operation without having to buy the whole farm. Finally, there must be some pooling mechanism to allow us to purchase interests in hundreds or thousands of farms and breweries without expending millions of dollars.

All of those elements exist in mutual funds today. If we presume a hypothetical "pig farm fund" and another that is a "grain farm fund" and finally a "brewery fund" and we were to purchase equal portions of each, we would have the potential to participate in the profit of each element of our imaginary economy without the ups and downs of any one part. When the pigs were selling high and corn was low, we would benefit from the profit of raising pigs. That element of profit would rotate through the high barley prices as the pigs reached oversupply and finally to the profitability of beer when barley was cheap and beer sales were up.

We would, of course, miss out on the booms as well and would have to put up with our friends and neighbors bragging about how much they gained in the new Pig Farm IPO they had recently purchased on the Internet through a discount stock trading firm. But when the dust finally settled years later, we would find that we had actually achieved a much better long-term gain than if we had chosen to participate only in a single element of our mythical economy. What we had done was minimize the business cycle risk and, at the same time, nearly eliminated the risk of business collapse. If a single pig farmer went under and lost everything, it would have little effect on our portfolio, but if we were an investor in that farm alone, it could be ruinous.

One more concerted activity is necessary to really be on top of the action here. It is extremely counter-intuitive so it needs to be put on "auto-pilot" to work well, but that factor tends to work in our favor. There is, as I have previously mentioned, a powerful tendency for us to buy into what ever is "going up." Once again, we need to have some type of sophisticated pooling of investment interests to make this work, but we are blessed to live in the 21st century and it already exists. Having the three imaginary funds listed above, pig, corn, and beer, to maximize our return and minimize our variance, we would set up an automatic rebalancing every quarter. For example, if PIG was up and both CORN and BEER were down, there would be an automatic sell of sufficient PIG shares and purchase of sufficient CORN and BEER shares to rebalance back to our original allocation. This process would be repeated every three month.

One more element is needed to set all this in motion: a vehicle that will allow transactions between the various positions without any significant transaction costs or taxation. Fortunately, for us in the 21st century, such vehicles exist and will be discussed in Section II.

Chapter 6 – Bubbles, Busts, and Fraud: The Violation of Trust

The Secular Bear

This discussion of the nature of markets and their behavior would not be complete without a clear warning about a strange phenomenon known as a *secular bear market*. The corn-hog cycle is an example of a cyclical market. The price decline or even collapse associated with a cyclical market is referred to as a cyclical bear. (Remember that during bad times the Yeomen would sell bears and bear skins at the market?) Timing and depth of such events appears to be fairly random, but at least when they happen, we understand the economic reason behind them. The secular bear is not so rational.

Secular bears are created by a breach of trust. Sometimes they involve out-and-out scandal as persons in places of responsibility and trust actually violate the law. More often, they are based on our assumptions about what we believe is, or will be, happening in the future. These violations of trust are so common throughout history that it is remarkable that we are "taken in" by them so often. Still, the very issue of their repetitive nature means there is something in us that is drawn to the "get rich scheme" of the perpetrator.

Bubbles, crashes, investor disgust, and secular bears are part of the landscape of investing. I would be as big a fool as any insolvent dot-com speculator if I were to tell you that it is possible to avoid being swept up in the wave of euphoria that comes from time to time, without warning, over the terrain of investing. What I can tell you are some of the certain signs that such a wave exists and then what an investor who "keeps his or her head when all about you are losing theirs" (Rudyard Kipling's *If)* can do at any given point in the wave to benefit from it.

One of the first important things to understand is that such waves are going on literally all the time. In my experience, I have witnessed one or more oil manias, real estate manias, stock manias, bond manias, mortgage manias, gold manias, silver manias, and even a movie mania and now a dot-com mania. If there is something that can be bought and sold with a potential market value higher or lower than currently exists, it will at some point be *securitized* and almost certainly have its day in history as the latest mania.

Securitized refers to the act of creating a security from a commodity or service. A *security* is a representation of something else which can be held as "security" for the ownership of the thing securitized. For example, when you loan money to the United States government, you are issued a piece of paper of some kind that represents that loan, or the *ownership* of a certain amount of money, plus interest, that currently is in the possession of the U.S. Treasury Department.

I will spend a great deal of time on this subject from a positive point of view, but for now, just recognize that we live in an age of *securitization*. That securitization provides oceans of liquidity and, in turn, capital that has allowed our economy to grow more in a year than the economies of all of Western Civilization once grew in a decade or even a century.

At the root of each speculative bubble is a fundamental belief in a couple of nonsense principles that somehow have become rooted in the human psyche. Oddly, the person most susceptible to ruin is not the professional speculator but the person who believes they have their feet planted firmly on the ground and are above such foolishness.

The first mythological belief that leads to ruin in a speculative bubble is the widely held conviction that somehow "the big guys" are getting some special deal in the world of commerce. When I have mentioned this as a myth, I have found such profound rejection that I have to conclude that somehow this is an almost religious belief.

Over the long term (the last 50 years for example), we have seen an average annual rate of return on the better-known equity indices of about 12% per year; thereby doubling invested capital about every six years. In order to have seen that nice 12% figure actually materialize, one would have had to stand firm during several short term 30% declines and a couple of 50% declines. If, instead, you had decided to have around 40% of your money in long-term government bonds, you would have seen a return of about 9% over the period, but your greatest short term drop in value would have been about 25%. Going a step further, if you find the concept of losing about quarter of your invested value in a short time a bit more than you are comfortable with, you could have stuck to short to intermediate government bonds. Your short-term losses would have been limited to about 10% in any downturn, but your long-term return has been reduced to about 4% per year. The backside to this impressive increase in stability, or drop in volatility if you prefer, is that your investment portfolio would now appear to have doubled about every 18 years. I say *appeared* because your *real* (after inflation) return has actually been *zero!* Inflation over that same 50-year period has also averaged 4% per year! In short, "no pain, no gain!"

If a relatively sudden drop of about 20% is a bit much to you, then you have no business investing. Put your money in the bank or short-term U.S. Treasury obligations, and be satisfied that after inflation and taxes you will have not only no long-term gain but also you will see no fluctuations in your day-to-day values! Of course, if you dare spend any of the interest, you will in fact see an erosion of your principal that is unlikely to be replaced but that is the price you pay either way.

Value is not changed by fluctuations in *price. If* you know the *value* of an investment and you believe in a free market system, you will also believe that the value of an item will be reflected in its price once the buyers return to their senses. In other words, if I have a portfolio of common stocks in companies that are steadily increasing the *utility* (value) of what they make, and the current price for that portfolio of stocks is well below the price that would be reasonable to pay for that increase in utility, buying that portfolio, or simply not selling it if I already owned it, would be a brilliant move.

Conversely, if I believe not in the *value* but in the *price* of my investment, as measured by the number of *dollars* on my statement, I would have a powerful incentive to buy only after I had seen the price increase for a long enough period to establish a "trend" and then to sell if I saw lengthy evidence that the "trend" was now downward! The first paradigm would induce me to "buy low" and "sell high," while the second paradigm would strongly entice me to "buy high" and "sell low."

Even before the choice of a specific investment is made, there is another critical issue. If you do not have a very clear image of the purpose for which you are investing, you are fairly likely to not achieve the purpose you want. It is very much like looking for a job and having no idea what you want to do. It's hard to imagine starting off from your home and just "heading out" with no particular destination in mind.

Investing without a purpose (other than to "see it go up") isn't really investing at all but merely a form of speculation. Sadly, this kind of speculation is not the stabilizing speculation of the hog speculator, but something called *destabilizing speculation*. Destabilizing speculation is an amateur sport that involves investing in something after the price has risen (which of course, if enough folks do it, causes it to rise further) and then selling out when the price is low (thus causing the price to fall further). If enough destabilizing speculators get involved in buying emotionally, we get a price condition in the market called a *bubble,* and when they all decide to leave, pretty much at the same time, we get a *crash*.

A secret to surviving such periods is to be very comfortable that you know the *"why"* that caused you to choose the investments in your portfolio to begin with and to be confident that the *"why"* has not changed. Of course, the original choice needs to have been made carefully enough to warrant faith not only in the investment management you have chosen but in the process and logic you used to make the choice in the first place. In other words, the secret is to avoid being a person *"who knows the price of everything but the value of nothing."*

The second secret is to simply recognize that the kind of price fluctuation we routinely have in the U.S. stock markets is absolutely normal. They don't happen very often, but when secular bears appear, the normal drop is about 45% and the length of time is commonly over 24 months from top to bottom. If that kind of decline is one you cannot stomach, then you should not have your invested money in shares of corporations.

Bubbles are subtle and dangerous moves in the price of a class of investment during which a mania develops. Sometimes they are generated by external events, but more often, they simply occur because of a combination of the powerful myths that are widely believed about investing and a lack of memory of the last bubble in that asset class.

George Santayana's warning that "those who do not remember history are condemned to repeat it" could not be more applicable to the series of bubbles, panics, and busts that have plagued us as long as there have been markets. The economic panic and depression of 1929 was very much an echo of the panic and depression of 1837. The Internet and S&P 500 bubble of the 1990s that ended in the market contraction of 2000-2003 followed the pattern of the railroad mania and collapse that ran from 1869 and bottomed in 1877. Even if we as a nation do not learn from these debacles, we as investors can.

Bubbles occur in different asset classes at various times, but they rotate from one to another in such a way that people fleeing the last unpleasant experience with the remains of their investment capital tend to become involved in the next "big thing" and, as a result, seem to move from one disaster to another. Bubbles and busts are created from fear and greed. The more emotion involved in investing, the more likely it is that there is a bubble currently forming and a bust is coming. That emotion not only can be negative or positive but also normally will be first one and then the other in order to create the bubble.

In order to have a bubble, certain elements must be present, and when they are, the creation of a bubble seems to be a near certainty. The unknown element is when the bubble will have run its course and burst. Just to confuse the matter all the more, from time to time along comes a sudden increase in the base price of a commodity or asset class that *doesn't* collapse, or at least doesn't collapse for a long time.

How can we tell when asset appreciation becomes an unstable bubble? Actually, you already have the necessary information if you have read the previous chapters. Asset appreciation is generated by increased utility. If the price of an asset is rising rapidly without a corresponding increase in utility, it is not going to last and is a bubble.

The characteristics that must be present in an asset class for a bubble to exist are:

- *It must be a "sure thing" and have no perceived significant risk of loss.*

- *It must be the subject of mass popular interest and speculation.*

- *It must either have no capability of creating reasonable utility (earnings) or have lost the capability because of oversupply.*

- *It must be the subject of mass inflows of cash from other asset classes.*

I will attempt to work through each of these characteristics here, but please understand from the beginning that bubbles are extremely hard to recognize when they are being created. In the second section of this book, when we get into the issue of asset class allocation, there is a discipline that has the potential to limit the risk of getting overly involved in a bubble, but it is extremely difficult not to get caught up in the mass hysteria that Charles MacKay describes in the book "*Extraordinary Popular Delusions and the Madness of Crowds.*"

Sure Things (Bullet-Proof Investments)

First, *there is no such thing as a bulletproof investment*. There are no "sure things" in the real world. Anytime you believe you have found an absolutely sure and secure investment, be confident that you have just been fooled. Perfect investment classes are about as likely as levitation or a perpetual motion machine. Interestingly enough, the perpetual motion machine has been the subject of speculative investment bubbles for as far back as there is a record of investing.

In 1982 gold had risen to $820 per ounce. To put that in perspective, in 2003 it would take about $1,640 to buy what $820 bought twenty years earlier, and the price of gold, even in the midst of a gathering world crisis, was just over $300 per ounce. In other words, gold in 2003 was priced at less than 1/5 the price it traded at twenty years earlier. In the years between 1971 and 1982, it rose from $38 per ounce to that high of around $820. The rise in price to $820 was followed by a rapid decline to half that value within a year. Twenty years later, it had lost 80% of the value offered in 1982 and was being artificially supported by central banks across the world to prevent economic disruption in South Africa.

Now before I rile any "gold-bugs" that might be checking prices, note that there are two prices for gold. One is the price at which you might be able to buy it from a dealer and the other is the price at which the dealer will buy it from you. The widely advertised prices aer those at which the dealers are selling gold, but the price that the holder of gold would get from those same dealers is commonly at least 10% and sometimes as much as 25% lower. Thus, if gold is listed at $340 per ounce, you as a gold seller would do well to get $300 per ounce for your holdings.

Oil prices (in 1996 dollars) were just over $10 per barrel in 1971. In the years 1973 and 1974 oil had increased to $20 per barrel with the advent of OPEC control of a critical part of the world oil supply. By 1982 the price per barrel had risen to over $50 ($75 in 2003 dollars). The consensus of pundits was for a price (in 1982 dollars) of $100 per barrel within a few years and the rush to invest money in oil and gas limited partnerships was on. Billions of investor dollars poured into wildcat wells, stripper wells, and anything that even vaguely looked like it had anything to do with oil. Following a precipitous decline following the peak in 1982, the price continued to fall until it was well below $10 per barrel in 1998 before rising to around $31 per barrel (West Texas Intermediate) in 2003.

Silver prices went from just under four dollars per ounce in 1975 to almost $50 per ounce in 1980. Following the spectacular increase, engineered by the Hunt brothers in an attempt to "corner" the silver market, the price dropped to $4.90 per ounce by 1982, while gold became the craze. The average price in 2001 was a little over $4.00. Translated into 2003 dollars, the 1980 price would have been about $100 per ounce.

There is a common thread in all these histories. The price of a commodity rises on some fear of shortage or crisis and then is hyped up by those who hope to profit from the sale of the commodity. The real bubble only comes though when the news media find pseudo-scientists who will proclaim the commodity's rise in price is justified by some future event. In the case of oil, it was the certainty that we would always drive seven-mile-per-gallon cars that looked like miniature versions of Buck Rodgers spaceships and technology would never improve in oil exploration and drilling. Gold soared because we lost faith in the American economy and believed that technology would not develop that would allow for gold to be mined more effectively. Silver "went up" simply because the Hunt brothers were buying all they could find. The many, many thousands of people who were burned in all those schemes really weren't guilty of "thinking" at all; they were just swept up in a mania of fear and greed.

Skipping over several other bubbles, the commercial real estate bubble emerged in the late 1980s. A construction boom gripped the country as commercial office building and apartment construction surged to levels that have not been seen since. In just about every major population center, commercial buildings were coming up like mushrooms as investors poured money into limited partnerships, real estate investment trusts, and direct investment partnerships. A humorous comment went around during that time that we had developed a new kind of architecture in the United State, *see-through buildings*! You could look in the front and see out the back because there was nobody in there. The price of commercial real estate collapsed in 1989 along with no small number of savings and loan institutions and numerous banks. Over a decade later, the price per foot of commercial real estate has not recovered in many areas.

Looking back, doesn't it seem strange that people would believe that it was a good idea to borrow money to build a huge office building between two other new office buildings that had no tenants? All it took was few good real estate limited partnership salesmen and a sufficient number of people who thought that getting tax write-offs was better than making money! By the way, it *never* works to invest with the primary concern being the "tax write-off."

As we emerged from the real estate debacle with new names on many banks and the price of commercial real estate at astonishingly low levels, the attention turned to computers, the fledgling Internet, and the stock market. The last major stock market collapse occurred in 1973-75 and most investors were blissfully unaware that it had even happened. Even the "Black Monday" crash of 1987 had largely vanished from the common memory. By 1997, stocks were the "sure thing" led by the S&P 500 Index funds and the infamous "dot-coms." The rest is an echo of every other asset class bubble and collapse. After peaking in early 2000, the S&P 500 Stock Index dropped about 50% by October 2002, and the Dow Jones Industrial Average went from a high of around 1200 to a low of 750 over the same period. The NASDAQ stock average plunged a stunning 85% from top to bottom.

Each of these asset classes had something in common. When gold was surging, the papers, television, magazines, and even the radio carried a steady drumbeat of praise for the "intrinsic" value of gold. In fact, except for the creation of jewelry and some industrial applications, gold has no intrinsic value at all. With the exception of the commercial applications, it creates no utility. Worse, it is expensive to store, and if you take physical possession of pure gold, you must subject it to assay before it can be resold! Silver carries the same restrictions.

Another important aspect of any pure commodity such as gold and silver is that as the price rises, old mines will become profitable again and be reopened. With the much-improved technology available today, even the old mine tailings can be processed to find significant quantities of gold and silver. It is simply not possible for gold to rise to a much higher price because if it starts to do so, the supply will increase as the mines reopen. Worse, banks around the world hold great quantities of gold that they would love to sell. Gold generates no interest or profit, and as I mentioned, is expensive to store.

Real estate was proclaimed as "bullet proof" because "God isn't making any more real estate." "Because the economy and the population is growing," the story went, "the limited supply of real estate in major cities will force the value of commercial real estate up." Of course what really happened was that we wound up with far too many buildings and far too much office space.

If we line up all these bubbles in time a pattern emerges. Cash flows that come from one bubble as it collapses often begin almost immediately to fuel the next bubble. Sometimes the cash flow would temporarily hold off in savings and money market positions, but eventually the flow would begin into something very different from the last asset class bubble.

Mass Hysteria and Lack of Utility

Every bubble starts with a price movement in an asset class. That price movement is accelerated and carried far beyond any rational level by the mass hysteria that accompanies every bubble. The mass hysteria hinges on some irrational "discovery" or claim that, on the surface, seems to make sense, but if investigated carefully, is absurd. The recent stock bubble produced prices in the largest companies in the S&P 500 that would have required earnings growth rates of 30% to 50% per year to justify. If somehow any of those companies had been able to sustain such an earnings growth rate, the company would have become larger than the entire United States economy in just a few decades. The bubble formed because prices on stocks were bid up because they were rising, not because the underlying companies had the capability of creating utility, or value, commensurate with the price being paid for the stock. While there is no way any of us can nail down the discrete cause of the price rise and acceleration, there is a direct correlation between the money flowing into S&P 500 Index surrogates and the degree the largest companies in that index rose above any reasonable valuation.

One of the goals at Enron was to be not only included in the S&P 500 but to reach a position where the unmanaged flow of money would accrue to Enron purely by virtue of being high in the index. Because more money goes to the larger companies by capitalization, Enron would see more money purchasing its stock and thereby increase the valuation of the executive stock options. In the short-term at least, the plan worked well. The same can be said of MCI-WorldCom and AOL, although we have no direct indication that they planned to rise to the top of the index in order to receive more capital.

Perhaps a better example of how such a mania works can be found in the Gold bubble of 1982. Gold bullion produces no utility. It does not pay the owner anything. It carries a value only in that it is highly malleable and is not a particularly common mineral in its natural state. The rush to gold was out of fear initially, as the world witnessed the United States appearing to lose its way as the President resigned, following the resignation and conviction for fraud of the Vice President. America lost the war in Viet Nam and was subjected to humiliation in the Middle East, as an alliance of oil producing nations were able to dictate national policy to what was previously presumed to be the most powerful nation on earth.

The silver bubble was generated when the price started up with no apparent reason, drawing more money that forced the price even higher. Silver also creates no value. It is just a minor commercial and jewelry metal with a limited availability in nature.

The real estate rush of the 1980s was triggered by accelerated depreciation and an absurdly high maximum federal income tax bracket. Because of the supposed tax advantages, a high-income investor could invest in a real estate limited partnership and only commit the money that would otherwise go to the Federal Government in taxes. In other words, it was a sure thing. Then, as the prices started to rise, people began to believe that it would always increase because of the scarcity of real estate. In the hysteria, few considered that no matter how little land there was available in a city, if no one wanted to pay rent on a building, it would generate no income and thereby be without value.

They also did not consider that in order to get those juicy tax breaks, the partnership had to borrow a lot of money. If there was no one who was willing to pay the rent on the building, then the property would be foreclosed by the bank or savings and loan. Federal tax law clearly states that if an investment had no reasonable opportunity to be profitable, any tax deduction associated with the investment would be disallowed. More than a few investors found themselves owing the IRS an amount that wound up being much larger than the investment they had made in the partnership after penalties and interest.

The hysteria associated with the dot-coms and the S&P 500 ignored the fact that many of the newly created companies had no plan on how they were ever going to make a profit. The assurance by the wise talking heads on television and in the print media that "low costs are the surest route to high returns" enticed hundreds of millions of dollars into S&P 500 surrogates. This drove the price of the largest of the S&P 500 companies to a level that could not be sustained by their earnings or earnings growth. The reasoning that "everyone is doing it so it must be good" is and was one of the principal marks of the investment bubble.

Massive Cash Flow

The final sign of a bubble is when "everybody is doing it." Almost without exception, if the consensus of investors is that something should be bought and bought immediately, then it has reached a peak price and is due for a fall. In each asset class bubble we have listed, there were massive and unprecedented cash flows into the asset class at its peak. Because the laws of supply and demand are not going to be repealed by political act (as the experiment called Communism in the Soviet Union proved), high emotional demand for any commodity or product will generate a high price. In fact, the rising prices tend to generate rising cash flows and the rising cash flow generates higher prices.

Eventually, most of those who are going to buy have done so. At that point, someone will have a need to sell. Perhaps the most significant turns in the market come at the beginning of a new calendar quarter. Pension funds and insurance companies are obligated to rebalance their portfolios at that point. If stocks have risen significantly, then the pension and insurance companies will be selling stock and buying bonds in about the second week of a new quarter. On the other hand, if stocks have fallen quite a lot in a quarter and bonds have risen, then they will sell bonds and buy stock.

The seller places the assets up for sale, announces it to the market, and is shocked to discover that the only offered price at which someone will buy is substantially below earlier figures. The seller, desperate for money, agrees to the price, even if it is 10% or 20% below what he or she expected. As soon as the transaction is posted on the exchange, an immediate decline sets in as fear grips those who bought at an even higher price than that being offered quickly attempt to get out of the asset class. Then the same cycle sets in on the down side. Here is where things become different though. Following the decline in price of straight commodities from gold to silver to oil, the price did not recover. Over a long period of time as advancing technology makes the recovery of any mineral less expensive, the price will tend to decline.

Even real estate is really not in short supply. Anyone who has flown across the continental United States will acknowledge that there is a lot of land out there with no one living on it. We tend to cluster together and drive up the cost of land because of our limited transportation ability. The reduction in the cost of information exchange may just change that completely! As the ability to communicate becomes more and more complete over a digital network, the time may just come when the location is irrelevant.

If the majority of homes had full wall three dimensional screens built in as well as smaller ones throughout the house, much, if not most, of the need to commute will disappear and we will be free to live in far flung locations while being able to gather together digitally for the interchanges we need to conduct business. To some degree that is already happening as a new form of community, the "exurb," forms away from the major metropolitan centers. A slowly growing number of workers are now "telecommuters" working from home for a corporate headquarters that may be on the other side of the globe.

In all of the asset classes where bubbles have occurred from mineral commodities to exotic large birds being raised supposedly for meat, the price collapse, when it occurs is at least 50%. In the case of commodities, the price decline often continues. There is a reason for that continued decline. When the price was high, new technology was developed to find and recover the commodity. After the mania passes, the new technology is further refined and the price starts into a long and generally irreversible decline.

There are a couple of exceptions to this rule. Because stock represents ownership in corporations and those corporations are actually creating utility, a bubble occurring in stock prices produces a different pattern. In all the bubble based stock price collapses that have occurred in the last two centuries in the United States, the general market price of stocks, as measured by the New York Stock Exchange composite, declined an average of 50%. Within the twelve months following the decline, the price rose by half. That did not take it back to its peak of course, because a 50% decline requires a doubling of value to return it to its former level. Interestingly enough, that doubling did occur within five years of the low point. Typically, the highest level the market reached was duplicated within 7 ½ years of the first peak.

From there, almost anything can occur. When the price of stocks is driven to irrational highs, it has a history of declining to irrational lows over the next few months or years. In the midst of the irrational highs, wise and learned people will create a justification not only for the irrational high but also for even higher prices ahead. Once the bubble bursts and the price falls to irrational lows, wise and learned heads (sometimes the same ones) will find justification for not only the low price but for a continued decline.

The issue here is that both sets of conclusions are irrational. We now know that real earnings of American corporations were declining in 1999 while the prices of equities were still increasing rapidly. Mass hysteria had set in and people were buying, not because of any perceived value but because prices were rising. Meanwhile, the "value" stocks, and particularly those of the mid-capitalization companies, were falling. Following the attacks on the United States on September 11, 2001, the averages reached lows that while well down from the highs a year and a half earlier, were not completely irrational. It was the revelation that a few companies had committed fraud in reporting earnings that completed the bust.

From that point in March of 2002, a panicked flight from the stock market in any form began that was as unreasoned as any bubble or bust before it. In July and again in October 2001, unreasoned selling was the rule and often by the same foolish investors who, again without reason, bought into the broad market index surrogates in 1999 and 2000. By the calculations of Dr. Edward Yardeni in October 2002, the S&P 500 was undervalued by just over 30%. If his calculations are correct, that same index would have to rise 50% to reach fair market value, right in line with 200 years of market history.

The critical point was that the average price of a stock on the New York Stock Exchange was rising while corporate earnings were falling through 1999 and early 2000. At the bottom of the secular bear, in October 2001, the earnings of the corporations represented in that market had been rising for a full year, while the prices of their stocks were falling. Emotional sentiments had driven the prices up to an unreasonable level and were now driving them down to one as irrational as the peaks to which they had risen two and a half years earlier.

It is often overlooked that Adam Smith, the author of *The Wealth of Nations* and widely hailed as the father of modern capitalism also wrote *A Theory of Moral Sentiments* and considered it the more important work. It is, in the final analysis, the sentiments of investors that drive the prices on the exchanges. At least in the short-term, the market is anything but efficient. The assumption that the market is always efficient and unemotional was one of the theoretical flaws that created the bubble and the bust that followed.

The South Sea Bubble

In 1711, the British Parliament granted *The South Sea Company,* exclusive rights to conduct trade with colonies in the new world not previously granted by the Crown of England. In exchange, *The South Sea Company* would assume the long-term debt of the Crown. As a result of the well known profitability of the established English colonial companies and the amazing wealth generated by the Spanish Colonies, the common assumption was that this new company would soon be generating wealth beyond anything previously known in England. *The South Sea Company* was a joint stock company, the predecessor of the modern corporation.

With the implied backing of the Crown and advertisements that hyped the "untapped riches of the new world," The *South Sea Company* had its initial subscription of shares not only filled but also oversold by multiples. The mania to purchase the shares was a classic example of mass hysteria, or as Mr. MacKay so aptly put it, "the madness of crowds." With the initial issue of shares such an astonishing success, the board of directors authorized the issuance of another subscription.

In the midst of what would come to be known as the South Sea Bubble, the original purchasers of shares in "The Company," as it was called by those caught up in the madness, saw their initial investment multiply by as much as 1000 times by early 1720, at least on paper. Sadly, one of the reasons for the absurdly high bid prices for the stock was the fact that very, very few wanted to sell.

Sir Isaac Newton, perhaps the most intelligent person who ever lived, has been reported to be one of the early investors. He saw the price offered to him for his shares go up until he concluded that it would be impossible for *The South Sea Company* to earn the absurdly high price of the shares even if it owned all the production of the Spanish colonies for one hundred years. At that point he sold his shares at great profit. To his dismay, the price of the shares on the open market continued to rise until he could stand it no more. He invested not only all he had made from his earlier sale but also borrowed as much as he could and increased his position. Two days later, the price of the stock began a steep decline, as owners of shares were unable to sell them to anyone at any price. Sir Isaac lost all he had invested and spent the rest of his life repaying the debts he had accumulated to buy the worthless stock. He forbade the utterance of the words "South Sea" in his presence from that time forward. He has been quoted as saying that he could plot the movements of the planets and the stars, but the movements of the market were a complete mystery to him.

All *The South Sea Company* ever really owned was an obligation to repay the debt of the British Government. One of the strange ironies of the mania and collapse was that in the midst of it all, the government debt *did* get repaid and the debacle allowed Great Britain to avoid default on its debt. What people were unwilling to pay in taxation to resolve their collective debt problem, they were willing to lose in a speculative bubble. In the United States today, astute consultants have, apparently correctly, advised states that their citizens are quite willing to provide substantial financing for government programs if it is disguised as a speculative venture with an extremely low probability of payoff, but an amount of payoff that is spectacular. We call it a state lottery.

The similarities between the Enron scandal and the events of 1719-1720 are amazing. Both John Law and Ken Lay appear to have been genuinely good men with the best of intentions who set out to create commerce and wealth where little had been before. Both legally created a trade in what previously had been government monopolies. Both were apparently unaware of what the greed of those around them could do to a financial institution operating outside of regulatory checks. Both were successful in *securitizing* what had been fixed assets and in securing public participation in a new market. Both though were, in the end, undone by efforts to keep the price of company shares high even as insiders were selling frantically before the house of cards came tumbling down.

The lesson to learn is not that owning stock in corporations is a bad thing, but that people have a powerful tendency to get deeply involved in either the euphoria of a bull market, or bubble, *and* the melancholy of a bear market, or market collapse. Quite the contrary, in the book *Stocks for the Long Run*, Jeremy Siegel demonstrates that for the past two hundred years in the United States, over any twenty-year period, the collective value of the stock of American Corporations has outperformed every other asset class available.

Perhaps the most valuable lesson here is found in the title of the book *Extraordinary Popular Delusions*. We desire to give the price of an issue or a market index a life of its own as if it were a living physical being. We refer to the variations in price as if they were physical objects operating under the laws of Newtonian Physics. Newton himself warns us that such presumptions may lead to ruin but the popular delusion remains.

The Panics of 1845 & 1873 – The First Internet Boom... and Bust!

The collapse of the dot-coms and the ensuing revelation that several corporations had been involved in either deceptive or out and out fraudulent accounting in the beginning of the 21st century was hailed by the press as a shocking and unexpected revelation. In fact, it was a rather classic case of the reality stated by George Santayana, "Those who do not remember history are condemned to repeat it."

Between 1860 and 1870, due largely to the necessities of war, the miles of railroad in the United States had doubled. The driving of the "golden spike" at Promontory, Utah, in 1869 had excited the public imagination with the vision of being able to send packages, mail, or even people across the continent in a matter of weeks instead of months. With the excitement of the public imagination by the newspaper writers of the day came a post war rush to purchase stock or bonds in anything even vaguely associated with the enormous profits that were surely just around the corner in the newly connected nation that now stretched from sea to sea.

In order to understand the implications of the advent of the transcontinental railroad and its relation to the Internet, it is necessary to understand what commerce had been like *before* the railroad boom.

Without the railroad, goods, people, and communication moved principally by ship or riverboat. That was all right if a store was either on a very major river or a seaport town, but as the population moved west and away from the ports it became harder and harder to do business. The principal means of transportation was the horse drawn wagon, the same device Caesar had used to conduct himself around the battlefield. The horse collar and wagon had been in popular use for over 500 years with only minor modifications. In Europe, the best roads were still those that had been laid by the Romans.

A general goods store could do business at most about ten miles from its front door as it easily took a full day to make a twenty mile round trip. If that store was not on a navigable waterway, it in turn depended on wagons coming cross-country to supply it with the merchandise it sold. To order that merchandise, the storeowner had to send word back to the manufacturer, often hundreds or even thousands of miles away, by that same, slow wagon/riverboat/sailing ship means of communication. Money was in short supply and in even shorter supply as one ventured out to where the farmers were creating farms.

These factors together caused the goods sold at the local general store to be priced at levels that would be considered outrageous today. The produce or stock sold by the farmer or rancher also had to transition those long miles on unimproved roads and trails, thus reducing the profit to the farmer even as the same primitive methods increased the cost of everything he bought.

Early in the Civil War, the strategists in the North determined that the ultimate outcome would be based on logistics. Several innovations that had existed, and probably would have eventually been adopted, were rushed into production by the necessity of war and the availability of money that only comes in time of threatened national survival.

It is in times of national crisis when a threat is perceived to our very survival that the greatest strides forward are made in technology, and it is in the war that normally concludes the crisis that the technology breaks out from the realm of experimental to actual. Even as we in the early 21st century are benefiting from and having to learn to deal with the changes wrought by the computer, the gas turbine (jet) engine, and microwave communication (all invented in the 1930s and

WWII), so the world of the late 19th and early 20th centuries had to deal with the inventions and technology created by the crisis that ended with the American Civil war.

The new innovations that swept across the developed world following the Civil War were centered on three much related technologies. The prime invention that had changed everything was the vastly improved reciprocating steam engine. By our standards today, the many tonned steaming behemoth with about the horsepower of a modern diesel truck engine looks anything but portable. What it replaced though was wind or rowing power in the case of water transportation and *real* horsepower in the case of land transportation. Just as important, a steam engine could be broken down into its component parts and transported to where energy was needed to run, for example, a sawmill or factory, and rebuilt on the site. Before the advent of the portable steam engine, one either had a waterfall or one did not have a factory or anything that remotely resembled one.

The second innovation was a concept that had been around but did not really catch on until the war: mass production. Prior to the Civil War, individual weapons were works of art made carefully by craftsmen. As the North entered the war in earnest, the opportunity to claim the Federal money being offered for rifles encouraged the assembly line factories that would eventually change all that we did. As amazing as it is today, a soldier's weapon in 1860 was made from uniquely crafted parts that required a weapon-smith to forge individually should they break. With the advent of mass production, the parts on the weapons became interchangeable and immediately replaceable in the field. This wondrous innovation could not have taken place without the energy source of the steam engine and soon was applied to the steam engine itself.

The third technology was in many ways even more amazing than the railroad or the replicable rifle. The primitive technology of the telegraph would eventually lead to the telephone and ultimately, to digital communication a century later. An interesting spin off of the telegraph is that Alexander Graham Bell invented both the telephone and the phonograph after having been a telegraph operator, and with that experience as his base, went on to invent the improvements that would take the technology of communication into the 20th century.

All of these technologies would prove themselves in the future to be the world changers they promised in the late 1860s and early 1870s. Unfortunately for the investors caught up in the promises, time was required before the promises would be fulfilled. Railroads had a fundamental problem that was little appreciated by the masses of speculators who were sure that fortune was just around the corner in railroad related companies.

The same mania had gripped the English market in the 1840s. John Francis in his book, *History of the Railways* published in 1850, quotes a newspaper article of the time that well summarizes the prevailing belief:

> "...the length of our lives, so far as regards the power of acquiring information and disseminating power, will be doubled, and we may be justified in looking for the arrival of a time when the whole world will have become one great family, speaking one language, governed in unity by like laws, and adoring one God."

In the predecessor to the IPO (Initial Public Offering) the sale of "script shares" in advance of Parliamentary approval for a railroad created obligations that exceeded the national income of Great Britain. Shares were sold that immediately jumped to a price of five hundred times the initial offering for railroad lines that went nowhere but to a wilderness and thereby had absolutely no hope of ever turning a profit.

The venerable *Economist* magazine in its October 1845 edition published a declaration so enduring it could well have been republished word for word in the year 2000:

> "The market value... depends, not on the opinion as to the ultimate success of the undertaking, but rather how far circumstances will tend to sustain or increase the public appetite for speculation. Nothing can show this more powerfully than the fact that we see nine or ten proposals for nearly the same line, all at a premium, when it is well known that only one CAN succeed, and that all the rest must, in all probability, be minus their expenses."

In 1845 when the house of cards began to fall, all of the excesses of any bubble began to be revealed. It was found that senior officers of railroad companies had used the capital raised for their private luxuries and that lesser officials had misappropriated funds to speculate in script. Criminal charges, public arrests, trials and numerous legislative investigations followed. The final collapse came in 1847 as other aspects of the economy were either neglected or overextended in the railroad mania. A minor change in names, dates, and places could have brought the headlines from the mid 19th century onto the papers of the beginning of the 21st century.

The end result, though, was as different from the appearance of doom in 1847 as the collapse was different from the delusions common in the mania of the early 1840s. As a result of the excessive and foolish mania that established railroad lines to every corner of England, Great Britain had the most efficient transportation network in the world for the next half century. The immense economic success of the Victorian Era can be at least partly credited to the notoriously efficient British Rail System.

When the railroad arrived in America, it found a land far more difficult to unite with the twin iron rails. It was 1869 before the two coasts were linked, but that link was reported with great fanfare in newspapers across the land. The story had been *telegraphed* from one side of the nation to the other in a day's time. It ignited the imagination of speculators who were blissfully unaware they were about to repeat the events that occurred in England a mere quarter century before.

Every company that floated shares in any venture that had anything to do with the railroad was immediately flooded with subscriptions. Railroads were once again built to places where buffalo were the principal residents in an eerie echo of the "roads to the wilderness" built in the English mania. In the rush to be in on the riches, it was overlooked that a single rail line now linked the East and West and that alternative routes were certain to be expensive to the extreme.

A specific fact generally overlooked in the American railroad mania was that the American West was not level. Surveyors put railroads in not to run through every small town, but to run where the engine could pull cars. That meant that many of the roads headed west did not go where even the sparse population lived. As the speculators were anticipating their profits from commerce, it was no small impediment that the people and businesses that were expected to generate that commerce were generally not where the railroad could serve them!

What followed was the Panic of 1873, a rout that so resembled the panics of 1720, 1845, and 1929 that it seems almost to have been acted out by the same people! Once again, arrests were made, Congress investigated, investor disgust drove the shares in profitable companies into collapse, and the prophets of doom proclaimed the end of investment. Wise academics proclaimed that the damage done to the economy by the waste of good money on worthless railroads would stunt future growth into the foreseeable future.

What really happened following the capitulation of the amateur speculators in 1877 was quite different. By today's definition of a "depression," America didn't have one. While the Real Gross Domestic Product of the United States (GDP) peaked in 1873 at $113 billion (1996 dollars), by the end of 1875 the economy had recovered to a real production of $118 billion. During the years of boom and bust and recovery from 1865 to 1880, the real GDP *doubled*. In an era when the main means of transportation was still the horse and the American people devoted a very significant part of their output to restoring unity to the nation while paying off a staggering Civil War Debt, the actual output of the nation rose at a rate that exceeds all but the very most developed nations of the world over a century later.

The table that follows illustrates the actual Gross Domestic Product of the United States of America during and following the mania and the panic:[3]

Year	Nominal GDP (billions of dollars)	Real GDP (billions of 1996 dollars)
1865	$9.14	$82.20
1866	$8.88	$83.60
1867	$8.51	$84.50
1868	$8.48	$88.00
1869	$8.29	$92.20
1870	$8.49	$99.20
1871	$8.77	$103.00
1872	$8.88	$107.00
1873	$9.24	$113.00
1874	$8.92	$112.00
1875	$8.99	$118.00
1876	$8.75	$119.00
1877	$8.88	$123.00
1878	$8.69	$128.00
1879	$9.48	$144.00
1880	$11.10	$161.00

In H.W. Brands book *The Age of Gold* (P. 446) the end result is clearly stated:

"*The results were little short of miraculous. Between 1869 and the end of the nineteenth century, the American economy grew as no economy had ever done before and very few did after. From a laggard in the race to industrialize, trailing Britain, Germany, and France, the United States became the leader of the pack, with a manufacturing output that, by 1900, surpassed the three European powers combined. The growth wasn't uniform over time: wrenching recessions in the 1870s and 1890s briefly set the economy back. But in each case, the hiccup gave way to renewed growth, and the engine of national prosperity roared again to life, hurling the nation ahead faster than before.*"

----

[3]Louis Johnston and Samuel H. Williamson, "The Annual Real and Nominal GDP for the United States, 1789 - Present." Economic History Services, April 2002, URL: http://www.eh.net/hmit/gdp/

According to the National Bureau of Economic Research (NBER) the index of railroad stocks dropped from a high of $40.06 in April of 1875 to a gut wrenching low of $23.59 in June of 1877. The index had topped in 1872 at $45.20. In the ensuing five years the price had plummeted 47%. The drop over the two years ending in June 1877 was over 41% alone.

The story doesn't end there, of course. An investor who either presciently bought into that basket of railroad stocks in June of 1877, or merely remained invested as some obviously did, would have seen the price rise from the dismal $23.59 to $55.86 over the next five years. That astute investor would have seen an average annual compound return of 16.53% per year.

The significance of these numbers is that first, the market value of the railroad stock continued to fall for two years after the Gross Domestic Product of the United States began its recovery, and second, it is clear that even as the railroads were *overpriced* in 1872 and even in 1875, they were dramatically *underpriced* in 1877 following the over 40% drop in share prices.

If, as I strongly suspect, the fall in market prices that began in 2000 and has continued into 2003 is effectively a repeat of the railroad mania and panic of the 1870s, then it would be reasonable to expect to see a doubling or greater in the indices of stock prices over the next five years. In other words, an opportunity exists during the irrational disgust that follows a commodity or stock bubble to increase one's wealth by contrarian investing.

The Next Bubble

As each pricing collapse that follows a bubble works its way out, the flight from the collapsing prices, itself the cause of the price decline, provides the opportunity for the charlatans to emerge in a new form. As people were seeking the double digit returns to which they had become accustomed in bank certificates of deposits, there were the Charles Keatings and the Michael Milkens lined up to sell them high yield (junk) bonds in the bank lobby.

Anyone who is guaranteeing a return of more than the current return for the 10-year Treasury note is either legally or illegally cooking the books. Millions of dollars have been lost to conmen who will "guarantee" returns of ten or twelve percent. If a ten-year Treasury note is yielding 4%, no one can earn a lot more than that without a substantial risk of loss.

Meanwhile, the cash flow into legitimate bond and money market investments has broken all previous records (massive cash flow), and people are bragging at cocktail parties about how they have had their money in short-term or even long-term bond positions and thereby avoided the loss in the stock market (mass popularity and popular appeal). Given that inflation is running about 2% now and forecast to rise to 3% next year, holding those low yielding bond investments is actually causing a loss in buying power after inflation and taxes to those masses of people rushing to the "safety" government bills, note, and bonds (an asset class that has lost its ability to create utility because of oversupply).

Let's presume that inflation and interest rates rise as the economy continues its recovery. Given that presumption, the holders of those "guaranteed" interest positions will find that selling them prior to maturity will create a substantial loss. If they hold them until they mature, inflation and taxation will have eroded their investment to a lower level than they paid for the investment. In other words, all the elements of a bubble in "guaranteed" low yielding notes and bonds are already in place. Only time will tell, but it will be a real surprise if the masses are right this time after being wrong so often for so long.

Fraud and Deception

Any speculative mania will have at its base the very fundamental element of *greed*. Greed is a subtle vice that begins with the desire to secure oneself from the uncertainties of life and fortune. Once that apparently virtuous desire is unleashed it far too often becomes a monster leading on to a susceptibility to charlatans.

Those who create schemes that are designed at their very root to take money from the unsuspecting and unsophisticated commonly start with an idea that actually has some merit. I strongly suspect that some of the perpetrators of these schemes begin by believing in their vision of how the idea will work so strongly that they, by power of that intense belief, convince others to join them and contribute money. As the game progresses, any rational person could recognize that the original idea has failed, but the deluded originator of the scheme is still charging ahead and accepting money as though it is working. In the deluded mind of the perpetrator, it may actually be working.

It would be nice to think of all such things as devilish plots hatched up in a smoke filled room by evil men intent on stripping money from the innocent, but it is rarely that simple. The unreasonable income or growth of capital promised by such schemes simply would never stand up to any investigation. The victims of the schemes are as much the perpetrators as are the originators. The greed of the originator and his unreasoning belief that what he is doing will work out to everyone's good is matched by the greed of the "investor" and his or her belief that they are now one of the privileged "insiders" who make all the money while the foolish common people stand outside with their simplistic savings and slow gaining investments.

Another commonality of these schemes is that there are still a faithful few who persist in believing that if the "great man" who led the scheme had just had a little longer to work things out and had not been cruelly "shut down" by the authorities, they would have received the riches promised. They are people who have so wrapped up their belief system in the riches they dreamed of receiving quickly that they are unable to let go of their emotional belief.

In 1920, Mr. Charles K. Ponzi created a scheme that would later bear his name, as it was reenacted thousands of times over. Ponzi publicized the fact that due to a revaluation of currencies, one could purchase a postal coupon in Italy for local currency worth about one cent in the United States, and that coupon could then be redeemed for six cents in America. With that simple fact as a basis, he went on to offer notes to investors on which he promised to pay 50% interest in only three months time. Within a year he had gathered over $9,000,000, a truly staggering sum in a time when a $35,000 house was considered a palatial mansion. Even after successive runs on his business, the *Securities Exchange Company*, he had only paid out just over $7,000,000, and just as many investors were lined up to give him money as were lined up to get theirs back as he was hauled off to jail.

In fact, the trading of postal coupons would never have worked simply because the transaction costs would have greatly exceeded the five cent profit. The United States Post Office, as it turns out, would accept no more than ten of the coupons from a single person or entity anyway. That issue was beside the point, as there is no evidence that Ponzi ever actually bought or sold any of the coupons. The few people who contacted the Postmaster to inquire about Mr. Ponzi's scheme were informed that there were literally no Italian postal coupons being redeemed in the United States. When Ponzi was queried about the apparent discrepancy, he replied that he had found a way to conduct the trades overseas so they would not violate American Postal Regulations. In actuality, he was not trading any postal coupons at all.

A simple visit to the nearest post office would have been sufficient to demonstrate that the Ponzi scheme had no hope of working, but literally tens of thousands of people still deposited the minimum of $1,000 with Mr. Ponzi's company, believing that 50% interest per quarter was a realistic possibility.

The Ponzi scheme was repeated a few years later in Florida, as people in New York bought land in Florida sub-divisions that were literally under water. During the Oklahoma Land Rush days, the "Boomers" were people who sold land they did not own. During the 1980s the Ponzi scheme, albeit in a barely legal form, was repeated with real estate and oil and gas limited partnerships. In some form or another, the scheme is going on all the time, and unsuspecting investors are being efficiently stripped of their money by con-men (and women).

I recently spoke at length with a couple that had just lost well over a million dollars to a "Ponzi scheme." In a time when mortgage rates were the lowest they had been in almost forty years, uniformly in the mid-single digits, this couple's tax preparer, a well-respected Certified Public Accountant, suggested they contact a local "financial planner" who was employed by a prominent Wall Street brokerage firm. The CPA was impressed that several of his clients had been receiving "guaranteed" interest payments amounting to 12% per year from what turned out to be mortgage partnerships being sold by this stockbroker.

After visiting with the broker, they were introduced to the purveyor of this partnership who drove them around to several prominent buildings in the city where they lived and showed them the mortgage documents he held on those buildings. The couple was thoroughly impressed and invested over a million dollars though the "financial planner" stockbroker. Within a month the money started coming in. Indeed, their invested $1,300,000 produced a check each month in their mailbox for the exact amount of $13,000. They were sure they had "hit the mother lode" and finally got in on an "insider deal" as they put it.

It never occurred to them that the mortgage markets are really quite frugal and rational, and that *if* the 12% interest rate on the mortgages was "for real," then it would have only been because the mortgagees (those borrowing the money) were either fools of the first order or in such sever financial straights that they would probably soon be in bankruptcy. More, had these mortgage obligations they thought they were purchasing been actual, they would have received about the same rate they could get in the broad market, even if the rate on the obligation was theoretically 12%. In other words, mortgage obligations, like any other interest rate bearing security, will provide an actual yield to maturity at any point that is equal to what the general market rate is at that moment.

This may sound a bit complicated, but this is how it works. If the going rate for commercial mortgages is around 6%, and the mortgage they are, for whatever reason, locked into bears an interest rate of 12%, then the market value of that obligation will be about 1.67 times the face value. That calculation comes from the fact that for every $1,000 one invests in a mortgage bond at the going new-mortgage rate of 6%, one will receive $60 per year. Thus, it is reasonable for someone to be willing to pay $1,000 for every $60 they will be receiving. If an obligation like the one our couple was purchasing has a 12% face "coupon" then it would be reasonable for them to pay about $2,160,000 for that monthly interest income of $13,000 rather than the $1,300,000 they actually paid.

Now, it just might be possible for them to have paid the money they did and legitimately receive the checks they received, but only if two things were true. First, the company paying on the mortgage would have had to be in financial straits, making it a "junk" or high-yield mortgage. Second, the payment would have been both the interest *and* a substantial return of principal, as commonly happens with mortgages. The combination of the two is a deadly deal. The payer could well "go under" leaving the investor holding what might well be a worthless note, or if somehow the distressed company paying on the mortgage managed to survive until the mortgage was paid off, the investor would discover that they had been spending their principal and were then broke!

Meanwhile back at the ranch (this couple actually *did* have a "hobby" ranch where they lived) the checks were showing up regularly each and every month in their rural delivery mailbox of the couple. This steady series of checks went on for about six or seven months, and then one month the check did not come. After waiting for a couple of days beyond the normal delivery date, the wife called the broker. A secretary answered the phone and told them that they had been receiving a number of calls and that the broker was checking on the problem. She waited a few more days and again called the trusted stockbroker. This time another secretary answered the phone and informed them that the broker had changed companies.

The wife immediately called the partnership headquarters and received a pleasant answer that there had been a foul up at the transfer bank, they were working on the issue and the check should be forthcoming, but to give them at least a week to get it worked out. The wife, much relieved, went about her business for the next week, only mildly concerned. After about a week and a half she again called. This time she received the feared multi-tone announcement that the number she had called was no longer in service.

She and her husband immediately drove to the city where the partnership was headquartered and where they had seen the buildings and the impressive documents. The partnership headquarters was locked and clearly abandoned with a prominent "for lease" sign displayed on the door. They drove to the brokerage firm where they were told that the broker had "gone independent" and was now using a prominent discount brokerage firm as his clearing agent. They also discovered that their accounts had transferred with the broker.

They were finally able to find the broker working out of his home. He assured them that there was some kind of mistake and that he was working hard to find out what was wrong, but that he was confident that their money was safe. They proceeded to an attorney's office where they found themselves in a room with several other "investors" who had experienced very nearly the exact same scenario.

Our couple, the CPA, and the broker, who held himself out as a "financial planner," were all victims of a classic Ponzi scheme. The person who set up the swindle was paying the early investors with money coming in from the late investors. The mortgages were merely old copies of mortgage documents he had obtained from the courthouse dating from the days of double-digit mortgages on those buildings. The perpetrator of the scheme had "completed the offering" and gone on "vacation" three months before the money ran out. He was smart enough to leave three months' payments in the account and a full staff behind. My understanding is that his fingerprints and everything else about his identity are linked to the real identity of a child who died at a young age in a distant part of the country.

At first glance it seems to be ironic that they gravitated to the partnership in mortgage obligations because they considered the "stock market" to be too "risky" for them. From their perspective, mortgages were secure and real estate was secure; therefore, the investment they were making was "secure." This perception was amplified by the fact that the salesman was endorsed by their trusted CPA and was employed by a major Wall Street brokerage firm.

Actually, their so-called "investment" was totally insecure. Their desire was to have a 12% return on their investment. Based on history, that is a pretty stout return but has been historically possible if an investor was willing to have a rather volatile portfolio of what *Ibbotson & Associates* refers to as Small Company Stocks, more commonly known as "Mid-Caps" today. The kicker is that they would have to have been able to tolerate some pretty significant volatility in their daily market values. They considered that volatility to be a "risk" and thereby avoided the only asset class that could have reasonably been expected to satisfy their expressed need.

They then turned to an asset class that has historically returned about half the long term return they wanted and were delighted to be promised the full return they desired. The myth they believed was that the "big guys" are able to get the good deals and the "little guys" (themselves) are left with the leftovers. In fact, the "big guys" get the same returns from the same places the "little guys" could use. The professionals simply have more patience, accumulate more capital over a longer period of time, and most importantly, *do their homework!*

While there are no shortages of people who simply refuse to recognize this so soon after being burned, the dot-com mania, particularly with regard to the Initial Public Offering (IPO) market, was a Ponzi scheme without a Ponzi, unless you count the analysts at the investment banks who were selling the IPO's to the public.

Enron was a Ponzi scheme with a group of leaders who moved the debts off the books and retained the earnings on the books. Of course, it is apparent now that the earnings they retained on the books were often created by trading with themselves. Jeffrey Skilling took his money and bailed out at the appropriate time. Kenneth Lay shows every sign of having been unaware that he was at the top of a money pyramid that was about to collapse. Andrew Fastow was probably another deluded and irrational perpetrator. His background was in marketing where "perception is reality," and the whole idea of having a person from marketing as the Chief Financial Officer of a corporation is an amazing concept. Although he apparently profited greatly from *his* actions, he was still there when it fell, indicating that he was clueless about the end result that would inevitably accrue from his deception.

I could go on with examples like WorldCom, AOL, and a host of others, but before we depart from this subject, I want to add one more. In order for there to be a Ponzi scheme, there has to be a general belief about things financial that is unrealistic at its base. Each mania has its own irrational underpinning that is unique to that time, but they all have something in common. Once something irrational and untrue is repeated often enough in public, the academic community will often come in with a "proof" of the reasonableness of the belief which reinforces the belief and leads to the mania.

There were three basic untruths that were widely propagated and believed leading to the speculative frenzy preceding the dramatic fall in stock valuations. The first was the fraud perpetrated by some major accounting firms as they entered the "consulting" business in order to be well-paid for advising companies they were supposedly auditing on how to phony their earnings. The second was the drum beat of higher expectations sounded by major Wall Street brokerage house analysts on stocks they privately stated were "dogs," even as they were being paid based on the sales of those stocks. Both of those areas are being dealt with under criminal law and in civil courts.

The third source of misleading information came from many pronouncements that there was no need to research or pay fees to invest because the "market" was inherently efficient, and paying fees to investment advisors and managers for investigating and planning was a waste. The end result was to convince not only the public, but also many investment professionals of the validity of that statement. The rush of investors to "discount" brokers and "no-load" mutual funds at the market top has only been matched by the exit stampede from the same areas as the prices bottomed. In fact, looking back from the bottom of the valuation collapse in early October 2002, an examination of the one hundred largest mutual funds over fifteen years old reveals that there is only a weak correlation between long term return and fees and that correlation is that *funds with higher returns had a tendency to have slightly higher fees.*

Do high fees mean high returns? No. If I do a search for higher fees I get no indication that it had much of anything to do with returns. What I do find though is that the lowest internal fee funds, largely from Vanguard, cluster in the bottom half of performers over the fifteen-year period. There is very little direct correlation between the internal cost of mutual funds and the long-term return of the fund. About 38% of the funds performed better than the S&P 500 Index, and about 62% did not have as great a return. A close examination of that 62% of funds with lower return reveals that many of those funds had a substantial quantity of bonds and cash in the portfolio, thereby reducing their volatility over the period. Others were sector funds that are in a sector-like technology that is currently taking a beating. All this says is that the simplistic belief that "low cost equals high return" generated by the marketing from a mutual fund family and reinforced by a series of questionable semi-scientific studies (often financed by that same mutual fund company) was incorrect. That untruth was one of the critical elements in creating the bubble.

Chapter 7 – A Value to Depend On

One of the values in our society that has changed has been the concept of change itself. Until the last 50 years of our history as well as in the vast majority of the world, *change* was and is anything but a positive concept. Today, a good definition of the culture of the Western world could be summed up simply by saying we are a people who have given up on the idea of a *better past*. The very nature of what we consider valuable and thereby worth paying for has changed so much that a great rift has opened between much of the rest of the world and us. Even in Western Europe, the birthplace of much that we call American, writers and speakers refer to us as "impetuous" and "hasty." They criticize our desire to move on to new and better technologies and, most of all, our cultural ability to change our institutions and companies seemingly almost overnight to accommodate those new capabilities. The nations of Western Europe often seem to equate greater stability and individual economic security with progress. We in the United States equate greater opportunity with progress.

One of the most critical questions each investor should ask is whether our definition of progress, revolutionary change, or the Western European and Japanese definition, greater economic stability and security, is the one that will prevail. If our relatively new definition is merely a fad and we will either reverse our position or come crashing down as the fools some Europeans believe us to be, then investing should be directed to European companies and those in the United States that are purveyors of the old "tried and true" methodologies. If this new value is in fact a more effective view of "what works," then the American value system will go on to become world dominant and is the place to have one's investments.

This is not a short-term question. Investing, if it is truly investing, has to do with changes in long-term values. It really comes down to a simple proposition. What we have defined as a virtue, *opportunity*, is frightening to much of the rest of the world. Opportunity involves change. Opportunity involves risk. Opportunity springs from one of the most fundamental values upon which our nation and our culture is founded, *liberty!*

The most fundamental of our national documents is not our

Constitution, although it is the guarantor of that value, it is the Declaration of Independence. Before we even knew what form of government we would finally thrash out, we knew what was important, and it still has the ring of truth to it over 200 years after it was penned in a world we would barely recognize today. "*We hold these truths to be self-evident: That all men are endowed by their Creator with certain inalienable rights, and among these rights are life, liberty, and the pursuit of happiness.*" We would see nearly a hundred years pass before even the states that we call united could reach an agreement on the meaning of those words. It would take a war so horrible in its scope and devastation that a century later the passions it awoke were still raging through the land. It would require the deployment of federalized National Guard troops to Little Rock, Arkansas, almost two hundred years after that document was signed, to begin the hopefully final process of realizing the fruit of those words, but we have persevered. Abraham Lincoln eloquently wrote as we realized the depths of the struggle needed to bring reality to those words, "*And now we are engaged in a great struggle to determine whether government of the people, by the people, and for the people will long endure on the earth...*"

Government can provide the protection for our lives; it can even provide the opportunity for liberty. Government cannot *give* us liberty though. It can only provide us with the right to take it. We have the *right* to vote, to shape our government, to determine our collective future, but less than half of us take the time and more importantly, the *responsibility* to educate ourselves and *exercise* that right. The Declaration of Independence and the Constitution that followed it cannot guarantee us or our children or our children's children any rights at all, unless we are educated and prepared to assume our responsibility as citizens of a free nation.

In nations as close to us in philosophy and even geography as Canada or Western Europe, the term *liberty* is still used disparagingly. It has the connotation of "to take liberties," meaning to do or act in such a way that one exceeds one's proper place in society. The struggle between the Yeomen and the nobility continues there to this day. In the United States we have a value they consider an offense, *liberty*. Are they right or are we? We believe that a nation where *all* are given unlimited opportunity to rise as far as their talent and their determination will take them will be a nation that releases a capability to create a level of wealth unbelievable to the rest of the world, and all who desire to do so and pay the price of liberty can share in it. They believe that the passions of individual people must be contained by society to limit the potential damage they might to do others by rising too far, too fast. They believe that negation and evolutionary progress towards greater protection from failure is the key to happiness and contentment.

Only history will tell if we or they are correct in our approach to this fundamental question about the nature of who we are as humans. I have had many people question me over the years about whether it is possible for our corporate earnings, national standard of living, and general growth to continue. There is a very vocal and active faction within our own country that favors reversing our growth in the name of sanity. They fear we will run out of something or we will so upset the order of things that we will bring the wrath of nature or economics down upon us. I do not agree with them and can offer much evidence that we are not running out of anything, but are finding and making more of all that we need and want than we can even use. But, I am not the objective judge.

On one point, though, I will take a stand and let that be the judge of our course. Democracy works. I have no idea why a large number of people whose intelligence and education by definition are average can make better decisions to govern ourselves than can a few highly educated people of superior intelligence, but they do. If we begin by agreeing that democracy works better than any other decision making method, then let us look at how people are voting on whether we or our critics are correct about the future.

Western Europe has a truly admirable cradle to grave welfare system that will provide nearly free medical care, vacations, long-term treatments, and even income for those without gainful employment. Canada's system is very much the same. The common man's paradise has been realized if security for the necessities of life is his goal.

Very few Americans emigrate to Europe to become citizens or even permanent residents, yet the waiting list for immigrant visas to the U.S. from Europe seems to grow longer every year. Few or no Americans are applying to emigrate to Canada, despite the guaranteed healthcare and retirement benefits offered just across the border in a friendly English-speaking nation. Canadians, on the other hand, are steadily migrating to the United States in such numbers that Canada has had to put on a recruiting drive in Asia to maintain its population levels. Those people are voting with their feet. They are casting the most expensive of votes. They are venturing into a strange land where the social safety net is notoriously weak but where the opportunity, the liberty, is almost unlimited.

I have had the opportunity to travel to Western Europe and Canada and have spoken with the people there who wish to be here and those who do not. I have had the wonderful opportunity to spend time with those who have come here, both legally and illegally, and then made the decision to stay in this chaotic uncertain place we call America. Even among those who stay behind there is an admiration for those who had the courage to risk everything to go to America. Among those who have cast their lot with ours, there is a sense of pride and accomplishment they believe exists nowhere else in the world.

Thus, one of our "whys" is answered. Why is it that we as a nation have the fastest growing economy on earth? Why is it that our productivity grows at a rate unimaginable in the rest of the world? Why is it that in less than a working lifetime, we have brought the medium standard of living of those officially in "poverty" to a level higher than the medium standard of living of the general populace only forty years before? It is because we have chosen to sacrifice a degree of economic security for the greatest degree of individual freedom and opportunity in the history of mankind, and in doing so, we have loosened the most powerful engine of prosperity in the world.

We Americans today have progressed from an economy of agriculture through an economy of industrial production and into a brave new world where the capital is measured in the capability of people's minds. We have entered into an economy of ideas where information is the raw material used to produce those ideas. We have the ability to employ the rest of the world to enact those ideas, and in doing so, raise the living standards and freedom of the entire planet. The best and most energetic minds on our planet are standing in line to join us. That is the "why" behind our success. It is a "why" we can depend on.

Section II – Effective Investing

Chapter 8 – Reasons for Investing

Entertainment

I want to explain the valid reasons for investing here and I want to explain how to effectively put together a portfolio that has the potential to accomplish your objectives. But, before we go on to the valid reasons for investing, I want to address another reason. Entertainment is what people do who "play the market." Short-term trading, buying on hunches, and trips to casinos, all fall in the same category—very expensive entertainment. During the long run of the 1990s bull market, I read several well-documented articles (and financial statements) indicating that the profitability of the "discount" stock trading firms was substantially higher per customer than the old-line brokerage firms. The concept of encouraging high frequency buying and selling of stocks was clearly profitable, but not to the trader!

I have seen long-term holders of diversified, managed portfolios with returns that were delightful to behold. The problem for some with that manner of investing is that *it is boring*. The happiest investors with whom I have had the privilege to work were regular people who had thoroughly diversified their investments into a series of well-managed portfolios for a long period of time. Even in the major decline at the beginning of the 21st century, their long-term returns were still well up in the double digits per year. What did they do to achieve such astonishing results? They didn't try to be entertained!

The successful investors I have met, as well as the luminaries whose wisdom I have read, have universally presented a clear set of principles that constitute a path to effective investing. They, too, have insisted that knowing what it is to invest rather than simply gambling on a price is one of the keys to success.

Security

We are born insecure, and as we grow older we find new sources of insecurity to fear. I once heard a comment probably lifted from some learned academic that rings true in our age as in no other in history: *"The greatest fear held today by most people is winding up old, alone, and broke."* For the first time in history, we, in the "developed" countries, no longer have sudden death from invaders, famine, or disease as our perceived greatest threat. The four horsemen of the apocalypse, war, famine, disease, and pestilence seem quaintly dated to another time or another part of the world.

We live in a society where the death of a single child from violence is reported across the country in a priority that was once reserved for deaths of kings. As tragic as the events of September 11, 2001 were, the number of people who died in that cruel act was so few in the scope of even just the American population as to be statistically insignificant. The impact of the event was the resurrection of a threat our ancestors faced that we believed had been relegated to the history books. Our efforts to secure our physical safety have been among the most important of our investments over the past two centuries. We have largely eliminated the threat of infection and now face our number one source of death in self-created risks such as auto accident or inappropriate diet. Our second most likely cause of death is the genetic malfunction of cancer. We are in a utopian world where death other than from self-imposed causes is most likely to come at a very advanced age and be from the "natural" aging process.

According to the overheard comment above, and my personal experience, given the removal of many of the sources of threat to our physical being, we find ourselves faced with a new threat. The fact that we may well live to a ripe old age is of little use if in that old age we wind up living at a dramatically reduced standard of living. In other words, now that the *length* of life dreamt of by our ancestors is, for most of us, within reach, the *quality* of that life becomes the threat.

As recently as a couple of generations ago and in the more primitive societies today, that threat was limited by the fact that most did not live long enough to be a burden. The few that did were greatly outnumbered by either their descendants or the younger members of their extended family. Most people (and I do mean *most*) never had to worry about being old because very few made it to what was then the exalted status of *elder*. As our ancestors settled down and began the long path of civilization, the repositories of history, the very *books* of the people were the elders. More, they had a proven skill at the most important issue of life, *survival*.

There are a couple of very basic issues in this relationship. Because there were very few *elders,* they were a rare, and valuable commodity and they carried the accumulated wisdom on how to deal effectively with the recurring threats to survival. Today, the fastest growing segment of our population is in the euphemistic category of "senior citizen." Even the accumulated wisdom of those "senior citizens" is not valued as our rate of technological change has rendered much of that wisdom not only obsolete, but in the view of many younger people, actually counter productive.

The end result is that we still have institutions that were started in an age of rare elders, such as social security and defined benefit retirement annuities, but their existence is threatened by the age imbalance created by those technological advances. That leaves us with the very real situation in which we find ourselves. With rare exception, we can no longer depend upon an ever-expanding population of younger people willing to provide for our well-being beyond our "productive" years.

The issue of providing for our financial security is in our hands.

Wealth

The purpose of investing is to create *wealth*. The word "wealth" evolved from the Middle English word "weal" and has an even older root in "well." The origin of the word came from having a fresh water spring that "welled up." One who held such a spring, even before the understanding of property lines, was *wealthy.*

The concept of the "well" as opposed to the "cistern" is illustrated often in ancient writings as "living water" as opposed to "dead water." In the very cradle of civilization, the concept of being in possession of a well is vital to the survival of the agricultural community. In Old English as well as in early Indo-European, the word for "wall" and "well" are the same. In order to move from the nomadic ways of the hunter-gatherer and pastoral tribes, the agricultural community must bind themselves to a stationary location through their investment in the soil that would grow their food. Deprived of their mobility, the only defense they had against other tribes that would destroy them and take that food was to build walls. In order to build the walls, they must have a source of water inside the walls. In other words, if you did not have a well you could not have walls, therefore well equals wall.

Even today, the presence of a well or spring on a piece of property raises the value substantially. Wealth implies a depth of resource that has some form of protection. Think of the difference between a spring and a well. Both produce water, but one may or may not be there when the weather turns dry. Springs, too, have the problem of things falling in them. Drinking water from a spring without filtering and purifying it is asking for trouble. A well is assumed to be dug or drilled deeply enough that it has tapped into underground water that is both uncontaminated and consistently available. The top of the well is either well walled in or at least covered to keep out things we don't want to drink.

There is more to the idea of *wealth* than just having money or even "net worth." Wealth implies that there is something owned that produces income the way we expect a well to produce water. There are ways that one can produce income that actually have little to do with wealth. A *cistern* looks a lot like a well but merely stores the water that is poured into it. In a period of dry weather, the cistern will run dry. Hopefully the well won't!

The idea behind "wealth" then is to have something that will provide a stream of what you need to live. In our society and culture, it is *wealth* that has become the wall that we depend on for protection. Ultimately, most of us have a dream that we will someday be able to pursue a higher calling. We are looking for Eden. We desire a place and a situation where we can pursue the growth of our souls without toil. We yearn for relief from the curse recorded in the book of Genesis, "You shall toil and earn your bread by the sweat of your brow." We seek a life where we first *have* wealth, and then, that some trusted person or institution would manage our wealth to ensure we have the income, or *money*, we want and need to continue our lives.

Money is quite possibly the most sought after and least understood element in our lives. From the very tangible things like *shelter* and *food* to the least tangible item *love*, people, when asked for a definition, can easily give at least a subjective impression of what it means to them. *Money* is a different matter. When people are asked for a definition of money, their answer is likely to be something like, "What I never have enough of." or "What I use to buy things." Those definitions are very nice, but they leave out the fact that we use money to *save* as well as spend, or at least some of us do! They leave out the issue of money as a means of measurement or even as a means of valuing time! John Kenneth Galbraith wrote a book on the subject of *money*, and by the end of the book neither he nor I seemed to have a much better understanding of what money really is.

The term *money* comes from the minting of coin on *Mons* Juno in ancient Rome. Precious metals had long been used as a medium of exchange, but the concept of having a universally accepted form appears to have originated in Ionic Greece.

The Ionians were Greeks who had emigrated from the peninsula and islands of present day Greece to the islands and coastal areas of Western Asia Minor. These newcomers realized that two old and well-established empires were their neighbors, Egypt and Persia. The Ionians determined that they were ideally suited to be in the business of commerce between the empires, and between those empires and the rest of the Mediterranean.

In order to facilitate trading, and thereby their profits, the Greeks came up with the idea of being an international provider of a standardized medium of exchange. The Ionians concluded that minting coins with a specific guaranteed weight and composition was the solution. Their coinage became the first international monetary standard, and the Ionians found greater profit not only in increased shipping but also in becoming the minter and banker for the ancient Mediterranean world.

The first coins were discs of a naturally occurring metallic alloy, electrum, composed of a specific mixture of gold and silver. Unfortunately, in a precursor to the monetary depressions that would shock the world again and again for the next three millennia, the need for this new money outstripped the availability of the metal and the civilizations of the ancient world soon turned to more readily available currencies.

With the collapse of the Ionian trading monopoly came the end of the first international currency. Much later, the Romans saw the value in having a standard of value not only for precious metals, but also as true money that had a given value separate from the metal from which it was made. As I said earlier, the Romans were very little into innovation, but they were masters of copying what others had invented and duplicating it effectively. Just as Microsoft has never been accused of being a hotbed of innovation, they have been very effective at standardization and mass production. In the end, it is normally not the inventor of a technological innovation that creates the greatest utility but the person or organization that finds the way to mass produce the new concept effectively and efficiently that does the most good and earns the greatest profit

Prior to money, the only way to establish what could be exchanged for something else was by barter. Barter works well enough as long as you can actually get face-to-face with the other party and haggle a bit. The problems start to crop up when you want to buy something far away. The Romans needed to buy food in Egypt and to provide their legions with something that would have pretty much the same value in Persia as it did in Britannia. They did it very much the same way they established order throughout the rest of their empire; they made a law. The Romans gave us the concept of a government of laws rather than men, and it is by some of those laws that money came into existence.

The Roman coinage was not subject to barter; it had a value based on the credibility of the Roman Empire. The emperor's visage was on the face (literally) of the coin and to deface (literally) the money was to defile (again literally) the emperor. In other words, because the emperor was the deified symbol of Rome and his face *was* the face of the coin, removing part of his *face* with a *file* was to deface the emperor's image with a file, a crime punishable by death. In effect, to attempt to remove part of the precious metal of the coin was to render the coin valueless and to potentially face death.

The net effect of this law was to create money that was actually more valuable than the underlying metal from which it was made. That, by the way, is one of the critical aspects of money; it *must* be worth more than that from which it is made. Money is very different from a useful, or utility, commodity. Money is a *concept* just as joining a finely knapped flint rock with two sharpened sides to the end of a staff is a concept that we call a *spear*. Money only exists in that reality we call *intangibles*. The value we attribute to money comes not from the material from which it is made but from the value we attribute to the authority or institution that stands behind the stated value of the money.

So, what is money today? As recently as a hundred years ago, the standard for currency of all kinds was something called *specie*, meaning *in kind.* Even the paper money of my childhood in the 1950s and 60s was entitled "Silver Certificate" and stated on the certificate that it represented "one ounce of silver on deposit in the treasury of the United States of America." The ratio of silver to gold was set at thirty-five ounces of silver to one ounce of gold, or more simply, the internationally accepted Breton Woods Agreement fixed the price of gold at $35 to the ounce.

Around 1971, that agreement broke down. Like other laws that attempt to dictate economic conditions, it simply did not work. At least two elements combined to create the collapse of that agreement. First, the Johnson Administration, a Democratic presidency with the backing of a Democratic majority in Congress, attempted to spend quite a lot more money than they were bringing in through taxes. They, in effect, flooded Southeast Asia with American dollars through the Viet Nam war while at the same time pumping dollars into the American economy through The War on Poverty and The Great Society.

As the number of dollars circulating grew faster than they were being earned in the United States, the real buying power of that dollar began to decline. In the United States, the price of goods and services began to rise, slowly at first but then faster. At first the rise in prices actually seemed like a good thing, as most people feared *deflation* far more than *inflation*. The fear of a return of the monetary shortage and deflation of the period following World War I in the 1930s was a specter not easily banished from the memory of Americans. After all, the Great Depression of the 1930s *did* come on the heels of World War I, and because we had just finished the second installment of world war, the fear was very real that it would happen again.

As we entered into the 1970s, the strains on the world financial system began to show. The dollar was the anchor to which all the other major European currencies were tied, and the dollar had been abused. France had been quietly collecting dollars, largely from our expenditures in Southeast Asia. In 1971, France presented America with a problem from which there was no easy escape. France demanded gold for the dollars it had accumulated. The secretary of the treasury under President Richard Nixon, John Connelly, warned that delivering the quantity of gold demanded by France would seriously deplete the gold reserves of the United States.

Jeff McClure

Their decision to break the Breton Woods Agreement set the currencies of the world free to float against each other. In a short period of time, the value of the dollar declined substantially against other major currencies of the world. At the same time, the prices of the things we buy in America began to rise faster. That same year President Nixon declared a wage and price freeze in an attempt to stabilize the value of the dollar. The result was an almost immediate fall in the economy. Upon withdrawing the freeze, prices jumped overnight.

In the United States, a death spiral of inflation had started. Rising prices of goods and services created an expectation of more price increases. The major American corporations were largely unionized, and the unions demanded pay increases with each new contract that had high inflation expectations included in the calculations. In order to meet the demand for higher wages and benefits, the corporations were forced to raise prices, thus completing the circuit of a condition known as *structural inflation*. By the end of the Carter Administration, a new term had entered the economic lexicon, *stagflation*. Even as the prices continued to rise, the economy was sinking into recession.

With the election of Ronald Reagan and the appointment of Paul Volker as the chairman of the Federal Reserve, an imperative to stop inflation was in place. Chairman Volker ratcheted up short-term interest rates to match the double-digit inflation that was now thoroughly entrenched in our economy. The battle to bring inflation under control would continue until the end of the 20th century.

Here, in the early years of the third millennium, we have learned the dangers of *inflation* but are again aware of the dangers of *deflation*. Perhaps we have finally learned from history because we have remembered it.

Today, without the legal restrictions of the Breton Woods Agreement, the dollar has once again become the reference and reserve currency of the world. Throughout most of the 20th century, whenever international instability became evident, the price of gold against the dollar rose sharply. But, by the end of the 20th century, international crisis failed to affect the price of gold. Rather, the international economic crisis that began with the collapse of the Indonesian currency in 1998 caused the price of the *dollar* to rise, while gold actually *fell* in value.

The price of gold peaked at about $820 per ounce in 1982. The price of gold in the early years of the 21st century was equivalent to a price of about $100 per ounce in 1982 dollars. I have heard it said from normally reliable sources that the majority of individuals who hold gold bullion as an investment purchased it at over $750 per ounce and are merely waiting for it to come back. In order to break even, they will have to wait until gold gets to over $1,500 per ounce. Considering that gold fields all over the world could be profitably worked at $400 to $500 per ounce, the chances that we will be seeing triple that price are close enough to zero for our purposes.

Over the decade ending in mid-2003, the price of gold has declined from well over $400 per ounce to around $260 and then with great assistance from gold traders, pushed up to the mid-$300 range again only to fall back. If we factor in inflation over the decade, the actual return on spot market gold bullion has been about a *negative* 6% per year!

Even the attack on September 11, 2001, on the World Trade Center failed to boost the price of gold substantially. In essence, these events confirm that the economic stability and military power of the United States have created the first nearly universal *money* since the fall of the Roman Empire.

The Roman currency started as a measure of a precious commodity that could be trusted. It developed over time into something much greater, a measure of *value* backed by the economic and military power of an empire. The U.S. dollar shed its relationship to any precious metal over thirty years ago yet has become the world wide standard for measure of value. The very nature of the measure of money has changed dramatically in the last fifty years.

The change has not ended. In the 1970s, I was fortunate to be able to live and work in Europe for three continuous years. As my family and I traveled about on our holidays there, we found the dollar to be nearly universally accepted. The form that was accepted was the greenback paper *Federal Reserve Note*. Last summer, we were again in Europe and were surprised to find that the paper dollar was not welcome in most places we visited. Rather, from the international airports to the innkeeper in a remote village on an island in the Hebrides, what they wanted us to use for money was a Visa card.

That plastic card with the magnetic strip on the back was universally accepted as money wherever we went. We, in essence, paid in dollars, and the vendor of the goods or services we were purchasing was paid in the local currency. Visa assured the vendor that he or she would not find that they had converted the dollar into the local currency at a rate disadvantageous to either the vendor or us. More, the transaction was deposited into their bank account in the local currency that same day.

From the local gas pump that takes your credit card to the inn in the Hebrides, money is rapidly becoming a digital item. We may still denominate the money in the local currency, but the denomination is becoming irrelevant. Wealth, capital, and money are changing very quickly into something the world has not seen before. Whether we like it or not, the money we want to "well up" from our wealth will be in the form of digital electronic signals. The very investments we use to create that wealth and from which the money needs to flow will be digital in nature. There was no small number of people who objected as the U.S. transitioned from a currency of hard metal to one of paper. Again, many of us will have difficulty trusting or accepting a digital form of money, but it is happening, and we can either adjust to it or unhappily live with it. It is better that we should understand what is happening and how we can benefit from it, rather than hiding from the changes that are becoming a universal reality.

Our misunderstanding of the nature of money is of more than academic importance. When we think of money only as what we can spend, we can easily make critical investment errors when money is used as a measure of *value*. If we were to receive a monthly or quarterly statement defining the value of our residence in terms of dollars we would be unlikely to sell our house simply because the value was "down." In fact, because we are far more astute in dealing with the prices of *tangibles* such as a house, we tend to have a desire to sell when the price is *up* and a reluctance to sell when the price is *down*. Unfortunately when we receive statements defining the liquidation values of an investment portfolio, we do have a tendency to do exactly the opposite!

One of the more serious errors made by amateur investors is their interpretation of the numbers on the *statement* issued periodically that reports a recent raw market liquidation *price* of their portfolio. There is a natural tendency to assume that the *dollars* represented in that statement constitute a pool of money. If, indeed, the numbers on that statement represent stored *dollars*, any reduction in the numbers of dollars from one period to the next is legitimate cause for alarm. *Dollars* do not just "go away." For a pool of dollars to be reduced there must be either spending or theft!

Of course, in reality, the fact that the reported *dollar value* of an investment portfolio declines is no more significant than if you were to receive an appraisal from the local taxing district on your home indicating that the valuation had declined from the previous year. The house is still there and is still just as much a house as it was last year. No theft occurred and no part of the house was sold. Where then did the dollars go?

In fact, the house was never "dollars," neither last year nor this year. The appraisal district simply is reporting how much a home similar to yours might be worth on the real estate market. The quoted dollars on your investment portfolio statement have exactly the same meaning. Unless something else happened, you did not either "lose" money if the appraisal is less or "make" money if the appraisal is more.

Of course, the long-term objective of any investment portfolio is to create those very dollars that are either realized as income or from the sale of the investments. How do we go about creating this money, this *wealth*? On the surface, it appears to not to be too hard. After all, if you had enough money in a bank savings account you would have a pretty good income, or at least it would seem so. In fact, what you would have is a slow return of your invested money.

A savings account is a *debt* vehicle. What we receive in return for the deposit of our money is a piece of paper, or certificate indicating that the bank is holding something of value in our name. That representation of value, which can be exchanged for money, is what we call a *security.*

Perhaps the best examples of debt securities are the bills, notes, and bonds issued by the United States Treasury. Unlike a savings account or a bank certificate of deposit, the market value of the Treasury bond will vary until maturity, but like the debt instrument that the certificate of deposit really is, the end return of the initial purchase price is effectively guaranteed by an agency of the U.S. Federal Government.

When a Treasury bond is auctioned off by the Treasury Department, the firms that bid at the auction effectively set the interest rate.

They are making an estimate of what they think inflation and taxes will subtract from the value of the bond over the time to maturity when the purchase price is refunded.

Shortly after the turn of the century in the year 2000, I did some practical research on that issue. I determined the interest rate of a thirty-year Treasury bond issued thirty years before, in 1971, and entered the annual interest payment into a spreadsheet. Then, I subtracted an estimate of income taxation and adjusted what was left for inflation. After adjusting the initial $1,000 that was paid for the bond in 1971 for inflation, you would have received back, in the year 2000, about $250 in 1971 dollars. The interest received over the thirty years, adjusted for inflation and taxes, was worth just under $750. In other words, what you had been receiving over the years was not *gain* from the $1000 purchase but a slow return of 75% of your purchase price. Your total return after holding the bond for the full thirty years, had you not spent any of the interest, was almost exactly *zero!*

Loaning money to the bank gets you a rather lower rate than loaning money to the government for 30 years with the result that you would have actually *lost* value, and rather substantially. According to *Ibbotson Associates, Stocks, Bills, Bonds, and Inflation,* had you purchased 90 day Treasury bills beginning in 1926, and spent the interest as you received it, every dollar you loaned the government would today be worth about ten cents in buying power relative what it would have bought back in 1926. If you had carefully reinvested all that interest over the 74 years, you would have a neat $14.00 for every dollar you loaned the government. Unfortunately, your dollar only buys about one tenth of what it did back in 1926, so your real value is about $1.40. Then of course, there is the issue of income taxes. If we rather optimistically assume that you somehow were able to defer the taxation on that interest you received, and that you are in a sort of middle of the road tax position, you would have almost exactly one dollar left after liquidating the bond. If, on the other hand, you had paid taxes along the way, you would be left with about seventy cents from every dollar you had loaned the government.

In other words, loaning money to even the government is a losing proposition over the long-term. If you are a commercial lender, the only way you are going to make money is to loan to the people or companies at a higher rate than you are borrowing it from people or companies. If a bank used only its own money to make loans, it simply could not make enough money to justify the use of the capital. Professionals are supposed to already know that, but it is something the rest of us need to learn.

Like the water in a storage tank, there is a reason for money in the bank or some other institution where you loan it out for the short-term. It is to smooth out the unevenness in cash flow and to have as a reserve in the case of an unexpected event, but it *is not creating wealth!* Money loaned to secure institutions is all about preservation of value but does nothing to create it.

Saving money does not create wealth, nor is it intended to. Japan has had one of the highest savings rates in the world for the past decade as their economy has teetered between recession and depression and the value of their corporate empire has declined 90% against that of the United States. Meanwhile the U.S. has had one of the *lowest* savings rates in the world and at the same time increased our collective wealth at an amazing rate.

Saving money is vital, but it is like storing corn in a silo. The corn is not subject to the danger of a bad crop, but as any farmer will tell you, there is a little less usable corn in that silo every year until, if you leave it long enough, it finally will become worthless *dust!* Planting corn, or even using it as feed for hogs and cattle subjects us to the risk of short term loss, but it is only by taking that risk that wealth may be created!

Banks create wealth all right, but they are in the wealth creation business for their *owners,* not for their depositors. The way a bank creates wealth is to provide utility to those depositors and for the borrowers. The services of a bank are *valuable,* so we are willing to pay for that value. Why are they valuable? The economists have a word for that "why." Value is created when we add *utility.*

Chapter 9 – Utility

Utility is what we create when we make something useful. I have a solid wood table in my office across which I hold discussions with my clients. At some time in the past, that table was part of a tree. The person who first cut the tree down added value to the wood. As it was removed from its stump and trimmed, it became portable.

Its value was further increased as soon as it was run through the sawmill and converted into boards. The boards were dried to prevent warping later, and then shaped, sanded, and joined together to become a table. The table was finished with a water resistant "finish." Now, the tree has become something that is quite useful, but it still is not worth as much as it will be. The table must then be transported to a location where there are willing buyers who want to have an attractive piece of furniture on which they can spread out papers and review them while sitting comfortably across from other people. Once that is done, the table is ready to sell.

In the case of my table, the original price of the tree, or even the tree trunk, was probably around $20. The final finished table cost over a thousand dollars delivered to my office. What was added to the table that is worth so much more than the tree trunk we started with? In a word, the answer is *utility*. A well-made and practical table in my office that is useful in a business sense and pleasing to the eye is worth many times the *value* of a log in the forest.

Three elements were combined to create the utility of the table. The first is a hard to describe quality called entrepreneurial effort. In other words, the person or persons who had the idea of creating tables out of trees and put effort and money into that idea added value to the equation.

The second element is *capital*. In order to cut down the tree saws were needed. To move it from where it was cut to the sawmill, trucks had to be available. Someone had to provide a sawmill and all its equipment, and there are a host of other tools and supplies that must be bought to finish the table. Finally, the equipment to move the table from where it was made to where it can be sold and used must be provided.

The last element in creation of utility is *labor*. To utilize the tools, people who were willing to work and have the appropriate skills must be employed. They too form a type of capital, as the tools require training to operate and someone had to invest time and money to create a level of skill. As our society evolves, the value of human skill has become perhaps the most important form of capital. A hundred years ago, a very large portion of our population was involved in what is referred to today as "common labor," meaning muscular work requiring skills that were "common" to nearly every person. Those jobs that required training were usually relatively simple. Henry Ford found it to be quite cost effective to hire new emigrants to America and train them on how to perform a single task on an assembly line.

Today, most of the employment in American is "skilled," meaning that it requires a high degree of sophistication on the part of the worker. "Unskilled" tasks are quickly being taken over by automation, or the task is exported to another culture where the standard of living allows the employee to be paid a wage that may be high to them but would be abysmally low to us.

We, as workers, sell our time multiplied by our skills in exchange for money. Most of that money is used to provide for our day-to-day lives. Unless we are entrepreneurs, we are unlikely to earn more money from entrepreneurial activities, and that only leaves our ability to invest some of that money in some form of capital as the source of our income in the future when we either cannot or do not wish to continue to sell our time.

Real Estate – The Original Equity

Ultimately, any property held for investment is only as valuable as the free cashflow it will generate. In an agricultural society, the value of the land was "produced" by the crops grown on it (often appropriately called "produce"). After feeding the workers (mostly family) and paying the demanded portion to the local taxing authority, selling the produce at the fair market was the source of two things. First, it provided a reserve of value in the form of some valuable commodity accepted as money. Second, it was the profit that was literally plowed back into the land as seed and perhaps capital improvements such as barns, irrigation ditches, drainage ditches, roads, and the many other things that made the land itself more productive.

Those improvements are "capital." Today we call them "capital improvements." This capital was invested in the farm, which itself was a form of company. In order for any active capital investment (like a farm or a modern corporation) to thrive, a significant part of the "return on capital" is reinvested to create yet more capital.

As time and economic sophistication increased, the farmer might well be interested in more than what we refer to as "subsistence farming." He might want a better bed or a cabinet for his kitchen or perhaps a stove to replace cooking in the fireplace. It doesn't take much imagination to trace that process from the farmer who wants a bed to the many niceties that fill our houses today. In order to purchase these things from those who make them or merchants who transport them to a place where the farmer can buy them, the farmer must have sufficient produce, or production, from his farm to have enough extra to sell to the public.

Obviously, the capital improvements he is making on his farm, from the plow, to the horse, to the barn, are means of accomplishing these things. The problem is that if he must accumulate the extra profit from the sale of his produce before he can pay for the barn, he is operating at a lower level of productivity and will thereby take quite a lot longer to be able to buy that new bed. The solution that emerged was for the farmer to borrow the money from someone or an organization that was pooling the profits of the farmers. Thus, the bank was born.

Banks – Loans from a Company

If the farmer, rather than converting his profits above that which was needed for survival into some form of wealth that he could store on his farm, instead deposited the profits in some form of money in a bank, and the other farmers did so as well, quite a lot of money could be accumulated. He could then pledge the capital and land that he owned as security and borrow the money to buy the barn. Presuming that the barn did indeed make him more productive now that he had a place to store the fodder for his animals and perhaps was even able to keep his cows out of the weather, the additional income from this increased productivity would serve to pay off the loan over time *and* provide the extra money for the bed *now*! Note here though, the farmer must first *own* the land for this to take place. If someone else owns the land, the bank has no collateral to recover its money if the farmer fails.

Additional advantages might even come from the improvement in standard of living brought by the bed, stove, and whatever else he might have purchased. First, by getting better rest and perhaps eating better, he and his family might be able to work longer and more effectively. Second, his health and welfare would be enhanced by the better food and the fact that he could tend to his cattle out of the winter weather. Perhaps the greatest advantage of this loan would be that the demand for the furniture and kitchen appliances would increase the profits and opportunities for those who were making all the items the farmer was buying to improve his life and productivity.

The craftsmen and merchants, now having increased profits from the increased demand, would also want to place their money in the bank and have the ability to take loans to increase their capital as they bought new and better saws and equipment and built larger and more effective buildings in which they would make their goods.

Eventually, some of the craftsmen, or even the farms, would either grow or combine with others to form larger companies to achieve something called "economy of scale." A craftsman building furniture had quite a capital investment in his saws and lathes, but he could not use them while he was finishing a piece of furniture. If another craftsman who did not have the equipment were to combine efforts with the lathe owning craftsman, they could make better use of the capital investment.

It was just such a process that led from the manufacture of automobiles by a quite large number of craftsmen at the beginning of the 20th century in America to the current relatively few, but extremely large, corporations that make automobiles for the American market. Linking back to our farmer, an even fewer number of companies now make tractors for farm use compared to hundreds in the early 20th century.

Unproductive Capital – the Investor's Peril

Before we move on to corporate finance and the opportunity to pool our money with others to share in the potential for wealth created by increasing utility, we need to take a small detour over to the less prosperous side of the tracks. Whether I own a farm, a business, or am working for a corporation or company, I can benefit from investing some of the *money* I earn through selling my time and skill to others. How I invest that money becomes a critical decision if I am to have any hope of living above a very basic standard in my "senior" years. Remember, before we get into the details, that *money* is generated from the creation of *value*. *Value* comes from the creation of *utility*.

If, for example, I purchase a house for $100,000, and it is my intent to rent it to someone to receive income, how much must the monthly rent be for me to have a fair return on my investment? If I pay cash for the house, all I need to do is look to long-term bonds for their interest rate to have an idea of what I could get without the risk and hassle of dealing with renters and repairs. Let's say I could get 6.2% from a portfolio of 30-year bonds equating to $6,200 per year with little or no hassle and work.

If I presume that the annual cost to me for owning that house is about 5% to cover repairs, real estate taxes, and insurance, then I would need to get about 11% per year in rent to have exactly the same income as I would get from the bond portfolio (11%-5%=6%). Then of course there is the difficulty of calculating the labor that I put into being the landlord. If I only paid myself about $100 each month for my time, I would need to get $1,200 per month in rent to equal the return on the bond.

From time to time, either because of the local economic situation or because of the need to repair and clean up after the last tenants, the house will be empty and generate no rent. If I were to plan on the house being rented 95% of the time, I would be up to a necessary rent of about $1,263.

Consider then, that the same person from whom I am asking $1,263 per month for rent could quite conceivably pay 5% down on the house (presuming they qualified for one of the government assistance programs) and have a house payment of less than $1,000 per month. Of course, the renter might not have $5,000 down payment on the house, and they might indeed have a credit record that precludes obtaining that mortgage. In that case, there is an additional risk that I am assuming if I accept that person as a tenant. The tenant may not make the payments on time, or at all! In that case, I have the rather substantial extra expense of evicting the tenant, attempting to collect the back rent, and probably expending quite a lot more than my estimated amount to clean up the mess they leave behind. The situation becomes even worse if I have a mortgage on the house myself. I am then obligated to make the payment whether or not I have the rental income.

When I have explained this to people who have asked my advice on purchasing "rental property" they almost always respond in very much the same way. They present the claim that the property "will appreciate." Then they normally ask the question, "What about the tax write-off for depreciation?" In other words, they believe that the property will appreciate in value while they are getting tax benefits because the Internal Revenue Service believes it is depreciating.

Now, before you get too deep in this, think about the last time you heard of the IRS giving away tax breaks for losses when the losses were really *gains*. The reason that the Internal Revenue Code allows for depreciation of improvements on real property is because it *depreciates* over time. *If* a house is thoroughly maintained in like-new condition over a period of three decades or so, the odds are that it will have an increase in sale value that almost exactly equals inflation. On the other hand, if the neighborhood deteriorated or if the maintenance was less than perfect, the sale value will not keep up with general inflation but will fall significantly behind.

I have actually added up the costs, including the much vaunted tax write-offs, on single-family rental properties over lengthy periods of time. So far I have found, without exception, what the owner received back almost equaled exactly what they invested. That only applies *if* they had a reasonable number of rental properties to work with. On individual homes with mortgages, more often than not, I have found the owner actually lost a fairly substantial amount of money over a long period of time.

The problem here is that they created no *utility* in the house. They simply paid fair market value, took the risk of bad renters and a declining neighborhood and then sold a house that was twenty years older, and that much out of style and worn out.

Again, almost without exception, they have come to me bragging about the "killing" they have made with their real estate. In one case, the owner had bought the house at $23,000 and had seen it increase in apparent value to $350,000 over a forty-year period. Actually, it hit the $350,000 mark at about the 30-year point when the owner moved out and was still at about that level. Over that last ten years, it had provided rental income to the owner at about $1,500 per month. A quick run through a financial calculator reveals that the house has grown in value at a compound rate of 6.83% per year. Unfortunately for all of us, there are small matters like taxes and insurance to consider. When those are taken into account, the compound return on the house has been about 4% per year. Interestingly enough, that was almost exactly what general inflation ran in the United States over the four decades.

Now, let's look at it from a different perspective. Let's say I was a builder with construction crews. Further, let's assume I could build a house with a market value of $100,000 for about $60,000. I have indeed improved on the utility of the lot if I put a house there! If I could build that house, then I would be entitled to the $40,000 profit. As a matter of fact, if you wanted to just buy a house and rent it out, I would be glad to build the house, make the profit, and let you have the hassle.

I have a client and friend in the building business. He refuses to build single-family residences, but beyond that, he notes what a local economy needs in the way of developed real estate and then builds it. If there is a business boom going on, he will find a large lot in a business area and build a business building. As he is building, he has his employees hunting down companies and individuals who either have leases coming up for renewal about the time he will have the building ready to occupy or hunting for people who need more space or who just want to move in. If he has made his economic estimate correctly, he will find an abundance of tenants and have leases filling the offices before he finishes the building. He keeps it leased up for about a year and then sells it based on the value of the rental cash flow he has established. He is a professional. He makes money on virtually every project. He adds utility where it is most needed and he is rewarded with a good profit.

Bonds – Loans from the Public

When larger companies want to borrow money, they find it more effective to go directly to the people with the money than to the bank. The way they do this is to issue and sell *bonds*.

In many cases, the borrower (bond issuer) has the option to "call" or pay-off the bond at one or more dates before maturity and will commonly do so if interest rates have fallen. Should the loaner of the money, (the bondholder) want to liquidate the obligation; the bond must be sold to another party. This is normally done on the bond market.

If interest rates at the time of sale are higher than they were at the time the investor purchased the bond, the value of the bond will be lower. In other words, unless a bond is held to maturity, there is a substantial risk involved in owning it. Of course, the nice thing about a bond is that unless the issuer of the bond defaults, the dollars that will be received over the life of the bond are known in advance. What is not known is what those dollars will be worth after inflation and how much of an inflation loss will be taken on the principal.

The other thing that must be factored in is the risk that the borrower will simply not be able to pay off the loan. Even the most financially stable and secure companies are quite capable of succumbing to mismanagement, bad luck, or a changing marketplace. Sometimes those failures occur quite suddenly. If you were to examine the companies listed in the Dow Jones Industrial Average ten years ago, you would notice that more than a few of them have simply ceased to exist. I don't think a Woolworth bond would bring you much today, but a decade ago it was considered one of the most stable companies in the nation.

Corporations and the Creation of Capital

Each of us is totally dependent on commercial corporations to create the things we need to survive. That is a blunt and, for some, very scary statement. From time to time groups of rather paranoid people make a futile attempt to remove themselves from this system by forming a commune and valiantly striving to go it alone, growing their own food without any assistance or "unnatural" services or products. What they discover, or more accurately rediscover, is that pre-industrial agricultural communal life is short, brutal, and miserable. It is not long before someone becomes ill or injured and the need for modern medical assistance becomes very apparent.

There is another issue for those who wish to "return to a natural state." They conveniently ignore the fact that they do not have to expend a great deal of time and energy defending themselves from either animal predators or other "natural" groups who might find it more cost effective to take resources by violence than to create them by labor and innovation. They benefit greatly from the sophisticated law enforcement and national defense institutions. Those institutions in turn are themselves dependent on corporations to exist. The companies of business owners that followed the Yeoman tradition into every area of service and goods production have improved our lives to the point where today we live at a standard of living beyond the dreams of even the nobility of a few hundred years ago.

Corporations are the principal source of those "things" we depend on for our very lives. Even the services provided by governmental entities from local to federal are largely paid for by taxes from corporations and those who work for those corporations. Beyond that, nearly everything those governments use to provide such services are purchased from corporations.

The improvements in our standard of living above that of the primitive communal tribe are virtually all a result of corporation-created products and services. That improvement in our lives is *useful* and thereby described as *utility*. It is far more effective for me to purchase food at the local grocery store with money I receive for selling my services than it is to attempt to maintain the rather substantial garden it would take to feed my family. The series of corporations that are involved in growing, transporting, processing, and finally assembling food for my purchase are all created with the intent of making a *profit*. That profit is the property of the owners of the corporation. The owners are the shareholders.

If the corporation has agreed to accept capital from the general public by selling shares on the open market, then you or I can purchase those shares through an initial public offering (IPO). The most important question here is often unasked by investors. If this company is such a wonderful idea and destined to be so profitable, exactly *why* are the current owners so eager to sell it to anyone willing to purchase shares? IPO investing is a highly speculative and dangerous area for investors unless they are already intimately familiar with the business that is selling itself to the public.

If the underlying reason is to raise capital so the company can buy new equipment or buildings in order to take advantage of a proven opportunity, then the offering may simply represent a legitimate need for capital to increase the profitability of the company. If, on the other hand, the prospectus reveals that the owners are not planning to purchase much of anything new to expand the profitability of the company but are simply planning to sell *their* shares to the public, then one has to wonder why people intimately familiar with the future prospects of the company find it to be in their best interest to sell.

Buying a share in a corporation places the buyer in the position of being an owner of the enterprise. The way the system works for publicly traded companies is that the entire corporation, or at least that portion that is held by the public, is for sale on the open market every day the stock market is open. The tremendous advantage provided by that system is the instant liquidity for both the buyer and the seller. The tremendous disadvantage is that same instant liquidity results in the sale price of a share of the company being posted every day the market is open.

While over the *long-term* that price per share tends to average around some kind of rationality, in the short-term the price per share may be either absurdly high or unreasonably low. That leads us to the question that has plagued investors as long as there has been investing, "Just what is a given company worth anyway?" After many years of research and experience I have concluded that answer to be so varied and random that it is quite a gamble to even hazard a guess. On the other hand there are people and organizations who have become quite good at making that guess. Finding and using them is one of the critical keys to investment success.

Chapter 10 – The Nature of Invested Money

The Mysterious Change

When money is invested it is no longer *money*. That fact is perhaps the single most misunderstood issue about investing. To return to the analogy of the farmer, a seed once placed in the ground to germinate is no longer a seed, but a *plant*. Because of the high *liquidity* of the stock and bond exchanges, we harbor the profound misconception that investments in stocks or bonds or even more so, funds of stocks or bonds, are *money*. Money is *not* capital, nor is capital money. Money certainly does constitute potential capital, but it is not capital any more than a bag of seed corn is a corn crop.

Yet another example of how money changes when it becomes capital is the concept of "priming" a pump. When I worked on ranches years ago, we had hand pumps that lifted water to pour out into a trough that served both as a washbasin and a place for the livestock to drink. In those old pumps, water was held in the well shaft by a series of leather disks. If the pump was very old or not recently used, the leather disks would dry out and shrink. Once they shrunk, they could no longer hold the water from running back down the shaft. By pouring in water from the top of the well, each disk was "wetted" by the priming water and could then pump water up the well shaft.

I have experienced coming to a hand pump in a field where I was working, so thirsty that I could have drunk about anything. There sitting by the well was commonly a quart jar of water. That quart of water was almost exactly what I needed to quench my thirst. If I drank it though, that would be all the water I would get. When I returned to the well later, again thirsty, I could pump all I wanted and no water would flow. On the other hand, if I, instead of drinking the quart of water, poured it down the well, after a bit of pumping, good, cool, fresh water would come flowing from the pump. Once I had drunk my fill, I would then refill the quart jar, screw on the cap, and put it back securely where I had found it.

The pump would usually continue to work all day without further priming, but the next day I again would face the choice of priming or drinking. Each time I had to take the risk that something in the pump had failed or the water table had dropped below the level of the well, and I would get nothing in return for sacrificing the quart of water at hand.

That water, once poured down the well, was really no longer water; it was "prime." When we country folk referred to the quart of water next to the well, we did not call it water; we called it "prime." The liquid in the quart Mason jar was no different than any other water, but it had been reclassified because it had a different purpose. Still, each person using the well had a choice as to whether to consider the jar to be full of "prime" or "water." We all knew that whatever it was called, it would quench one's thirst, and we all knew that once poured down the well there was no calling it back. Once it was poured out, it was no longer water; it was "capital," although we certainly would have never used such a term.

Another oddity of language is that the "prime" in a pump today is commonly called a "head" as in a "head of steam." That pressure is what gets things moving in modern pressure machines from ocean going ships to turbine generators. As I mentioned earlier, the word "head" translates directly to "capital."

Once you have purchased something with your money, it is no longer money. If you purchase food with your money, you would never think to still consider it money, but for some reason, once a person purchases something they consider to be a fairly liquid investment, many people still tend to think of it as money. If a person buys shares in some form of corporate investment, the money is gone. What that person now has is shares. Now those shares may have a quoted price at which someone recently sold other shares like them, but that does not make them money.

A New Element: Time

Reverting to the farming analogy, if you were to price the corn that you planted yesterday in your garden, a new element would appear in the equation: *time*. As long as the corn was indeed a grain called corn, it had an immediate value. We could grind the corn into corn meal and turn it into an edible substance in a matter of a few minutes. We could also exchange it for other things we wanted ranging from tools to eggs.

Conversely, we could plant some of the corn. (Here is where our parallel with investing comes in.) We might choose to purchase, clear, cultivate, and fertilize a piece of land and in that case, as we planted the corn, we would be active investors. We could also give our corn to a farmer who was noted for being quite good at growing corn. In return, we might receive an interest in the corn crop or even in the value of the farm itself. The best, if perhaps strained, analogy would be that of giving the corn to a farmer of some note in a corn-producing venture. Because he had a good and innovative method of producing corn, we might give him quite a number of bushels of corn, not only to plant in the ground but also to sell in order to provide tools, fertilizer, and perhaps even his own food while he was producing a new crop. Presuming that the farmer planned to have a high level of production based on having a really large corn farm and he gathered corn from a large number of people, that example might be a good analogy for corporate investing today.

At any given moment, our partial interest in the farming enterprise could be measured in bushels of corn, but in reality, our interest, called shares, would not be corn. In fact, if all the bushels of corn the farmer had on hand been tallied at any point, the odds are that he could not refund the corn to the investors.

Now I am going to throw some numbers at you, so hang on. In the United States of America in 1998, a single corn plant produced, on average, 400 grains of corn. Of course, every seed does not produce a successful plant and there are quite a few expenses that go into corn production. Let's just say, for the sake of our example here, that only one in twenty of your corn grains were actually planted. The rest went to the long-term purchase of land, equipment, buildings, and vehicles.

Now, let's say further that because of the cost of "doing business" including purchasing fertilizer, fuel, food for the workers, and other costs, only 5.6% of the corn produced was "profit." In that situation, for every grain of corn you invested with the farmer, there would be an *average* return of 1.12 grains of corn *per year*. You will note that I said *average* because in some years the cost of operating the corn farm would be much greater than the crop produced and in others, there would be a bumper crop. It turns out then that the number of 1.12 grains per year is only valid if you allow him to replant the profit for at least seven years. Then, you note in your corn prospectus that the farmer has also advised you that in some cases, when there is a severe drought for example, it may well be twice that long before you could reasonably expect a 1.12 grain per year return, or *you may receive nothing back at all.*

The most important thing to remember once you have invested your corn is that it is no longer corn. Even if the corn were planted in *your* garden, as soon as it is in the ground, the corn is no longer edible. In exchange, you have given up your corn to the ground and cannot expect it to have grown to more kernels of corn until the time comes. Because rain will not come in some years, and in others a storm will wreck your crop, you learn that in order to have a profitable corn crop, you must expect to see ups and downs over several *years.*

A new element has come into play as soon as your corn is planted. You planted the corn to achieve a profit, but you did so understanding that the profit was not to be immediate. Farmers understand that the word "gain" is associated with "long-term" as in "years of waiting patiently." Investors in modern exchange markets need to understand the same wisdom.

Investments are the same; we convert our money into a totally different thing and then we need to leave it alone, barring some unexpected event. Effective investing always involves a longer period of time than saving or speculating. In some circumstances, highly sophisticated investing involves a set price at which the decision has been made in advance to sell out. In most cases though, we hire a manager and give him or her a period of time to produce.

Chapter 11 – Invest in People, Not Things

An enterprise consists of three things: people, capital, and product. Without any one of these things, the enterprise does not exist. If any one of the elements is flawed, the enterprise is doomed to failure. This principle applies to the largest corporation or the smallest attempt at profitable business. In order to understand the basics of what makes for a good investment and what does not, let us examine them in reverse order.

Product

Any enterprise into which you are considering investing needs a profitable product that can be identified and priced. Now that seems like quite an obvious statement, but the various manias and bubbles of history have proven that investors often are far more aware of the price of the share than they are the nature of the product. The reverse is the legendary wisdom of Warren Buffet as he sorts through companies that often are commonly known names and makes the decision to purchase either an interest in or even the entirety of one that seems so mundane as to be foolish. He has let it be well known that the first thing he is looking for is a company that sells something people are willing to buy. Then, he is interested in knowing that the price the company is getting for that product is profitable to the company and is likely to continue to be profitable into the future. This requires that the company have some kind of a unique ability or right to that product, or a means of producing it more profitably than other companies.

If another company can produce the product more cheaply, it is unlikely to continue to be profitable to the company making it now. Once a product is sold based mainly on *price* it ceases to be a unique item and becomes a *commodity*.

Personal computers went from being a unique item, with great difference in quality and capability, to a commodity in a very short time. Dell Computer Corporation managed to do two critical things in that critical period. Michael Dell used a business model of directly selling the computers to the public and businesses, thereby avoiding the cost of a commercial distribution network. Dell does not have to make a computer and hope someone will want to buy it. The computer is made only after a customer has ordered it. With the speed of change in that particular commodity, that concept alone saved a great deal of waste. Also, by not using "resellers," Dell was able to effectively "pocket" the potential profit that would otherwise go to the salesperson and the store. Some of that was offset by the selling cost Dell pays to its own sales division, but the combination of those two things would almost be enough to create success.

The second element was as crucial as the first. Dell managed to first create in reality and then create in the minds of its customers, a name-brand quality reputation. The willingness and capability of "making it right," and the willingness to take back the merchandise if the customer simply did not want it, produced a loyal clientele who simplified their lives.

Those elements do not make the shares of Dell either worthy or unworthy of purchase, but the elements of product and profitability are there. Dell has a product that has evolved from selling a "better" computer to providing better service to creating an experience for its customers that brings them back.

Once the mass of investors, both amateur and professional discovered that Dell had the corner on this form of innovation in a rapidly expanding commodity, the shares of Dell Computer Corporation soared with the overwhelming demand to own those shares. Unfortunately, the masses buying the shares still mainly did not know why they were buying those shares other than the classic reason that "they are going up!"

In early 2000, the price of the stock on the open market was about eighty times the record earnings the company had just reported. In other words, if the company continued to sell computers at the fastest rate it had in history, it would take *eighty years* for a purchaser of the company to receive a *zero* percent return on capital. Three and a half years later with the share price at half that seen in early 2000, the consensus of the 21 analysts who rate the company is that the earnings will grow at a 15% annual rate over the next five years, and even at that rate and the halved stock price, it will take a decade for an investor to recover the price in earnings. That, by the way, is indicative of pretty much a fair market price for a growth stock.

Capital

Access to capital is crucial if a company is going to be worth more in the future than it is today. In other words, the company must either have a very substantial amount of liquid capital itself or be in the position to get that capital through either a bond or stock offering. Of course the problem with the bond or stock offering is that a large number of other people will be taking a part of that added worth if it comes. "Value" investors generally look for a company that already has the capital as well as the protected and profitable product.

Growth oriented companies are in constant need of capital and will commonly have new stock offerings. If indeed the company has a better mousetrap and needs to purchase the equipment and facilities to make those mousetraps, then all the shareholders, new and old alike, will benefit from the new capital. If the growth of the company is not as fast as the inflow of new capital, the value per share will actually decline as earnings per share are "diluted" by the issue of shares.

Growth is tricky. No matter how good the mousetrap might be, there are a finite number of mousetrap buyers in the world. Dell Computer Corporation, among many others, was priced for quite a long time at a level that could only be justified if the company grew at 50% per year. As long as the computer-buying boom went on with dramatic innovation in computer software and hardware each year, Dell could grow at that rate. Eventually, the ability to come out every few years with a dramatically new set of software requiring new computers to run it had to end. As the creation of new software applications that mandated new computers slowed, Dell, even by taking market share from other companies, simply could not grow at 50% per year. As soon as the earnings growth slowed to "only" 15% per year, the stock price dropped rather dramatically (about 75%).

People

Here is the crucial element. Other computer companies were able to produce computers that were at least as good as Dell's. Some of those companies even had some truly exceptional service at one time. Several came and went that appeared to be able to produce computers and sell them at lower prices. What they did not have was the vision and the management capability of the leaders at Dell. Popular belief, right or wrong, centers that virtue on Michael Dell himself. The same was said of Jack Welch at General Electric. In both cases, the man at the top took a "might have been" company to success while around them other companies trying similar operations either failed or were relegated to the sidelines. There is little doubt that Bill Gates was the driving force behind Microsoft or that Andy Groves created Intel as much by leadership and management as by creating chips.

For over three quarters of a century, the Congress of the United States has seen a loss in seats by the party with the President in office in the mid-term elections. In 2002, both the Senate and the House of Representatives saw the Republican Party gain seats while a Republican President was in office. Rightfully, that credit belongs to George W. Bush. To what degree he personally planned the strategy that brought this historic election shift we may never know, but we do know that he was the one who approved it and executed it, and he was the one who selected the staff that made it happen.

The lesson here is a simple one; people create value. They may use things, but things do not create value without people to make it happen. People are the employers of capital to either create value through utility or not. A company may have relatively limited capital and a product that is quickly becoming a non-profitable commodity, but if that company has exceptional leadership, it has the potential to rise above those limitations and establish itself by creating value in another area, thereby banishing its competitors and enriching its owners.

The Pareto Principle

Vilfredo Pareto lived in the late 19th and early 20th century and made a great contribution to our understanding of large-scale human behavior. He noted that about 20% of the people owned and operated about 80% of the means of production in a free enterprise system. That rule seemed to apply to every developed nation he examined. As we have moved forward, the Pareto Principle has appeared in nearly every measurable enterprise. In large sales organizations, it is considered normal for 20% of the salespersons to account for 80% of the sales. If the organization is very large, even the 20% may be broken down into two groups with 64% of the sales actually coming from only about 4% of the sales force. The same ratio, albeit with variations, applies to engineers, mechanics, military officers, and managers.

The principle can be taken even further. In extremely large groups, about half the added value created by management can be credited to an extremely few persons, sometimes even one. I doubt that Bill Gates is the only person who is critical to the success of Microsoft. Steve Ballmer has proven to be the other person in this case, and there may be even a few more. The issue here is that there are relatively few people in any organization or profession who have the demonstrated ability to create value far beyond their peers. The challenge is to distinguish the right few from the trivial many.

Observation has led me to believe that in the world of investing at least some of those few can be identified. It has been my experience that among a group of professionals, a mature manager will tend to establish him or herself, relative to his or her peers, so that he or she adds value to any process. It has also been my experience that once that manager establishes a relative position over a period of five to ten years, he or she tends to remain in that relative position as long as the environment is not altered.

It is important to note here that I did not refer to *things* as being able to arrive at a level and stay there. Apple Computer Corporation lost market share and value once Steve Jobs left. The common belief was that the culture of Apple would somehow sustain the company, and the price of the stock even rose as Mr. Jobs was forced out. Whether or not one likes or agrees with his methods, it is clear now that successful visionary leaders such as Steve Jobs *do* make a great deal of difference in whether or not an enterprise is successful.

Michael Dell's ability to take risks, learn from his mistakes, and adjust the nature of the product to sustain his profitability in the face of a rapidly changing marketplace is one of the great examples of managerial leadership under the most stressful of circumstances. I have little doubt that if somehow Michael Dell were to transfer from Dell to Gateway (a circumstance unlikely to the point of absurdity), within a few years Gateway Computer Corporation would be the one to beat, and Dell would fade into "has been" obscurity.

The problem remains of how to identify those managers who can add value to a portfolio at a time and at a price that is not ruinous. No matter how good a leader and manager either Bill Gates or Michael Dell are, the mere fact that they are the prime value-adding element of their enterprise makes them dangerous. First, they have a following that tends to create a rather overvalued condition for their companies.

Second, should they leave or become unable to continue through personal crisis, sickness, or death, the value of their companies would plunge precipitously. As there might be absolutely no warning of such an event, they not only add value to the investment but also add risk out of proportion to that value.

Chapter 12 – Diversify, Diversify, Diversify

The First Level of Diversification: Companies

The lesson learned from the horror stories of Enron, MCI-WorldCom, Adelphia, and even stalwarts like Dell, Microsoft, Intel, AT&T, and General Electric is that bad things can happen to any company. Less well remembered is the incident in Bhopal, India that ended the viability of Union Carbide, at one time one of the bluest of the blue chips. Woolworth Corporation was one of the 30 Dow Jones Industrial Average stocks at the beginning of the 1990s and did not exist ten years later. Texaco's downhill slide started with a taped conversation about "black marbles." At one time, Polaroid was one of the leading technology companies in the world. The shock of Owens-Corning's decline from over $40 per share to $1.50 wasn't headlines unless you were dependent on it. Burlington Industries, once a foundation piece of the American economy, traded at $18 per share in 1998 but dropped to a penny stock in about two years.

In example after example, people who were sure they were smarter than the average investor found themselves holding shares devalued by 80% or more and have expressed to me that they are "waiting for it to come back."

Twenty years ago in a much more simple economy, the minimum portfolio size was generally considered to be twenty companies in different industries. Today, I would tend to raise that number to around thirty-five. Even then, unless you are a full-time investor with education, experience, and the temperament to not get attached to a particular stock, the odds are against you. In fact, in all my years of experience, I have yet to see a personally managed stock portfolio that had a return over time that would be even marginally acceptable to a professional.

There is a fact here that is widely ignored. If an individual who is managing his or her own portfolio were able to buy and sell stocks in such a manner as to consistently outperform the average professional portfolio manager, they would be able to make a good seven figure income by doing just that. Contrary to the media hype, professional investment managers either perform or are fired.

The *Wall Street Journal* published an article in April 2002 indicating the average individual equity investor managed to eke out a 4.1% average annual rate of return from the beginning of the year 1984 through March 2002. Meanwhile, again according to the *Journal* article, the Standard & Poor's 500 Stock Index had averaged over 14% for the same period. That level of difference between a broad index and the performance of an individual investor is quite consistent with my experience. Amateur investors are competing with professionals. When that happens, the professionals tend to win. Whether it is golf, basketball, or stock and bond investing, professionals have a dramatic edge over amateurs. They have the time, the money to research, the education to know what has worked before, and the staff to assist them. Even then, good professional investors will tell you that they are fortunate to be right 60% of the time when they buy and sell.

From time to time I have had the opportunity to interview managers who have consistently turned in excellent returns over long periods of time. They all are firm believers in looking at all that is known about a company and knowing that they are still only looking at a small piece of the pie. The only way they can avoid being caught up in a loss on a number of companies simultaneously when the unexpected occurs is to have a large enough number of individual positions so that they are not exposed to the risk of loss when a few seemingly unrelated stocks have the same problems. One recently gave me an example that seemed obvious in retrospect. He said that he had simply not suspected that every publicly traded corporation that used a given audit firm, in this case *Arthur Anderson & Co.*, would decline simply because of its choice of auditor but it happened.

Even geography can be a risk in a portfolio. The investor who has a portfolio of real estate in the form of rental properties commonly has them in a very limited geographical area to facilitate management. The sudden loss of a single large employer in that area can devastate that real estate portfolio. The same applies to shares in corporations. An investor who owns shares in individual corporations may actually have a better understanding of the corporation in his or her local area and thereby have an advantage over the professionals. On the other hand, that very advantage will be more than offset by the risk assumed through geographic concentration. Anything from a natural disaster to a regional economic decline could reduce the value of the entire portfolio during a time when the average stock on a national basis was rising in value.

Another advantage that an individual investor might have that would be negated by concentration would be industry. A medical research executive or even technician might far better understand the medical research and development industry than would the general public or even the professional analysts. The risk would be that a government policy change covering the means and amounts paid for medical care could dramatically affect that entire industry. The same could well happen to any industry from airlines to machine tools to retail sales. Diversification across industries, geographic region, and individual companies is the most basic level of diversification needed to avoid unnecessary risk in a portfolio.

The difficulty with this principle is that I have yet to find the individual investor trying to manage a portfolio that has paid much attention to those factors. Unfortunately, the same complaint applies to the portfolios I have seen that were managed by stockbrokers.

The Danger of Fixed Annuities

Before we leave the principle of diversification, I want to discuss a very little understood danger that is centered in the area of non-diversification. In a bear market for stocks and half century lows in interest rates, the sale of fixed annuities has mushroomed. Sadly, the misconceptions about them are as severe as in any other area of investing.

Fixed annuities are a loan to an insurance company. Unlike a bond, this loan allows the borrower, the insurance company, to set the interest rate they will pay you, the one loaning the money to them, and then change it when they want to. They commonly come complete with a substantial penalty for early liquidation, and normally have a "free" annual withdrawal amount, typically around 10%.

The attractive feature for many investors is the *"guarantee"* associated with the principal and some small interest rate. Sadly, the old truth applies there that any guarantee is only as good as the guarantor. An elderly couple that recently came to my office for advice had a tale of woe to tell that is all too familiar. They had entrusted the proceeds of the sale of their farm to their long-term insurance agent who had convinced them to place it in a "guaranteed mortgage trust" paying 12% per year. For several months the checks came right on schedule at

1% per month (does this sound familiar?). After about six months when the checks stopped, they discovered that the "trust" was a scam. They attempted to sue the insurance agent but were unable to extract any money as he threatened to declare bankruptcy.

The same insurance agent had taken their IRA money and convinced them that the place to be was in a fixed annuity issued by a company with a very impressive sounding name and, again, an unusually high interest rate. About a month after they bought three different annuities, the state insurance commissioner seized the company to prevent it from collapsing. The letter from the commissioner advised them that it could be a number of years before the company was "rehabilitated," and that after those years the commissioner might be forced to liquidate the company. That liquidation, they were warned, might take even more years. Only after all of these actions had taken place and whatever the commissioner had determined might be paid out had been paid, could they then contact the local state insurance guarantee pool administrator in their home state to determine if the policy was covered for reimbursement.

Simply put, any money you invest in a fixed annuity is in the hands of a single company and is commingled with that company's assets. If that company fails for any reason, you are just another creditor standing in line to get whatever you can.

One of the reasons I sincerely like variable, rather than fixed, annuities, is that the Investment Company Act of 1940 protects the investment accounts of a variable annuity from the failure of the insurance company. Mutual funds are similarly protected. If you stick to investment accounts that are registered under that act, you have one less major threat to worry about. I will discuss this in more detail later in the book.

The Second Level of Diversification: Asset Class

The Theory
"Determinants of Portfolio Performance" by Gary Brinson, appeared in the July-August 1986 issue of *Financial Analysts Journal*. The article reported the results of a study of 91 very large pension plans over a ten-year period, from 1974 through 1983. These pension plans were

some of the largest pools of invested money in the United States, and by examining their investment performance, Brinson hoped to ascertain what accounted for the variation in the investment results from one plan to another.

Brinson theorized that there were three things that contributed to the performance of each portfolio, security selection, market timing, and asset allocation. The study concluded that the primary determinant of performance was *asset allocation*.

First there is a fact: *Historically, stocks have produced value for investors at a much higher rate than any other available, reasonably liquid, investment type.* The study that produced that finding is published as a book, *Stocks for the Long Run* by Jeremy Siegel. Pension funds are composed of cash positions, bonds, and stocks. Brinson's study simply confirmed that placing more of the pension fund in stocks resulted in a higher long-term return. It also determined that choosing individual stocks for the pension portfolio made less difference than simply having a larger portion of the fund invested in stocks than in bonds or cash.

Unfortunately, that is only a limited answer. In 1952, Harry M. Markowitz wrote an article for *The Journal of Finance* entitled "Portfolio Selection". Markowitz noted that an investor was not only concerned with the potential appreciation of an asset but also with the variance in price of the asset. His insight was that combining different types of investments in a portfolio could reduce the price fluctuations that so frighten investors. Markowitz's work laid the foundation for Modern Portfolio Theory, which has since been enlarged into something called Capital Market Theory (CMT).

CMT is based on the observation that historically there are some types of securities that seem to have moved in quite nearly opposite directions from other types of securities most of the time. The race has been on since that discovery to find the ideal mix of types of securities, or "asset classes" as they have come to be called.

The first attempts at this ideal portfolio were to mix stocks in general and bonds in general. By mixing stocks and bonds in a 60:40 ratio, a portfolio was found to have about the same variance or "risk" as bonds, but get a substantially higher return than a pure bond portfolio.

Now comes the rub. As more and more managers created the same

191

mix, the results deteriorated! What had happened was a phenomenon that was more like quantum physics than anything else. The prices of things on the market are set by our collective desire to buy or sell those things. As managers attempted to rebalance their portfolios to the "right" asset allocation each quarter, they tended (and tend) to all do pretty much the same thing at the same time. The result was that bonds tended to become more volatile as more and more buying and selling was done to rebalance portfolios. At the same time, stocks became less volatile as managers with excessive valuation in stocks were selling and, when stocks were low, those same managers would tend to buy stocks to again rebalance.

That activity combined with the relaxation and ultimate deregulation of interest rates in the United States has gradually produced a tendency to make stocks and bonds behave more and more alike as time has passed. What has not changed though can be seen in the title of Harvey McKay's book *Amazing Popular Delusions and the Madness of Crowds*. Mr. McKay documents the stock mania of 1720 that came to be known as *The South Sea Bubble*.

Investors tend to rush into some given asset class and overvalue it while leaving another undervalued. A carefully planned mixture of asset classes has proven to have a tendency to smooth out some of the more severe bumps. Historically, we can see it has been possible to achieve that without giving up a great deal of return. I will have more on that a little further along, but first let's get some idea of what asset classes are.

Liquid Asset Classes

Within the liquid investments that constitute the stock and bond universe, there are divisions called "asset classes." Unfortunately, there are no exact, standard rules for what constitutes one class or another. What is known, is that the more unlike two investments, or asset classes are, the more they tend to behave differently. There are a few classifications that seem to be generally accepted:

• Value stocks are from companies who have assets that can be clearly valued and the price of the stock seems to relate to the value of the assets.

• Growth stocks are from companies whose valuation comes from the rate, or potential rate, of earnings growth.

•   Large stocks are from companies that are, well, *large*. The stocks in the S&P 500 Index, or the Dow Jones 30 Industrial Index are by definition "large." The folks at the Russell Company have an index of the largest 1,000 companies traded in the United States that seems to provide the best definition of a "large" stock.

•   Mid-Cap Stocks are defined by *Morningstar* as those stocks that comprise the next 20% of the total capitalization of their universe. As of mid-2003, that means companies that are valued between $1.4 billion and $8.3 billion. The Russell Company again has an index simply called "Mid-Cap" that seems to fit the bill quite well.

•   Small-Cap Stocks are those below Mid-Cap. A common index used to define the small stock universe is the Russell 2000. The Russell indexes track 3000 stocks with the smaller 2000 being considered "small stocks" and the larger 1000 considered "large." The Russell indices include about 98% of all the capitalization traded in the United States.

•   Long-term corporate bonds are commercial "loans" to companies whereby the company agrees to pay a fixed interest rate per year to the bondholder and will redeem the bond by paying back the "principal" at some point over ten years from the date of the loan.

•   Intermediate-term corporate obligations are generally considered to be those between three and ten years.

•   Short-term corporate notes are those three years or less.

•   Money market obligations are generally from thirty to ninety days in maturity. They are commonly referred to as "cash."

•   Long, intermediate, and short-term government obligations follow the same pattern as the corporate obligations but generally pay a lower interest rate as they are considered to be nearly free from risk of default.

Unfortunately, there are more definitions. There is global, foreign, Pacific Rim, European, Asian, and more, in both stocks and bonds. While some obviously believe these sub-classifications of "foreign" are important, I will take a pass on them and simply say that there are quite a number of stocks and bonds that originate outside the United States. If they trade in the United States stock and bond markets, they are required to comply with U.S. accounting standards. While that set of standards has gotten a pretty big black eye lately, it is still the most revealing and consistent set in the world. As of last report, there wasn't a rush of European and Japanese CEOs lining up to sign off on their financial statements.

It is a very good idea to realize that as soon as you leave these American shores, you are dealing in a whole new world of risk. Currency risk is bad enough when we try to figure out how it will affect the profits of American companies, but as soon as you start owning stocks or bonds that are actually denominated in foreign currencies, you have gotten into an area that is not only best left to the professionals but is scary even to them!

While I may catch it from some quarters, I am just not interested in learning the details of "foreign" investing. Leave that to the professionals. Even in a professionally managed portfolio, I am cautious. There is a whole new level of risk there, and I have yet to be convinced that any reward that may accrue is worth it.

This new class is what I refer to as "global." The globalization of business is a reality, and I believe that the businesses that are going to be the leaders of the 21st century are going to be nation irrelevant. Truly global companies publish in English, denominate in dollars, and trade typically on the New York Stock Exchange. They may be like Toyota and Nokia, headquartered in Japan or in Finland, but they do business all over the planet. Unfortunately, it is quite hard to find pure global investment funds or indices as opposed to "foreign" or even geographic region.

Now for the good part; historically, the further apart the classes are in characteristics, the less they act alike. For example, small value stocks and large growth stocks spend a significant part of their time headed in different directions. Interestingly enough, there are times when the ten-year return of opposite stock sectors is about the same, but they got there by such different paths that it is quite a shock to see them at the same place. The nice thing about that is their widely differing paths tend to have a smoothing effect on a portfolio if they are both represented in that portfolio.

Of course we have left out bonds here. Bonds are fairly straightforward when it comes to investing. There are short, intermediate, and long duration bonds, generally running out to about four or five years for short, five to ten years for intermediate, and beyond ten years for long. What that refers to is the length of time until the bond issuer is obligated to refund the principal of the bond.

Then there is the issue of quality. Again, it is fairly straightforward. The highest quality bonds are those that are obligations of the U. S. government, immediately followed by "government agencies" such as the mortgage bonds issued by Fannie Mae, Freddy Mac, and Sallie Mae. If you don't know what those mean, you shouldn't be involved! Some pretty impressive assets may back them, but there are traps here for the unwary and ignorant.

From there we have investment grade corporate bonds, sub-investment grade corporate bonds, and "junk" or "high yield" bonds. There is a consistent pattern to bonds though. The lower the grade and the longer the term, the higher the stated yield will be. The point is that lower grade bonds have a higher chance of default, causing you to lose some, or all, of your invested principal. The longer the time to the maturity date, the greater the chance that interest rates will rise and the market value of the bond will fall. High interest rates normally mean high inflation too, so you stand to lose more of your principal to inflation in that situation.

Bonds *sometimes* move in different directions from stocks. There was a time when that was considered a certainty. Now, bonds serve mainly as a potential stabilizer that (hopefully) smoothes the short-term variability of a portfolio in exchange for a lower rate of return.

Having said all that about bonds, experience has shown that mid-term bonds (out to about ten years) actually have done better over the long haul than long-term bonds! So, if you need a relatively low rate of return and want some stability in your portfolio, short to intermediate *government* bonds are potentially useful. Recognize though, that in a rising interest rate environment, you stand to actually *lose* money over the long term in government bonds. You may receive your principal back, and you may get all the interest, presuming you do not sell prior to maturity, but rising interest rates commonly mean inflation is higher than when you bought the bond or bond fund, and your principal and interest after taxes may well be worth a lot less than what you started with.

Finally, there are municipal bonds. Here again, things can get scary. "Munis," as they are sometimes called, are issued by municipalities and pay interest that is largely exempt from income tax. That does not mean that you will not pay taxes on capital gains nor does it apply to state income taxes unless the bond is issued in that state (sometimes). Many munis are issued in small quantities and are, as a result, not too liquid and can be very expensive to sell. Additionally, municipalities are far less stable than the U.S. government. Worse, you can be subject to income tax on your social security benefits and the feared Alternate Minimum Tax for excessive tax-exempt income. Corporations sponsored, but not backed by municipalities issue some municipal bonds. Those are just as dangerous as any other corporate security but are, frighteningly, often bought by elderly people who really don't benefit from the tax advantage and are in fact taking risks of which they have no concept. Generally speaking, municipal bonds are useful in a managed portfolio for upper income folks who do not need a great deal of return.

Before we leave municipal bonds, I must address the concept of insurance on those bonds. The "AAA rated tax-free municipal bonds" that have become so popular appear to somehow levitate above the mundane world of supply and demand. Often I seen interest rates on those bonds that, if found in a corporate bond, would clearly indicate the presence of "junk" or high yield and thereby below-investment-grade quality. Why are municipalities forced to pay such high interest rates if the bonds are "insured"? There is a fundamental principle here. If you find a high return on a bond, you have also found a high risk. First, in the event of a widespread municipal crisis resulting in the default of a large number of munis, it is quite questionable that the insurance companies would be able to cover it all.

The second difficulty with municipal bonds is that it is not unusual to find that an attempt to sell them prior to maturity will result in substantially less than the amount paid. The municipal bond market has no central exchange like the New York Stock Exchange. It often takes more than one company to get involved in finding a buyer. The fees for those services can be fairly substantial when compared to buying and selling stocks. In the case of many of the less-than-huge bond issues, it may not even be possible to find a buyer for a given municipal bond in any reasonable period of time. I have had people come to me in emergency situations where they desperately need to liquidate municipal bonds and found that the type bonds they wished to sell had the last market transaction reported weeks or months ago. We have normally found buyers but often at a substantially lower price than the current owners expected and only after substantial delay.

The combination of increased risk of default and illiquidity has resulted in a higher interest rate for municipals than would be expected from a cursory glance. In this country we have a hyper-efficient bond market. If you see a high rate, you may be assured the risk is there.

Once again, I risk censure as I have left out *real estate*! Developed real estate in the form of office buildings and apartment complexes is indeed a separate asset class. More, in the last two decades of the 20th century, real estate investments acquired liquidity and some degree of diversification through Real Estate Investment Trusts or "REITs." First, REITs are a relatively new phenomenon. As they have been developing over the past twenty years, they have matured so that the REIT of today is quite a different thing from the REIT of even ten years ago. It is hard to tell today if REITs will eventually provide the liquidity and capital for real estate and thereby transform the industry. It certainly does not bode well that the reduction in taxation on dividends does not apply to REIT income.

Meanwhile, REITs are just too new to use as a reliable asset class. Obviously that leaves the idea of direct investment in real estate. Again, my experience is that the professionals make money regularly doing that with large sums. Sadly, in many cases the people they make money from are the amateurs. Developing real estate is, by and large, a moneymaking business if done correctly. Real estate developers generally have their own money in the project and are often on the hook directly for money they have borrowed. In most cases, the REITs I have examined have purchased existing real estate and are intended to generate money for their investors by paying out the net rental income as dividends. A couple of problems arise from this model. First, a direct investor in commercial real estate receives an offsetting tax deduction each year as the property is depreciated. That offsetting tax deduction effectively reduces the cost of the real estate to the direct investor and thereby allows the direct investor to offer a lower rent charge to the tenant to receive the same net income. The REIT investor does not receive this benefit. The end result is that the income is lower on a REIT than commercial real estate in general.

Asset class diversification is a critical element in creating an effective investment portfolio. There have been times when a given class of stocks, or even bonds, seems to be the ideal investment as it rises well above the others. Of course, the reason it rises is that people have perceived it as the best class of investment at that moment. As surely as it pulls ahead of the other classes with similar long-term histories, though, it later will go out of favor and fall back behind.

Asset classes have had a long-term difference in appreciation as well. A large portfolio of stocks in smaller companies has historically provided a substantially greater appreciation than a portfolio of larger companies. That matches up well with our intuitive understanding that smaller companies tend to be more effective than larger companies. Of course with that higher long-term appreciation, we must expect a greater variance in price from month to month or year to year.

Bonds, over the long term, have had a substantially lower total return than stocks. They have also had a lower variation in short-term pricing. At the bottom of the scale, 90 day U.S. Treasury bills have had very little variance in price from a smooth line, but they have also consistently provided a *negative* real return after inflation and taxes!

The point to asset class selection and diversification is that by examining the historic return of differing liquid asset classes and subclasses, we can design a portfolio made up of a very large number of individual liquid securities, stocks and/or bonds, that historically has demonstrated the type of return that an individual investor desires to accomplish defined, planned goals. We can also adjust that portfolio's assets to minimize (but not eliminate) the short-term variance of the portfolio.

It is prudent to note that when I say "short-term," I am referring to any period less than about five to seven years. The more aggressive the portfolio, the longer "short-term" becomes, because the variances tend to not only be greater in portfolios designed for higher return, but they tend to be longer as well! In other words, more aggressive (higher expected return) portfolios will tend to fall faster and stay down longer than less aggressive portfolios. That is the price we pay for that higher return.

Asset Allocation & Rebalancing
One of the most basic understandings of portfolio management that has come from all these academic studies is that not only do

different asset classes behave differently but also we can and *should* construct a portfolio based on an asset allocation that fits our objective(s). Let's use the example of a stock portfolio that was comprised of an equal weighting of the following asset classes: large company value, large company growth, mid-cap value, mid-cap growth, and small-cap value. Had we started that portfolio at the beginning of 1997 and tracked it through the end of the third quarter of 2002 pretty much the absolute bottom of the historic bear market, our various asset classes would have looked like the dotted lines in the chart below.

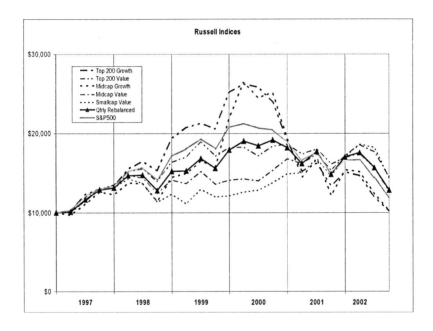

Figure 1: Russell Indices 1997-October 2002

It would have been very hard emotionally to maintain our asset allocation of equal weighting as the large (Top 200) and mid-cap growth classes increased from the original $10,000 investment to about $26,000 while the value sector of our portfolio just inched along with very little overall return. Even more difficult would have been the *loss* from mid-1998 through mid-2000 in the small and mid-cap value sectors. Had we joined the crowd and jumped aboard the large company and mid-cap growth mania, we would have found that after five and three quarters years we had exactly zero gain! Worse, we would have suffered through a nearly 50% drop from our highs at the end of the first quarter of 2000.

Even the S&P 500 Stock Index, which theoretically has a mixture of growth and value stocks, would have produced a drop of over 45% and an average gain of only 3.1% per year. Had we stuck to our guns and held on to each asset class, we would have done a little better at about 3.8% per year but we would still be down 37% from the high point.

Now for the good news: If we had carefully rebalanced our portfolios back to the same equal weighting at the beginning of each quarter, our average annual rate of return for the period would have been about 4.5% per year. That is nothing to get too excited about, but the drop from the high point would have been only 32%!

I will be the first to say that seeing our hard earned capital drop by nearly one third over the span of about two and a half years is not a pretty sight, but when it is compared with experiencing a loss of nearly half it looks pretty nice. Had we been in just the mid-cap or large company growth classes, the drop would have been well over 60%. Had we been unfortunate enough to have the bulk of our wealth invested in DELL or the NASDAQ index we might have seen declines of between 75% and 80%!

A couple of things jump out at us from this example. First, chasing the fastest rising sectors or stocks is potentially painful. Second, riding a single index up… and down, doesn't improve things that much. Finally, it is pretty clear from this example that setting up an allocation that matches our needs and then returning to that asset allocation every three months has the potential to lower the volatility of our portfolio quite a lot *and* give us a better return. In this case, the quarterly rebalancing produced an improvement in average annual return of 1.4% per year. The good news in this is that by the middle of 2003, our rebalanced portfolio would have risen over 20% from the lows in 2002.

A word of caution is in order. What we used here are indices, and more specifically the Russell indices. You cannot invest in an index even though there is no shortage of companies trying their best to create funds that behave like indices. Sometimes those index funds miss the mark by quite a lot. A second caution is that neither taxes nor transaction costs have been figured into this example. In fact, it is possible to conduct an automatic rebalancing on the first day of the quarter, avoid ongoing taxes on the transactions, and do so without transaction costs, but I am getting ahead of myself here.

The Prize and the Catch

When Gary Brinson studied the elements that most affect the long-term performance of a portfolio and concluded that asset allocation was the most important element by far, he was studying *pension funds*. Unfortunately, there are some small difficulties.

First, we cannot actually invest in an "asset class." We are required to either select a sampling of some of the stocks or bonds that are part of the asset class or use a predefined basket of the individual securities from that asset class.

The second problem is even more difficult: in order to stay allocated appropriately, we will need to move capital from the asset class or classes that have appreciated more into those that have appreciated less on a regular chronological basis. Brinson's study focused on pension funds where there is no taxation on the reallocation and, as the pension funds were very large entities, the transaction costs were extremely low as a percentage of the fund. In the very real world in which we live, we are often faced with both transaction costs and taxation when it comes time to reallocate.

A third problem that may exist in a retirement fund sponsored by an employer is that all the asset classes may not be adequately represented, and there may be only very few well-managed positions to choose from.

The final problem, which I will address later, is that the act of rebalancing the accounts takes a substantial amount of attention and time. Unless you have an investment account or vehicle that automates the process, you are forced to really be on the ball to get it done on the first day of the quarter. Missing it by even a few days can be hazardous as it is not uncommon for there to be major moves in asset classes a few days into the quarter as the pension funds do their manual rebalancing. The holders of 401(k) and other similar retirement accounts receive their statements a few days after the quarter ends as well, and they tend to make most of their moves toward the beginning of the second week of the quarter. One of the crucial issues in getting the improvement in return we see here is to actually make the move within a day of the end of the quarter.

One of the challenges of financial planning and effective asset class management is overcoming these obstacles. In nearly every case it can be done, although it sometimes takes a little original thinking.

The Third Level Diversification: Manager and Management Company

In the process of discovering that different asset classes behaved differently, Dr. Markowitz also noted that the higher the total return of a given type of investment, the higher that variance became, but the variance went up faster than the return.

Of course when we are looking back ten years for that group of higher performing portfolios, we have the problem of looking at performance that may have been generated by a manager who is no longer at the helm. We also may be looking at a specialized portfolio that just happened to be in the right place at the right time and got all that return in a relatively short period.

If we weed out the portfolios that have not had the same management for the decade and those which were focused in an asset class that just happened to be popular with investors, we are still left with a significant number of portfolios that have substantially outperformed "unmanaged" (index) asset classes. Here, I believe we see the Pareto Principle being played out in reality. By using a combination of Capital Market Theory and the Pareto Principle, it is possible to identify a series of managers in various parts of the investment universe who have for some reason provided a substantially greater return to their investors than have others.

There has been a great deal of effort put into analyzing the performance of mutual funds and finding some way to forecast which will be the better performers in the future. The continued failure of such efforts can, in my opinion, be traced to asking the wrong question. A mutual fund is a "thing" and as such does nothing by itself. Because it is the manager or managers who determine what securities are held by the fund, any superior performance will be the result of the manager's decisions.

One other element that must be eliminated before we can proceed is the element of luck. There are over 3,000 publicly available investment managers in the United States alone. With that many people managing stock and bond portfolios, some of them are just going to have been lucky and chosen the right place to have investments at the right time often enough to look really good.

The way I choose to weed them out is to simply interview them. What I have noticed over the years is that managers who have achieved their exceptional long-term returns by skill are not hesitant to tell me how they did it. More, when they tell me how they did it, the answer makes good sense. I have read the books on effective investing by the masters from Adam Smith to Warren Buffet. There are principles that emerge from their lives and from their practices. When I interview truly skilled and disciplined investors, they have, without fail, followed those principles. What they have that others don't is the discipline to not deviate from them *and* access to information, or a way of processing that information, that other people don't. In my experience, only about 1% of managers actually manage to do that very thing.

Here I have to draw on my own experience as well as the principle of diversification. I have observed that a given investment management company tends to do better in some asset classes than in others. Within an investment management company there may be literally hundreds of portfolios and managers, but typically only one or a few are exceptional. In my experience, even when there is more than one exceptional manager, a close examination of their portfolios reveals that a substantial overlap in investments is common. In many cases, when there are a number of good managers at a single firm, the excellence is in fact not theirs but comes from the superior skills of *their* manager!

Given that a senior manager is quite possibly critical to exceptional performance and knowing that the departure of such a senior manager may or may not be announced, it is unwise to have all, or even a large percentage, of one's investment portfolio under the control of a single management company. Ideally, you would have each market sector represented in your portfolio invested under the management of not only a different manager but also under a different management company. Because it is quite possible to have one's investments under a single entity for administrative purposes, while at the same time maintaining diversification in management companies, it is a good idea to do so. Obviously, if the only investment option one has is a company retirement plan, and the company has selected a single company to manage all the investment portfolios, you are stuck with that choice. If that is true, it may be wise to not put all your invested money in your company's retirement plan despite the tax advantages of doing so.

Generally, my recommendation is that having five managers from five different companies investing in five different sectors of the market is a good base for diversification. There are certainly exceptions, particularly if you or your advisor has the time and the ability to closely observe the manager and company, or if your liquid investment portfolio is only part of your total invested positions.

Chapter 13 – Create and Follow a Plan

Know What You Want

The first step in obtaining what you desire from your investments is to know what you want! Recognizing that investment values rise and fall, sometimes dramatically, the commonly stated desire of amateur investors that they simply want their portfolio to "grow" is not a good objective. If indeed they invest to "see their money grow," they are speculating and are likely headed for a fall.

One of the most damaging attitudes is the very common practice of investing only while the values are "going up" and either liquidating or avoiding investing when values are "down." The resulting behavior of "buying high and selling low" seems to make no sense at all until we consider that if the stated purpose of the investor was to see the values reported on the statements "go up" and they "go down" for any lengthy period, then the investment is certainly not doing what the investor paid for it to do! Given that point of view, it is perfectly rational to sell or liquidate the investment that is providing the opposite of what one expected. A person who has only thought about what they want in terms of "seeing my money grow" does not realize that if there is perceivable growth, then there will also be periods of "non-growth," and other periods of "negative growth," to use a rather inverted term.

In my experience, every investor has a distinct list of things they want and things they don't want as a result of the act of investing. Some of the things people commonly want are normally led by the desire for "financial independence," although it is stated in quite a number of ways. There seems to be a universal desire to be free to do what one wants to do with at least part of one's life. While we in the 21st century seem to take for granted that "retirement" or financial independence or whatever one wishes to call it is a natural state of affairs, that concept has been a virtual unknown for those not born into nobility or great wealth until the very recent past. Being financially independent and thereby having the freedom to pursue aims beyond those associated with survival, was solely the purview of the landed nobility.

Having and defining the goal, or goals, is the important thing. If we dare voice and even write down large, long-term goals, then we can begin to take responsibility for achieving them. The secret of success then, is at least partly found in having goals that are far enough in the future that one can ride out at least one or two "market cycles" of decreasing and increasing values. Most market cycles have played out over a period of about three to five years in the last century, or so. There are notable exceptions to that rule, and they must be taken into account. Most recently, during the period from the summer of 2002 through March of 2003, a five-year holding period might well have resulted in returns anywhere from zero to a loss for the great majority of equity portfolios. If one goes back seven years though, a reasonably allocated portfolio of stocks, held in well-managed funds, would have produced a gain in excess of what could be expected from a "savings" position. By going back ten or fifteen years, the gain on a well-diversified equity portfolio would have been quite likely in excess of 10% per year on a compounded basis.

That leads to a critical issue. Looking back from the market low in mid-2002 or even in March of 2003, presuming you were invested over that time, do you know what average annual compounded return you received on your portfolio over the preceding decade? That time frame took us through both a bull and a bear market and is a good measuring stick to determine how well you and your managers have done. If you simply don't know and don't have the data to find out or were not an investor over that time period, then examine the return of the managers you are considering in the light of that very stressful period. Remember, though, to compare them with their asset class not the broad market or even absolute returns. Bond funds, for example, did quite well as a rule during the period. But don't be deceived by high returns in the past, as the real engine for that bond growth was one of the greatest declines in interest rates in the history of our country. Falling interest rates mean rising bond values. Unfortunately, interest rates have a very definite floor below which they cannot fall. From the record low rates of 2003, the odds are very much that the next decade will see a substantial rise in rates and corresponding fall in value.

Define a Definite Objective

Knowing what we want gets us a step closer to success, but there is a necessity to define it clearly if we really want to have it. For example, a 53-year-old man might determine that his most important goal is to be able to have an income of let's say $70,000 without having to work. Converting that goal to an objective might cause it to be stated like this: "When I turn sixty-five years of age, I want to have an income equivalent to $70,000 in today's dollars without having to go to work."

That object, you will note, is stated in the first person and is very specific as to the exact thing ($70,000 per year) and the time (age 65). That is quite a different statement from something like "I would like to be able to retire some day." "Some day" never comes, and the word "retire" carries some negative baggage with it for most of us. On the other hand, the ability to do whatever we want to do with our life without having to sacrifice our time to an employer or business is, in essence, *freedom!*

Note that we still have not defined how much inflation will increase the number of dollars we will need to buy what $70,000 buys today by the time age 65 comes along. We don't know how much money will be needed in a retirement fund, how much will come from other sources or anything else about this objective. Those are not important to the objective yet. There are more than a few people who do not set long-term objectives because they don't know all the answers. In fact, we will never even get close to knowing the answers until we know the exact questions.

The fact that you are not able to make the perfect plan should not dissuade you from making some plan! Even if you are already *in* retirement, a carefully thought out and written plan will organize and pave the way to answering questions that you may not even know you need to answer. What will happen to the survivor when one member of a couple dies or becomes incapacitated? What income can our investment portfolio reasonably give us if we live to a very ripe old age? Where then should it be invested? These are questions that can either be deferred until the crisis comes from the failure to plan or solved before they are critical.

Then, if one has an idea of which asset classes are appropriate for a set of long-term goals and those goals are clearly identified, it is possible to "ride out" a bear market with some degree of confidence. Of course, in order to do that one should know in advance that bear markets happen, and normally happen when they are least expected. Going back to Harry Markowitz, in order to receive a return above that of guaranteed or insured savings, one must be willing to accept variability in the market price of the investments. If you determine that you need, for example, a 10% average annual rate of return over a ten-year period to have the money you need for a specific objective, a good stock fund portfolio over the ten years ending in the summer of 2002 would have done just fine. That is true even though the broad market prices of stocks fell by half from April of 2000 through the fall of 2002.

The issue is to know that you are in an asset class, or better, classes, which represent the creation of *utility*. If utility is created, then value is accruing in that asset class. If value is building, the price of the asset you own will rise, sooner or later. Remember, the new element that changes when money is converted to capital is *time*. When money is converted to useful capital (capital increasing utility), then the market price of that utility will emerge. It is like a wellspring. It may be temporarily blocked and thereby lose value but will eventually break out and rise. As a group, smaller companies tend to create utility at a higher rate of speed than larger companies. Larger companies, on the other hand, tend to be more stable in their market value *and* tend to have value still being produced by utility created in the past.

We are often stopped well before setting long-term goals by the frighteningly large amount of information about the future we think we do not know. In fact, we do not know *anything* about the future with any certainty. Children know little about how things work, so it is not hard for them to have dreams and set goals. As we get older, it gets harder and harder because we *think* we do know some things about the future. We gradually come under the very false impression that we know what the future will probably hold, and as we go along, we tend to get more and more pessimistic about it.

Consider that the future we "wise old" adults face is exactly the same future that children face. They are generally optimistic and enthusiastic about that future, and we are generally pessimistic. The children are right. We wise old heads are wrong.

The future is better than the past. At least, it will be if you want it to be. It seems to be a commonality across many centuries that as we humans age, we think of things as getting worse and the future as being quite limited in potential. First, history shows that with the exception of certain great disasters that echo across history such as occurred with the fall of Rome and the socioeconomic collapses of the 14th and 17th centuries, things are generally getting better for those of us who live in that civilization loosely called "the West." The standard of living we take for granted today can only be measured in multiples of that of half a century ago. Even the meager standard at which the median American family lived fifty years ago was multiples of that of a century ago. For some reason alien to my understanding, sometime in the 1980s the idea caught on that the "next generation" would not live as well as their parents. A quarter of a century later we don't hear that any more because it is simply untrue!

Plan the Route to the Objective

Inflation: The dilution of the dollar

Once we have goals and have defined those goals in clear terms with reference to a measurable standard and a specific time, we know where we are going and when we need to be there. The next step is to plan a route that will get us there when we want to arrive.

Let's refer back to the goal of having sufficient investment income to be able to live at a comfortable standard of living without having to work for it. We know a pretty good definition of where we are going, but let's put a measuring stick to that point. At 2.5% inflation, $70,000 in today's dollars will require about $96,500 in future dollars, thirteen years from now, to purchase the same goods and services. There are a number of ways to find that number, but the easiest is to use a simple calculator and multiply $70,000 times 1.025 thirteen times.

What we have defined is not an end point in our journey but a transition point. We have a good estimate of how much money our wealth needs to generate at the point when we wish to begin drawing on it, but we also need to consider that we hope to continue to live for quite a number of years beyond that point, and we will need to continue to draw from that wealth for at least that long. If there is someone or several persons whom we wish to continue to draw on that wealth, then it must sustain itself even longer.

What we are seeking is a rate of return that will allow us to draw the income we need from our investments while still allowing the average long-term dollar valuation of our portfolio to increase with inflation. In order to do that, we must start with an educated guess about what rate of inflation we will experience in the future. Over the second half of the 20th century, the average rate of inflation as measured by the Consumer Price Index (CPI) was about 4%. During the first half of the century, the rate was very similar but ranged from dramatically high in the first quarter of the century to an actual deflation in the second quarter.

To put that 4% in good historic perspective, a very large portion of it occurred at two times in the century. The first event was during World War I. Because of the expense of the war, the United States abandoned the gold standard for the first time since the Civil War. The result was very much the same as in that earlier war. We spent money on a war that was actually not at all in concord with the amount of money that was being collected in taxes. The result was a dilution of the national currency, or inflation. During World War I, inflation decreased the buying power of the dollar by two-thirds in a very short time. Following World War I, the Congress was quite sensitive to the threat of further inflation and empowered the Federal Reserve Board of Governors to take action to control inflation. The Great Depression of the 1930s was, at least in part, brought on by the actions of the Federal Reserve Board to fight the threat of inflation.

The second bout of inflation followed another round of expenditures for a war without putting the economy on a war footing. That war coincided with one of the most dramatic increases in social welfare expenditures in history. The war was in Viet Nam. The second war was the "Great Society" initiative. Once again, we spent great quantities of money that was not collected as taxes nor actually borrowed from the public. In a fashion, one could say that in both World War I and the Viet Nam War our government "cooked the books" to create money to spend on what it believed needed done. There is not a great difference between what Enron did with its finances and what the Treasury of the United States did in both time periods. If the dollar is effectively a share in the United States, then the results were similar.

While it is possible that our government will again enter into a war or a dramatic social expenditure binge without consideration of the cost, it is unlikely anytime in the near future. In both cases, we were venturing into economic territory where we had never gone before as we departed from a gold-based currency. We now have such a currency and have learned a great deal about how to maintain its value at a reasonable level. In fact, we are learning that a little inflation is a good thing. It took us a century, but I believe the lesson is now learned and will be well heeded into the future.

The CPI numbers do not well describe the actual increase in cost of living for a given family any better than the national average temperature describes the heat or cold of any given day for a specific location in America. Included in the CPI is the cost of housing. If a family chose to own a home for an extended period of time, their cost of living would quite possibly rise considerably less than the national average. The advent of children into the family is another factor that increases the cost of living dramatically. The backside to that is that once children leave home, it is not uncommon for a family to actually see a falling cost of living, no matter what the national averages say.

The lesson here is that once we begin drawing income from our portfolio to live without having to sell our time to an employer, we have a great deal of control over cost of living increases. Even if we return to a 4% level of general inflation, an event I consider unlikely, people who are financially independent may well have the ability to limit their personal inflation to around the 2.5% we are assuming here.

For other goals, inflation will be a different number. For example, the cost of a university undergraduate education has been rising at about 7% per year for the past twenty years. There are variants in that level of inflation in that it is possible to obtain a good quality four-year undergraduate degree by attending a community college for two years and then finishing at one of the lower cost state supported schools for the next two years. The cost of that route has pretty much paralleled general inflation over those decades. Meanwhile, the cost of an undergraduate degree at one of the more highly rated private universities has risen at double digit rates over the same period.

One of the most important things to remember here is that the rate of increase in cost must be figured separately for each goal you have in order to create a realistic objective and path.

Real Return: What we have to live on.

Let's proceed with determining the path to that most universal goal, financial independence. If we assume that 2.5% is what we must make in order to have a real return of zero, then we must determine what return we want to have on our investments above that number. If our goal was to have that $96,000 per year to live on thirteen years in the future, or even if our goal is to take the money we have today and generate a reasonable income from it, we at least have an estimate of how much it will need to make just to hold our own.

As time is a critical element in the growth of capital, we can either have capital now or have a combination of time and free cashflow to arrive at an investment objective. It has not been unusual over the years for me to have a person in their sixties approach me with around $30,000 to $50,000 and want to create a monthly income for themselves of $1,000 or more. Because $1,000 per month is $12,000 per year, even at the best historic long-term rate of return, they will run out of money within about six years. Sadly, some people have come to me with even less, not understanding at all the relationship between the amount of income they could reasonably expect to take and the amount of money they have.

Actually, the investor in his or her 60s with that $30,000 to $50,000 has a shot at making it if they are willing to deal with the reality of where they are. First, they are probably going to be eligible for full social security. Second, if they are willing to work and save like their future depended on it for the next several years, they might have a quite reasonable standard of living to look forward to. No, they are not going to have a yacht in the marina, but they are not going to go hungry, and they may just possibly get some reasonable supplemental income from those investments. The question is, as it has been through their lives, will they invest the money or will they go out and spend it on something?

Let's assume, in this case, that our model investor has those thirteen years until he or she wants to be able to walk away from work and not come back. The first thing I would want to know would be what other income would be coming in at that point. Social security might be part of the income to include in our analysis, or it may be that our model investor believes it will not be available. There may be other income as well. For this example, let's assume that the income we desire,

$70,000 in today's buying power and nearly $100,000 in future dollars, is going to come directly from our portfolio of investments.

Let's also assume that our hypothetical investor currently has $265,000 in his or her investment portfolio. Further, let's assume that through a combination of payroll deduction and employer matching our future retiree will be contributing $1,000 per month. Again, for the sake of simplicity, let's also assume that this is all in a retirement account that is exempt from current taxation.

Before I go on, I want to point out that we have just made a whole bunch of assumptions. In reality, it might well be that the monthly investment would be lower today but expected to rise with pay increases, if there are any. It also may be that if our goal was something other than income at retirement, then we would need to carefully consider taxation on the investment portfolio in the years between now and the year we want the money. Here again, if you are not interested in digging deeply into the details of that type of thing and spending a lot of time doing it, this is a good guide to what you should expect out of a financial planner.

So, we have $265,000 now and will be depositing another $156,000 ($1,000 times the months until we want to begin drawing the money out). What we really have to work with is a total of $421,000 and thirteen years of time. Some of that exists today as invested "capital" and some of it exists as the "time" our investor is planning to sell. The time they are planning to sell to create portfolio investments can also be considered capital. That capital has been created by an investment in education that has increased the value of the time our investor is selling to either an employer or customers if he or she is a business owner. The $1,000 per month is not all the income received from selling the capital (time) that was created, but is called the "reinvested capital" and forms the basis for financial independence in the future.

We now have a good estimate for what will be invested into our retirement account over the next thirteen years and we know the income we will need to draw from that retirement fund ($96,500 per year). Now the question that remains is, "What rate of return does the investment portfolio need to make for this all to work?"

Finding the answer to that question requires a little work. If you have a spreadsheet program on your computer, you can set up a problem with all the elements in it and through trial and error come to the correct answer within a few minutes. In this case, a 10% rate of return gets the job done very nicely. That amounts to a real return of 7.5% and inflation of 2.5%. A 10% average annual return for thirteen years takes our investment portfolio to $1,287,740. Drawing 7.5% of that per year gives us $96,500. (Actually, I ran all the calculations on a monthly basis, so the answer will be slightly different if you do it annually.) The portfolio must continue earning that 7.5% above inflation to provide for needed increases in income into the years of our financial independence.

It is important to note here that I have not included taxes, fees, or expenses of any kind in this method. What must be considered when looking at returns is the *return net of taxes and expenses* in determining what is likely to work.

It is a bit of a drill to set this up for each of your goals and then carefully position funding for each of them, but again, that is what a good financial planner is supposed to do in some form or another. It is no mystery why most investors do poorly. The skills involved in setting up a plan for being successful are not difficult to learn and the tools to accomplish them are in every Microsoft Excel spreadsheet, but those skills are not taught in school, even for those with a university degree.

Chapter 14 – Investigate Historic Returns and Allocate

The Trade Off: Return vs. Variability

There is a bit of wisdom here that needs consideration by each person who makes a plan individually. As long as one is investing regularly, the up and down variations that occur in the total market value of the portfolio from quarter to quarter or even from year to year are not a negative. That does not mean that one cannot lose money investing monthly, but it does mean that purchasing securities on a regular calendar basis with the same amount of money each period tends to create a higher return than will be recorded by a lump sum investment.

Now that I have opened the can of worms known as "dollar-cost-averaging," I need to finish off some of the myths about it. For starters, if the price of the security being purchased is rising, the lump sum investor will have more money in the end than will the investor using dollar-cost-averaging. The fact is that he purchased the security at a lower price. If the price was rising and he spread out the cost over a long period, then most of the later regular purchases were at higher prices and thereby gave him less gain.

What dollar-cost-averaging has done historically, is give the regular "payroll" or monthly investor a bit better return than the underlying investment reports. That is because he is purchasing some of the shares at lower prices and some at higher. The average return, for some pretty esoteric reasons, tends to be higher than the underlying investment.

What many people fail to consider, though, is that the reverse occurs as well. When an investor begins to liquidate a portfolio of securities, such as mutual funds, he or she will experience *reverse dollar-cost-averaging*. I suppose the effect should have a name of its own, like "dollar-price-averaging" or something, but the fact remains that a systematic liquidation of a portfolio to provide steady payments on a calendar basis tends to result in an average return lower than that of the underlying portfolio.

Another way of understanding this effect is to think of a portfolio

215

that averaged, let's say, 10% per year, over a ten-year period. If that portfolio experienced a reasonable amount of variance over the period, a person *investing* regular monthly amounts might see a return of 10.2% per year while a person with systematic *withdrawals* might experience a return of only 9.8% per year. The differences will vary according to the amount of variability of the portfolio and the amount being either invested or withdrawn. What this means is we have to not only consider what the long-term reported rate of an asset class may be but also take into account the short-term variations in the market values.

The most basic understanding here is that there is a relationship between the long-term return of a class of securities and its variability over the short-term. Harry Markowitz noted that the higher the long-term return of a type of security, or asset class, the greater its short-term variability in price and the longer one needed to hold it to have a high probability of achieving that higher return. In other words, the faster we want to go, the bumpier the ride will be, and the longer we need to stay in the car. Another way to see it is to understand that one can go quite fast as long as there is a long distance to go, but going 70 miles per hour in one's driveway is not conducive to long-term success!

The lesson in all of this is that when one elects to have goals, one also sets a long-term return. In order to achieve that long-term return, we will experience year-to-year variability in the market value of the portfolio, both up and down. The higher the return we wish to have in order to accomplish our goals, the greater that variability will be. The question is whether *you* as an investor are prepared for the variability that will come as a result of your goals.

The trade off here is fairly clear. Over the last ten years, which in many ways represents a nearly worst case scenario for stocks and a best case scenario for bonds, the average well-established, general large-stock mutual fund created a real return *(after inflation)* on invested money of about 6.7% per year, while the average stock and bond mixed portfolio averaged about 5%, intermediate government bonds averaged about 3.84%, and the average three month CD averaged 2%. Again, I want to emphasize that those returns are *after inflation*. The nominal returns (before subtracting inflation) are listed on the graph below.

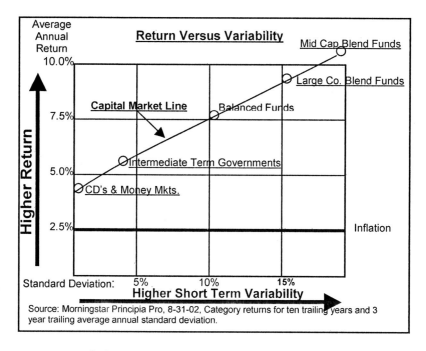

To put all this percentage stuff in dollar terms, a pure stock portfolio would have generated a total of $24,000 from an investment of $10,000 over the ten-year period. If we wanted to smooth out the ride and mixed stocks and bonds in a balanced portfolio we would have had only about $20,000, while an average portfolio of jumbo CDs would have provided about $15,000. Considering that the ten years we are examining was among the very worst for stocks and best for bonds in half a century, you can see that stocks for all their recent bad reputation would have created far more wealth.

For better or worse, the route to that higher return over that ten-year period took the pure stock portfolio up to $45,000 before it arrived at $24,000. The balanced portfolio peaked at about $25,000 before returning to $20,000, and the CDs calmly managed to stay just ahead of inflation with nary a bump. Of course, after we figure in taxes as well as inflation, we really didn't make anything in the CDs and had quite a sizable gain in the stocks. The price we must pay for growth is pretty clear here. The route to wealth is not smooth.

Market Timing

An obvious question arises at this point. Why not just liquidate one's portfolio when it is at $48,000 and hold it in a money market fund until the market hits bottom and then jump back in?

The issue of timing the market to jump out at the top and back in at the bottom of long-term price variations has fascinated scholars and investors as long as there have been markets. In fact, there were times in history when it seemed to work quite well, but it actually wasn't market timing that was working, it was something we today call "insider information." Given the wide dissemination of information about earnings, earnings prospects, economic indicators, and other pricing information that affect the price of securities in general or specifically, any widely traded asset class is priced at about where the consensus of investors believes it should be at any given moment. Most of those investors are doing their best to determine what the underlying company or bond will be worth months or even years into the future and from that, will decide the price at which they are willing to buy or sell the security today.

In order to be a successful market timer, you would have to know the future better than the consensus of investors who are active in the market. That is a tall order considering the sophistication and information flow of the "movers" who are watched closely in the day-to-day activity on the market floor. I have read some really fascinating theories over the years on "beating the market" through market timing. I also have had the privilege of being able to observe the portfolio of one of the most sophisticated and dedicated market timers I have ever known. He spends several hours each day and thousands of dollars per year on the data that pours into his home office where he carefully considers the meanings of graphs, statistics, and balances before making the decision to jump from equities to money markets and back again. He is even in a portfolio where there is no charge for his movements and no taxes on the exchanges!

Despite his many hours and expenditure of many thousands of dollars, the informal competition we have held over the last ten years has me substantially in the lead with my carefully allocated, "buy and hold" portfolio of mutual funds. After searching for twenty years, I am still awaiting the first market timer to present his audited portfolio, held over a decade or longer, that has outperformed a "buy and hold" portfolio of the same equities.

In short, market timing has never worked and, in my educated opinion, probably never will. The only people who make money from market timing are the folks who sell the market timing newsletters. Some time ago, I had a client who was quite serious about market timing. His story is sufficiently typical of timers that it bears telling. He started his timing efforts after experiencing the 26% drop in equity prices that occurred in about two months in the late summer and early fall of 1987. After some rather heated discussion between him and me, he told me he was convinced that it was possible to avoid that kind of drop in value by leaving the equities market when certain signals were given and that he had read an article on the subject and was going to do it.

Sure enough, soon his orders started to come in moving his portfolio from his equity funds to money market funds and back at interesting times. As 1988 and 1989 progressed and we entered into 1990, he indeed was pulling ahead of the value he would have been able to have with a "buy and hold" approach. I was impressed enough to watch his portfolio closely. Then, in August of 1990, Saddam Hussein invaded Kuwait. The equity prices on the world markets dropped precipitously. As there were no cyclical indicators that preceded this sudden change in valuation, the market timing indicators missed the fall. After the valuations had dropped about 15-20%, my client's timing indicator service advised him to "get out" and he did. As 1991 dawned and it became clear that we were quickly defeating Mr. Hussein's forces, the equity valuations not only returned quickly to their previous level but shot even higher in a very short period of time. My client reentered the equity market at a point substantially higher than where he left, as once again, the statistical indicators his market timing service relied upon had no way of judging the effect that war would have on equity valuations.

Several years later, in 1994, that client called me up to express his anger at the relatively low returns on his portfolio when compared with the market averages. Surprised by his call and quickly calculating that he was correct that his overall returns from for the last five years were substandard, I apologized profusely and promised to get back to him with an analysis. It was only after the call as I reviewed his account activity that I remembered that crucial error in 1990-1991. Despite all the "good" moves he had made over the years, that one mistake had cost him not only all the gain he had gotten from the timing activity but put in him in a position of being well behind the underlying return of the investments he was using for the same period.

Amazingly, when I called him back to explain that it was the timing move in 1990-91 as well as a couple of other moves that set him back, he could not remember making the switches. I had to send him copies of his orders to convince him that he had done it to himself. Afterwards, he abandoned market timing, probably to the betterment of his portfolio values.

Purely from my experience, I have concluded that there are times in a rapidly rising bull market when there are a number of "methods" that actually do enhance returns ranging from "momentum investing" to market timing. I have also observed though that any additional return gained from those methods appears to be more than lost when the general securities values turn unexpectedly downward. The problem with the unexpected turn is that it looks just like one of the random turns that come and go in every market. No one, and I mean absolutely no one, to date has come up with a foolproof method of determining which up turn or down turn is the one that will continue or is just another random fluctuation. Guessing where the next short-term market wave will take us is about as likely to be successful as trying to forecast where and how high the next wave will reach on an ocean beach. Both are examples of truly random activity and randomness is by definition, unforecastable.

Asset Class Returns

Average Annual Returns 1952-2002			
Asset Class*	50 yr Nominal Return	After Inflation**	After Tax*** & Inflation
Small Company Stocks	14.4%	10.4%	7.52%
Large Company Stocks	12.0%	8.0%	6.0%
Corporate Bonds	6.4%	2.4%	.67%
T-Bills	5.3%	1.3%	*-.13%*
* Ibbotson & Associates, *Stocks, Bonds, Bills, & Inflation,* 2002 edition ** 50 year inflation 4%. *** Tax calculated at 27% for income and 20% for long-term capital gains.			

The table above lists the four major asset classes tracked over the past half century by Ibbotson & Associates and published in their *Stocks, Bonds, Bills, & Inflation*. It is important to note that when Morningstar or any of the other sources of market valuation or performance refer to "small company" or "small stocks" they mean something completely different. The small company stocks by Ibbotson's figuring are about equivalent to what other index services call "Mid-Cap" or middle capitalization.

If you look carefully at the table above, you will note some very significant numbers. After taxes and inflation, Treasury bills have actually had a *negative* rate of return. Corporate bonds, with rates slightly higher than government bonds for the period, returned less than one percent. Although I have not listed them on this table, government bonds had a slightly *lower* than zero rate. After deducting 4% for inflation, large company stocks had a real return of 6% and small sized companies had a real after tax and inflation return of over 7.5%.

Most tables and sources I have seen start in 1926 and calculate from there to the present in order to present historic returns. I have chosen to start fifty years ago instead because we have a very different economy now than we had in the pre-World War II period. After WWII we were a dynamic, world leading, industrial nation, but during the 1930s we were still primarily an agricultural country emerging from a near third world status.

The last fifty years have taken us through pretty much the full spectrum of economic events, from a near deflation condition in the first couple of decades to double digit inflation in the late 1970s and early 80s; from low interest rates to high and back to low; from a time of economic stagnation when the stock market indices barely budged for over a decade to one of the biggest run ups, and busts, in the history of the market. Looking back half a century, we have a pretty good idea of what can happen, although there are always new events to come.

In our planning example, it is pretty clear that our hypothetical investor could have gotten that 7.5% real rate of return from either mid-cap or large-cap stocks. It is also pretty clear that even in one of the greatest bond market expansions in our history, he couldn't have come close to achieving his goals in the other asset classes.

Russell Index Average Returns Ten Years ending September 2002			
Asset Class*	10 yr Nominal Return	After Inflation**	After Tax*** & Inflation
Russell Mid-Cap Growth	8.07%	5.57%	3.96%
Russell Mid-Cap Value	10.99%	8.49%	6.79%
Russell 1000 Growth	7.99%	5.49%	3.33%
Russell 1000 Value	11.92%	9.45%	6.22%
* Morningstar Principia Pro, October 2002 edition. ** 10-year inflation 2.5%. *** Tax calculated at 27% for income and 20% for long-term capital gains.			

Here we are not only looking at the returns of different sized stocks at or near the market "bottom" in 2002, but also breaking out the difference between "growth" and "value." Without getting too detailed, "growth" companies are those which have stocks valued primarily by growth of earnings. A prime example would be Dell Computer Corporation. The "book value" of Dell is really rather low, but the earnings or profits of Dell have tended to grow at an astonishing rate as the direct marketing model of that company has dominated the personal computer market. An example of a "value" company would be Procter and Gamble. It is unlikely that one would buy P&G for its earnings growth, but the comfort of investing in a company that dominates the soap and toothpaste shelves of American stores from coast to coast is hard to beat.

Once again, there are a few things that jump out about these returns. First, it is apparent that the mid-cap value asset class is winning followed closely by the large-cap Russell 1000 Value. It is also clear that the growth side of the market is in painfully bad shape. If we were to back up about two and a half years though, we would have found that the lagging Russell 1000 Growth Index had an average annual rate of return, beginning in October of 1992, of a whopping 23.94% per year while the Russell Mid-Cap index had returned 11.75% per year from 1992. Worse, at that point, the Russell Mid-Cap Index was actually substantially *lower* than it had been two years earlier!

There is a lesson to be learned here that is very, very important to understand if you wish to be successful: *Asset classes go in and out of favor.* During one period, the growth side of the equity market will be the hero and the value side will sink into the pits. A few years will go by and it will be the value side that is all the rage while growth oriented company stocks are distained. There is no way that I have found to be able to accurately forecast which will do what and when.

The nice thing about this disconnect is that, except for the incidents when something external drives the whole market down, having both value and growth in one's portfolio tends to smooth out the ride, and sometimes quite significantly. It is tempting to observe the recent rise in the Russell Mid-Cap Value Index and conclude that is the place to have all of one's investments. It was also tempting to think the same about large-cap growth back in late 1999 and early 2000.

One of the hardest things to do for any investor over the long haul is to set an allocation based on long-term returns from asset classes and then stick to that allocation. The Brinson study pointed out that was the single greatest contributor to either success or failure for an investment portfolio and it remains true today.

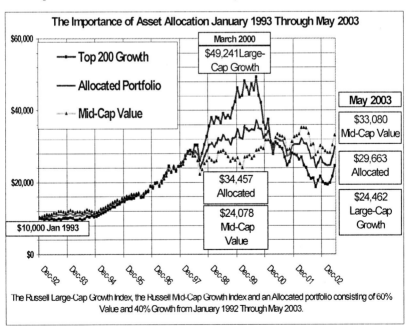

The Russell Large-Cap Growth Index, the Russell Mid-Cap Growth Index and an Allocated portfolio consisting of 60% Value and 40% Growth from January 1992 Through May 2003.

The graph above shows that mid-cap value appreciated faster than the Russell 1000 Growth Index for about the first year of the chart. The growth index then outperforms the value index for about the next seven years. Then, mid-cap value starts up and the large company growth index starts down. Having a balance of each in your portfolio would have clearly provided more stability than either one alone. Of course, there are times when both go down, such as in the fall of 1998, September 2001, and again in the second and third quarters of 2002.

At first, your impression might have been that the best thing to do would be simply to use mid-cap value for the whole period, but it would have been very hard to accept the loss from $30,000 in mid-1997 to $26,000 in mid-1999, while your friends and neighbors were seeing their large company growth accounts grow to $52,000. That is the problem. We seem to be hard-wired to go with the consensus, and that means that from time to time we will all tend to flood to one side of the market or the other.

The problem with this is that you cannot invest in an index, and I would recommend against it even if it were possible. Even attempting to invest in an index can be quite hazardous. Index surrogates such as the S&P 500 Index funds and market-traded funds that attempt to mimic an index actually change the behavior of the index itself. Additionally, funds that attempt to mimic an index do not allocate money based on how well the fund manager believes a company is being run or how profitable it is likely to be, but simply on the basis of size. For example, more money goes to the large companies in the S&P 500 and less money goes to the smaller companies. It is hard for me to accept that larger companies are inherently more efficient than smaller ones and should therefore get more of an investor's money. If anything, history indicates that the exact opposite is more likely to be the truth.

During the market "bubble" that emerged in 1997 and finally collapsed in 2001-2002, the dot-coms got the black eye, but they were long gone by the time the downhill slide really started in the spring of 2002. It was the massive sell-off from the S&P 500 index funds that brought the house down in the most dramatic manner. According to articles in the *Wall Street Journal* at the time, record in-flows of money entered the market in the first quarter of 2000 as we reached what we now know to be a rather substantial overpricing of equities in the United States. The *Journal* article also stated that about

63% of that inflow was deposited into index funds. The result was an overpricing of about 50% in the largest of the S&P 500 companies and a corresponding under pricing of mid-cap companies.

If this is a fascinating area for you, I encourage you to read *Asset Allocation: Balancing Financial Risk* by Roger C. Gibson and published by Dow Jones-Irwin, Homewood, Illinois, 1990. In it, Gibson creates a case that effective asset allocation not only provides a reduced volatility for a given amount of return but also increases the expected return of a portfolio over traditional investment styles. The returns we have seen over the past ten years tend to support that conclusion.

Back in Chapter 12 when I cited the Brinson study indicating that it found asset allocation to be the major determining factor in long-term return, I also noted that the study only considered three elements when looking at portfolio returns. What it did not consider was the manager of the portfolio. It made the assumption that one well-educated manager was pretty much like another. Brinson did look at individual security selection in the portfolios as a possible determinate, but did not consider whether the same manager had been at the portfolio for the entire period. It also limited the examination to pension plans. Pension plans often have multiple managers and generally have a specific and rather narrow mandate with regard to what can and cannot be done in the portfolio. Another quite significant issue in pension plans is that they are not influenced by tax consequences and do not have to deal with large inflows and outflows as investor sentiment changes.

In the real world of investing, publicly available, professionally managed portfolios, known as mutual funds, predominate. Once we determine the asset classes that have historically demonstrated the potential to accomplish our objectives, then we have to determine how we are going to utilize those asset classes. Now it is time to choose who will be in charge selecting the specific investments in each asset class.

Chapter 15 – Choosing Managers

Once More Unto the Breach

Vilfredo Pareto discovered that 80% of the means of production was owned by 20% of the people in every developed country he investigated. Later, others have expanded on that observation to note that it is common for 80% of the results above a certain minimum to come from about 20% of the producers.

I have personally observed again and again that principle to be true in every example where there is measurable productivity. I have had the opportunity to review sales results for a number of companies in different industries. In literally every case, 80% of the production comes from about 20% of the producers.

Each of us that have worked under the supervision of a series of managers can verify that the "Pareto Principle" applies to management as well as it does to sales and maintenance production. Some managers are simply better than others.

Before we start trying to choose investment managers though, we probably want to put to rest the question of whether or not we should be buying individual stocks and bonds for our own portfolio. I have been carefully auditing individually managed investment portfolios for over 20 years and am still waiting for the first of those portfolios to have an historic performance worthy of note. On June 21, 2001, Dalbar, Inc. published a study entitled "Quantitative Analysis of Investor Behavior" on individual investor returns beginning in January 1984 and continuing through December 2000. The three findings of that study, shown below, clearly make the case for professional management and the need most investors have for guidance from a professional investment advisor:

- The average fixed-income investor realized an annualized return of 6.08%, compared to 11.83% for the long-term government bond index;
- The average equity...investor realized an annualized return of 5.32%, compared to 16.29% for the S&P 500 Index; and
- The average money-market fund investor realized an annualized

return of 2.29%, compared to 5.82% for Treasury bills and 3.23% for inflation. Money-market fund investors lost money after inflation.[4]

I have yet to meet the investor managing his or her own portfolio who knew the trailing average annual rate of return of that portfolio. The inability to calculate the rate of return of one's portfolio means that perhaps the most critical factor in determining success or failure in time to do something about it is missing. As you read this, if you think that you are well above average, and *you* are sure you have a better return than the Dalbar report would indicate, I challenge you to actually produce an *internal rate of return,* or IRR, on your portfolio performance over the past five and ten years. If the term is alien to you, then you are beginning to see the problem. The only way a portfolio can be evaluated is to calculate the actual return, taking into account all the cash flows in and out of the portfolio. That is what we call an IRR.

As I mentioned earlier in the book, *The Beardstown Ladies' Common Sense Investment Guide* was an example of just the behavior that is reflected in the Dalbar study. On the cover of their book the ladies quote a "23.4% annual return" and include the sub-title *"How We Beat the Stock Market – and How You Can Too."* Their *actual* return over the time period (1984-1997) quoted in the book was 9.1% per year. Not only did they *not* "beat the market," they trailed it miserably. Over the same period, the S&P 500 returned 14.9% and inflation ran about 6%. In fact, they could have done as well as they really did, or better, by simply dropping their money in a local certificate of deposit. Their blissfully ignorant treasurer assumed that she could simply add the money they invested to the total return each month as if it had been gain.

To make the error worse, the return quoted is *simple* interest rather than compounded. While that may not sound like a serious error, note that 10% simple interest provides the same return as 7.2% compound interest. As the number rises the difference does as well. 23.4% simple interest is about the same as 14.9% compounded. In other words, the

---

[4] Press release "Dalbar Issues 2001 Update to "Quantitative Analysis of Investor Behavior" Report, Boston, MA – June 21, 2001. http://www.dalbarinc.com/content/showpage.asp?page=2001062100

return reported by the Beardstown Ladies was really about the same as the broad market but stated in such a way as to make it sound like much more. Unfortunately they did not really even get that rate of return. Market returns and the returns of mutual funds are reported on the basis of compounding. The Beardstown Ladies, like many another investor believed they were "beating the market" when in fact they were getting a long term return far below that of the unmanaged indices.

There was a time when it was possible to purchase a portfolio of blue chip stocks and basically take a "buy and hold" approach well into the future. That day is gone and is unlikely to return. There are probably no better-qualified persons in the world to choose a portfolio of financially stable and profitable companies than the editors of the *Wall Street Journal*. They are the judges of which stocks go into the Dow Jones 30 Industrial Stock Index, among others. If we assumed that they knew what they were doing at the beginning of the 1990s and at that time, banking on their judgment, bought the thirty stocks in that index then went on a ten-year vacation, we would be rather shocked today. Upon our return, we would have found that of the thirty stocks, only eighteen were still in the index. Some of the vanished stocks had been merged into other companies, but a significant number simply went out of business and disappeared, along with our money!

Now that we have (hopefully) settled the issue of whether or not it is a good idea to manage your own portfolio at the specific investment level, let's go on to finding managers for your investments.

In Search of the Significant Few

If we presume that Pareto's Principle is correct, then there should be a few investment managers who are truly exceptional. Considering that there are over 3,000 fund managers out there who are all well educated and many of who have more than five years of recorded public experience, we should actually be able to find *quite* a few.

Oddly enough, I have found many of the outstanding mangers I have used over the years by word of mouth. At conferences or in talking to friends or even individual investors, I will hear of a manager or fund that is reputed to be performing very well. In most cases when I investigate, I find that the performance is more illusory than real, but from time to time, I hear of truly superior performance, often from aseasoned colleague. When I find what appears to be one of the critical few managers with exceptional talent for investment selection, my next step is to set up an interview with the responsible party.

It is surprising to me to find that as I arrive at the office of a mutual fund manager I want to interview, that my visit is considered a very unusual event. It seems that actually expending the time and money to visit with a manager before turning my clients' capital over to his or her care is considered a radical move! At first I had trouble believing that almost no one else was willing to make the journey and take the time to interview the manager before committing the money. Then I thought of the tremendous sums of money both individuals and stockbrokers would commit to the stock of a corporation whose headquarters they had never seen!

Shortly after entering the business of advising people on how to invest their money, I was privileged to meet Tom Bailey, founder of Janus Capital Corporation and, at the time, manager of Janus Fund. I was thoroughly impressed not only with his historic performance as an investment manager but his philosophy that there were a few truly outstanding companies in the corporate world whose growth would shock the world, and that the critical element in selecting the best of them was to interview the people who were making it happen. He went on to say that the interview was followed by speaking with the team around the decision maker and on the work floor who could tell him quickly if the boss was a great as he claimed.

I was also fortunate to meet other legends in the world of invest-ment management, most of who have now passed from the profession but whose wisdom impressed me intensely. I was honored to listen for hours to Jack Kenney, a protégé of Phillip Caret, founder of Pioneer Fund in 1928. It was Mr. Caret who was reputed to have said, "You never know who is not wearing a swimming suit until the tide goes out." That prophetic statement could have just as easily been about the string of scandals at the beginning of the 21st century as about the scandals of the 1930s that he remembered. His version of buying into whatever asset class is currently out of favor was to say, "Buy when the blood is on the street," referring to the string of suicides in 1932 on Wall Street. Jack was the one who first said to me, "Good managers make good companies, but good companies without good managers don't stay good very long."

When I first started in the investment world, an individual, whether a broker or investor, stood a fighting chance of beating the professionals. The professionals and the amateurs were all working from pretty much the same information. Today, it is as hard to find the good investment managers as it was back then to find the good stocks. In fact, there are far more mutual funds and even more mutual fund managers today than there were commonly traded stocks in the past.

One more word of warning: the risk-reduction move of diversification across several asset classes can be almost totally negated by having your investment managers in the same investment management company. Each management, or mutual fund, company has a chief investment officer that runs the show. The managers at a given company will also all be using the same analysts. Because the people who work together in any investment office have to get along, even the managers will tend to think alike just because they are there. It is prudent to have your managers at different companies and, if possible, to have those different managers in different cities and regions across the country.

Having a large portion of your invested money at one mutual fund family is potentially a risky proposition. Spreading the wealth does take a bit more work, but it may save your financial future.

The Second String

After finding at least one good manager in each asset class and sub class that you want to use, we are faced with the next difficulty. Getting your money under the care of the chosen investment managers is sometimes difficult as they are commonly in secluded offerings of some kind, but even harder is planning for what to do when the manager leaves or fails!

One of the few things I can be quite sure of about the future is that the managers I choose today will need to be replaced at some point down the road. It is not unusual for a great manager to be in his or her 50s before they are identifiable as someone we want to use. The mere fact that they have done an outstanding job of managing money will tend to attract more money to them. At some point, it is not uncommon for them to either be overwhelmed by the inflow of new money, to get in a conflict with their supervisors, or to simply decide that it is time to call it quits while they are still ahead.

Sometimes the killer is simply pure hubris, as they come to believe the hyped magazine articles they read about their genius at stock picking. I have heard it said and observed that a fund manager's picture on the cover of *Money Magazine* is the kiss of death. One manager I thought highly of had his mug on the cover of that fatal document twice in one year! His fund went from the number one performer for the previous two years into a slump that only ended when he left for greener pastures.

It is critical to plan for that inevitable event. Several exceptional investment professionals have told me over the years that one of the principal differences between an amateur investor and a professional is that the professional knows why and when he will sell before he buys. He also knows what it will cost to get out of a position and where he will go with the money when he does. You may note that the talking heads on the daily stock-hype television shows are always telling you what stock or fund to buy, but they never seem to get around to telling you what or when to sell! You may also notice that most of the "guests" who come on the shows telling you to buy this or that stock already own it in their own portfolio or have a serious interest in seeing the stock price go up, which of course it tends to do after being hawked on investor television.

In our case, the first step is to be sure we know how to get out before we get into an investment fund. We need to identify, if we can, some means that will either minimize or, if possible, eliminate the cost of doing so. One of the most disturbing things about advising people to sell overgrown positions in order to rebalance their allocation, or simply to get diversified out of a single position that occupies the majority of their portfolio, is to hear them object to selling because of capital gains taxes. I commonly ask them, "Would you rather wait until the capital gains taxes on the sale are reduced or even eliminated?" You can imagine my surprise on several occasions when the answer was "Yes!" In some cases, that is exactly what they did. All they had to do was wait until the price went back down to, or below, what they paid for the stock and presto… no more taxes due! At that point, in almost every case when I approached them to see if they were now willing to diversify, they replied, "No, I am going to wait for it to come back."

Once we plan how to get out of an investment, we need to already have a new manager lined up and ready to be used. Leaving a bad or overvalued position is important, but staying out of "the market" while we search for a replacement is taking a serious risk that the prices will rise while we are on the sidelines.

Chapter 16 – Investment Vehicles – Keeping the Cart behind the Horse

Privately Managed Accounts

Hopefully, we have already determined that broad diversification across several asset classes using professional managers is an important issue in our journey toward investment success. Now the question arises as to how to achieve that broad diversification.

Mutual funds have become, well, *mundane*. It just isn't sexy to go to a cocktail party or even a church reception and tell your friends that you have your whole portfolio in *mutual funds*. For a while, a few years ago, when the whole concept of having "investments" was still pretty new, owning even a single mutual fund carried a sort of class. Today, you can get more respect by telling people you compost your kitchen garbage than by suggesting that mutual funds are a quality way to invest.

One of the recent and more sophisticated efforts to entice investors away from the herd is the lure of "privately managed accounts." In return for a rather substantial (from the investors' perspective) annual fee, people with less than stellar sized accounts are offered the "personal attention" of a skilled investment manager. The question, obvious to me but apparently rather invisible to the investor lured in by the promise of superior returns in a private account, is "If the manager is so good and thus so valuable, how can he or she afford to manage my account 'personally' for the rather paltry (from the manager's perspective) sum of money I will be paying each year?"

What will actually happen, in all likelihood, is that the manager will set up a portfolio and invest all, or nearly all, of the different investors' accounts in the same positions. In some cases, the manager simply co-mingles the money and, in fact, does have them all in one portfolio. Then, there is the issue of who is minding the farm when the manager is sick or on vacation. Soon it becomes apparent that if the manager was all that good, why isn't he or she managing hundreds of millions of dollars in assets for a mutual fund company?

It may come as a surprise to find that in many cases the "private" manager *is* managing one or more mutual funds. When the private account holdings are examined closely, it may also come as a surprise to find that the private account looks quite a lot like the mutual fund being managed by the same person!

Actually, despite my rather negative tirade against private accounts, there is a place for them. If an investor has a very substantial portfolio and does not need to generate high returns, then it may be useful to have the account privately managed for tax reduction, or more likely, because of the prestige of such an arrangement. The drawback is that the privately managed account is subject to a much higher level of *non-systemic risk* than is the simple mutual fund.

For starters, the large, privately managed account is, by definition, dependent on a single investment manager or firm. If that manager or firm makes some crucial errors, the potential loss is staggering. Because privately managed accounts, be they called "hedge funds" or "wrap accounts" or a host of other sophisticated sounding names, are forbidden by law to advertise, they operate in a shadowy world where they are sold by word-of-mouth. Only the readers of the financial news publications will even have the opportunity to hear of the failures of such funds that occur again and again.

Another problem with privately managed accounts is that they are rarely independently audited. Even if the investment portfolio manager is quite honest and sincere, the fact is that the private management of small accounts is simply not efficient, and all your eggs are in a single basket with only the manager watching the basket. At best, you will have mediocre results and at worst, lose your money. It is rare that there is any good reason to have a private manager unless you simply don't need a great return and you have a burning desire to put restrictions on the investments like "no gun makers" or "no cigarette companies" or some similar restriction. If the primary reason you are investing is to have a good return, be well diversified, or have a more simple life, private management is not a good idea.

Investment Companies

The original purpose of a "company," as formed by the Yeomen, was to combine investors' capital for some purpose, generally intended to be profitable. In one sense, *all* companies could be considered investment companies, but here we refer to companies formed for the specific and permanent purpose of investing in *other* companies. As we have noted above, investing in the shares of any publicly traded company carries with it the rather substantial risk of that company suddenly and unexpectedly experiencing a substantial loss of market value for any number of reasons that may be completely unrelated to the state of the economy, the industry, or the market. The most effective means available to limit or even very nearly eliminate that risk is to have a portfolio of shares from a relatively large number of companies across a large number of industries and geographic regions. The drawback is the cost and complexity of managing such a portfolio, not to mention the simple matter of having sufficient capital to own a portfolio with a large enough number of issues to be properly diversified.

An investment company is an entity formed to acquire and manage a portfolio of investment securities. The owners of the company are the investors, and they provide the capital used to purchase those securities.

There are three basic types of investment companies in the United States. First, there is the common and now quite well known investment company simply known as a *mutual fund*. The next, and not so well known, version of Investment Company is the *closed-end fund* traded on stock exchanges like any other stock. Finally, there is the *unit investment trust* or *UIT*. Actually, there is a fourth version that is sort of a hybrid between the mutual fund and the unit investment trust that we call a *series fund*. Even that hybrid comes in two versions that might be considered separate types.

Before I go any further, let me warn you that unit investment trusts can be very dangerous vehicles. They normally invest in a fixed portfolio of securities for a set amount of time. Unfortunately, it is not uncommon in my experience to find that they are both highly expensive and have hidden issues that are not readily apparent to the typical investor. In many of the cases I have seen, unit investment trusts were used to package trash securities that professionals would never touch. By packing them together in a UIT, the less-than-quality nature of the individual securities could be hidden from easy view. While there are good reasons for professionals to use them, it is rare, in my experience, to find them well used by the general public.

A very important point that I mentioned earlier and will discuss more later is that accounts registered under the Investment Company Act of 1940 are protected by Federal Statute Law from the creditors of any of the associated organizations or institutions. In other words, if the company that sells you the fund or the advisor or even the custodian were to go bankrupt, they, or their creditors, could not touch your money.

All mutual funds are not diversified and all are not open-ended, but for our purposes here I have chosen to only refer to diversified, open-ended companies as *mutual funds*. To be called "diversified," the Investment Company Act of 1940 requires that at least 75% of the fund must be so well diversified that no more than 5% is invested in any one company. Non-diversified funds are only required to diversify half their capital, and that other half may be as little as two companies. As you may well surmise, that would be a very unusual fund and would, in all likelihood, be drummed by the press. The exceptions that I know of are funds that actually specialize in owning Berkshire Hathaway! Having half the fund invested in Berkshire Hathaway allows investors who cannot afford the tens of thousands of dollars to purchase a single share to participate in Mr. Buffet's empire. There are funds that have chosen to concentrate their assets in a single industry, and sometimes in a single type of company in a single industry. These "sector" funds are for those who wish to invest in a sector of the economy and still have at least diversification across a number of companies.

Mutual funds, as I have defined them here, are "open-ended." That means that they are continually in the business of issuing *new* shares to the public, and must be ready, willing, and able to redeem shares every business day. When an investor purchases shares in an open-ended mutual fund, he or she is purchasing shares in much the same way one purchases shares in an Initial Public Offering (for a newly traded corporation) or a secondary offering (for a corporation that is issuing new shares to increase its investor capital). The difference with a mutual fund is that the fund will also buy those shares *back* from the investor at a price based on the end of the day valuation of the underlying securities held by the fund.

The advantage to using open-ended funds is that a level of risk and a level of expense are avoided. Closed-end funds often are priced in the market at levels well below what would be indicated by the price of the underlying securities. At other times, they may be above the current market value of the underlying assets. With movements in market value of the underlying assets being a mysterious and often random series of events, adding another inexplicable and random level of pricing to the equation is to add another level of risk.

Some speculators insist that purchasing shares of a closed-end fund when it is trading well below the value of the assets of the fund, is a good way to buy the underlying securities at a discount. While there is an element of truth to what they say, any deep value professional stock investor will tell you that just because the shares of a company trade at a discount to the assets of the company, there is no guarantee that some day the market will recognize the value and raise the price! The savvy investors in the market may well recognize that the current value of the underlying assets may be high now but believe that those underlying assets will be worth less in the future. Trying to outguess all the other investors in our highly efficient market system is a dangerous game unless you have legitimate information they do not have.

Another advantage to using mutual funds is that their performance is a matter of public record. There are no mysterious "pro-forma" results and the published information is extremely transparent and, quite importantly, audited. Because the requirements are pretty clear cut and it would be the death knell for a fund management company to have a mutual fund tagged for violation of the rules, hanky panky is almost unknown in the business of actually managing the mutual funds listed in the United States.

With literally thousands of separate funds to choose from, the opportunity to *use* the variety to work for you is both an asset and a difficulty. There are more funds and managers available than there are widely traded stocks. The trick is to use them intelligently. The most efficient way to gather information on them is to use a digital service, either online, or better, delivered for loading into one's computer. While there is quite a lot of information available from mutual funds on a no-cost basis, sorting through the data for over three thousand managers is going to be an undertaking of vast difficulty. There are several companies that provide summarized in-depth analysis of individual funds. It may be a surprise to you to find that they tend to have widely differing recommendations on which funds are "good" and which are less good or even bad. Having followed those recommendations for as long as they have existed, my experience is that a fund that Morningstar rates as "Five Star" in March may well have dropped to two or even one star six months later.

"Which mutual funds should be in your portfolio?" is not the question to ask, and if you are asking the wrong question the opportunity to get the right answer is quite elusive. The question is "Which *managers* do I want to use to access the *asset classes* I have chosen from my *financial plan?*" As I have mentioned many times already, having a financial plan finalized *before* choosing investments is one of the critical elements for effective investing.

Step one is to determine what managers are operating in each of the asset classes you wish to use. If, for example, you wish to have a mid-cap value investment as part of your plan, you should start your search by identifying all the mid-cap value managers available with sufficiently long public records to merit further inspection. In the past, I have been comfortable with a five-year record to review as that commonly took us through a full market cycle. However at the beginning of the 21ˢᵗ century, I find myself looking for a longer record to get us back beyond the raging and very unusual bull market and the equally fierce and unusual bear that followed. At the very least though, I want to see how the manager performed *against his or her peers* in the asset class over at least an up market and a down market.

Searching for a mid-cap value manager, you would discover, begins with determining exactly what constitutes mid-cap value. Different rating services and different indices use different criteria. Presuming you find a definition you like, you may then discover that it is rare for a mid-cap value fund to announce that it is a mid-cap value fund! For example the prospectus may state something like:

"The XYZ Mid-Cap Value Fund seeks capital appreciation. The fund normally invests at least 65% of assets in equities of companies with market capitalizations ranging from $500 million to $5 billion. Management typically invests in securities that it believes have strong appreciation potential based on the following factors: changes in economic and financial conditions, new or improved products or services, changes in management, or improved efficiencies."

Mutual fund companies bend over backward to not restrict

themselves to an excessively narrow definition of what they can do. That "65%" notation is what allows the fund to refer to itself as a "mid-cap" fund, but the rest of the statement is pretty much boilerplate. Of course they are going to try to invest in stocks that "have strong appreciation potential." It would look pretty silly to state that they are going to buy stocks that they really believe haven't a chance in the world of appreciating! Of course they could state that they will attempt to purchase stocks with high dividends or a host of other things, but you can be sure that the objective will always be that the management will attempt to do great wonders. Some will make statements like "Management will attempt to purchase stocks that are undervalued." Again, that does seem to be the purpose in managing a value fund...

In running a screen in Morningstar software for funds with the Morningstar Category "Mid-Cap Value," I found about 311 funds. Unfortunately, quite a number were duplicates of each other with either slight or significant variations in name. It was certainly surprising to find funds in that mid-cap category, though, that Morningstar had listed in the "Large-Cap" square in their "style box" and whose name included "Large Cap." Another problem is the irregular habit that rating companies have of restarting the tenure of a manager if he or she hires an assistant.

It might be that the real manager *is* the assistant and the old manager is sort of "emeritus" in which case that would be a valid change. In many cases though, I have found that the "old" manager is still managing and has simply brought on an assistant to cover for him or her for vacations and sick days. In most cases, the assistant is serving as an understudy and will eventually take over the running of the fund. The only way to determine that issue is to call the fund company and speak with the manager or the assistant manager. Do not take the word of a marketing phone bank salesperson on this issue. I have often discovered that not only does the person answering the phone not know the answer (although that will not keep them from giving you very confident misinformation) but also, commonly, they are not even in the same city as the manager! In some cases I have found that the phone-answerer is really working for a different company to which the job of dealing with the public has been "out-sourced!"

You may think it is strange to actually speak with the manager on an issue like this, but if you were going to entrust your economic life to the performance of a manager, it would seem strange *not* to speak with him or her. *Very few* mutual fund investors attempt to contact the fund manager(s) and very few even know who he or she is! You may find it impossible to contact a manager who has been on the cover of *Money Magazine,* but remember what I said about that. Again this is based on my experience, but if a manager is famous enough to be recognized on the street, odds are he or she is now managing more capital than can be effectively managed by one person, and you are actually getting the second string working for you anyway.

That may or may not be bad. If the fund manager is really a good manager of people as well as securities, then the performance may actually be enhanced by several assistants who each manage a portion of the portfolio. I have been told by managers who learned their skills at a major mutual fund firm that at least one famous mutual fund manager really was doing very little actual stock picking as his fame rose. Rather he had hired and trained a stable of managers, each with a small specialty section of the fund, and he managed the managers. It makes little difference whether he was managing the managers or managing the purchases, he did have a performance in that portfolio during that time frame that was amazing.

One of the most disappointing issues that comes up in these long and laborious searches is to find a portfolio that has had the same manager for over a decade, has a performance record that is truly excellent, and then to discover that the fund is not available to the public! In that case, the real fun starts as the search for a portfolio that *is* available to my clients begins. In some cases when I have found managers that I believed to be truly outstanding investment professionals, I actually contacted other management companies asking them to contract with the manager in question to make such a mutual fund available to the public. From time to time they have done so and thus provided us with the services of the outstanding manager.

What you want is a series of managers who have outperformed their asset classes and the vast majority of their peers. You will need to measure them against an appropriate index. For example, in the late 1990s the mid-cap value indices were seriously declining while the S&P 500 was rising. It would have been totally inappropriate to measure a mid-cap value manager against the large company indices, and particularly the S&P 500, which at the time was seriously over-weighted in large company growth stocks.

As you research managers, it is also important to find out who is the manager's boss and how much he or she has to do with the success you are seeing. This is another case of needing to do some deep investigating before investing. The environment in which the manager is operating is a critical element in the success you have noticed. In some cases it is not the listed manager at all who is creating the results but the manager one time removed up the chain. Also, while you are looking, don't stop with a single chosen manager for each asset class. Sooner or later that manager you have chosen will leave, have the environment change, have a personal crisis, or simply be overwhelmed with new money flowing in. When that day comes, and it eventually will, you will need to have your next move already planned out.

Finally, and I am going to dive into this one again later, you need to determine the manner by which you can easily transfer capital from one manager to another. In any given time period, it is normal for the investment value you have allocated to the various asset classes to vary greatly. On a regular chronological basis, you absolutely need to reallocate your capital back to the original balance. If you fail to do so, you will eventually find yourself extremely over weighted in the faster growing, and thereby more volatile, classes. When, and I say again, *when* the assets reverse position, you will find yourself losing quite a lot more of that unrealized gain than will be comfortable if you do not rebalance. It is emotionally *hard* to take capital from a sector of the market that has been rising rapidly during the rebalancing process, so I strongly recommend you set it up so it occurs automatically on a calendar basis, ideally quarterly.

Here arises a difficulty. In the next chapter I will delve into the mysteries of taxation and fees, but there are many investors who have hurt themselves because they delay or stop rebalancing out of a desire to avoid payment of capital gain taxes on the appreciated securities. It is good to remember a saying I once heard early in my career, "The nice thing about paying capital gains taxes is that it means you had a gain." There are only two sure ways to avoid capital gains taxes on appreciated securities. The first, and most common, is to take a loss elsewhere or wait until the gain disappears in a declining price. I have a lot of trouble understanding why someone would want to lose a hundred dollars to save the fifteen or twenty-dollar tax due on the gain, but it happens. The second way is to wait until you die and your estate gets a "step-up" in cost basis on the stock. Once again, I have it on good authority that the loss is greater than the gain. Worse, I have seen both played out at once! I have seen investors who, in an attempt to avoid taxes, locked up an investment until they were dead. Unfortunately, between the time they decided not to sell in order to avoid taxation and the time they died and it passed to their estate, the price declined on the investment so there was no gain anyway!

Reallocate your portfolio and do not let the fact that there *may* be a cost to do so deter you from doing what needs to be done to provide you with the rate of return you need. Remember, the reason for the investment is to have more money in the future. An increase in value may require that taxes be paid on the gain. There are ways to avoid that, and we will explore them, but meanwhile, do not let taxation drive your investment choices too hard. The first thing we have to do, before we even consider managing the taxes, is to have gains or income that might generate taxes. One sure way to avoid taxes is to have no gains. Again, it is not worth it!

The last type of mutual fund I want to explore here is the *series fund*. The series fund appears very much like a series of separate mutual funds, but for administrative purposes they are registered and administered as if they were a single fund. Within the series fund are a series of "sub-accounts", each with a different investment objective, normally different managers, and in at least some cases, different management companies.

A variant on this is the fund family that has within it a series of managers from different companies. This is quite different from the standard fund family you find with Fidelity or Vanguard. Having the ability to use managers from differing companies around the country while staying in the same fund family is a rare and, from my perspective, very satisfying concept. While this second version is technically not a "series-fund" for legal purposes, I will include it in the definition here for simplicity.

That is what makes the series fund useful and interesting, at least in my view. If, and this is a critical *if*, a series fund indeed has a series of excellent managers and management companies within its boundaries, one can have the advantages of having a well-diversified portfolio of mutual funds in the various asset classes one needs without having the bother of either opening and maintaining a number of accounts at different companies or opening a brokerage account with the attendant fees and difficulties.

Ideally, the series fund should not manage its own sub-accounts. The purpose of such a fund is to get the diversity needed to create an effective investment portfolio without having to range far afield. The series fund typically allows for exchanges between sub-accounts without charge in a manner similar to a mutual fund family. The difference is that the series fund allows one to transfer between sub-accounts of different mutual fund management companies while staying, for administrative purposes, within a single fund.

While I am going to dwell on taxes far more in chapter 17, it is wise to note here that if you have a portfolio of mutual funds, or other investment companies, and you do not have the portfolio within either a qualified retirement account (such as an IRA or company retirement plan) or a variable product (discussed later), you will be subject to ongoing taxation on the funds. Each year, near the end of the year, mutual funds are required to distribute substantially all of their realized short and long-term capital gains as well as any interest or dividends. That means that in late December, a mutual fund will "declare" and distribute dividend and interest income, and capital gains. Normally, those gains and income are reinvested immediately back into new fund shares. It does not end there though. As the shares drop in value from the distributions that have come out of them and new shares are purchased in the fund at the reduced price, something called a "taxable event" has taken place.

In January, an IRS form "1099-DIV" is issued to you, and you are then liable for the taxes on the reinvested distributions. In some years, particularly in a long market decline, the taxable income may be insignificant, but in other years, it will be a sudden and quite unexpected surprise. A few years ago, I went over a portfolio brought in by a potential client and calculated that the income taxation on their mutual fund portfolio over the years had reduced their net return by an average of 5% per year over the previous fifteen years. When the portfolio was quite small, the taxation did not make a great deal of difference in the overall picture, but when they approached me, the portfolio had grown to over $200,000. Their additional tax liability that year was just over $10,000 on the distributions from the fund. Because they did not actually receive any income from the fund, they had to take the $10,000 from their savings and were not happy about it.

They asked their CPA what they could do to avoid the problem in the coming year. He suggested they take the $600 per month they were investing, plus an additional $250 per month, and instead fund a savings account to be used to pay the taxation on the fund in the following year. For some reason the idea of stopping their long accustomed investing habit and paying the Internal Revenue Service more than they were currently investing each month was a less than desirable solution. For whatever it is worth, we *were* able to reposition the capital with minimum costs into positions where the taxation was minimized and they became much happier.

Qualified Retirement Accounts

It might seem that Qualified Retirement Plans (QRPs) would belong in the next chapter, but even though we are going to spend time on them there, they are really vehicles that hold investments and need some consideration as such. I am going to discuss here not only Qualified Retirement Plans (QRP) such as the well known but little understood 401(k), 403(b), 401(a), and other corporate oddities, but also the many variants of the Individual Retirement Account. To save time, I will refer to them generically as QRPs. For our purposes, the term Qualified Retirement Plan refers to any retirement account qualified under the Employee Retirement Income Security Act of 1974 (ERISA) or held as an Individual Retirement Account (IRA). Those include the standard deductible, non-deductible, Rollover, Transfer, Roth, SIMPLE, and SEP IRAs.

A QRP may have an administrator chosen by your employer as its custodian or it may have, in the case of many IRAs held in a single mutual fund family, a branch of the fund manager's company as the custodian. In many cases, it may offer a reduction in taxes in exchange for a tax penalty for early withdrawal. The critical thing for the purposes of this chapter, though, is that one can hold multiple investment products in a single account and movement in that account will not generate taxes. Within that account, in many cases, the transfer of capital from one manager to another may be done with little or no cost. That makes the issue of rebalancing much less expensive and cumbersome.

Of course, there is the problem of having good diversification. If your employer has chosen a single mutual fund company to provide you with the various investment options, you are stuck with what you have. Unless you can effectively petition your employer to provide you with a less concentrated set of choices, you will have to live with what he or she has given you. Meanwhile, if there is matching, take it!

Even if you are forced to use a single mediocre investment management firm, a 50% match on your investments gives you a head start that is going to be very hard to beat! That is a real plus and more than makes up for a less than ideal manager choice. Even if the tax advantages of the deduction are questionable, such as when you might be in a higher tax bracket in retirement than you are when working, the employer's match generally makes up for the difference. Using a QRP when there is no matching deposit or using the QRP for amounts greater than the ceiling on the match is something that should be considered only on a case-by-case basis. Here again, having a financial plan is the critical element.

Retirement plans may be excellent ways to avoid taxation on exchanges and ongoing income, but they are not exempt from the same careful research and planning that the rest of your financial world deserves. The managers in a QRP are as important to investigate as those in a taxable mutual fund portfolio. At least in a QRP with your employer, you should be able to get detailed information about each investment from your employer. That is the law, although it is not well honored in many cases.

Once you leave the employer, you should quickly transfer your retirement plan to an IRA. Then you will have the ability to manage your portfolio using a host of investment options. You will also, at least under the law as of the time of this writing, have the ability to transfer your IRA to your spouse on a tax-deferred basis, and to your heirs under most circumstances with the lion's share of the tax deferral intact. This is a complex area and, once more, I strongly suggest you confer with a properly qualified and certified tax-planning specialist. See chapter 19 for the details.

Variable Products

Here I am going to open up a can of worms that could fill a library. If you are going to make your own plan and manage your own portfolio of, hopefully, diversified, managed investment accounts, then you will need to do more study than I could cram into this book. If instead you are going to use a professional planner, then what I will reveal here will make you an educated client capable of evaluating the advice you are given. That is, in my opinion, the ideal position.

There are two types of variable products. One is variable life insurance and the other is the variable annuity. Both have their place in the world of investing, and can be quite effective and efficient if utilized for their intended purpose. Unfortunately, they are both far more complex in their structure than any other type of investment company vehicle. The complexity is not generated by some perverse creator who wishes to simply make things as hard to understand as possible, as I have seen in UITs created by brokerage houses to make a simple act into a monster of obscuration, but because of the blindingly complex Internal Revenue Code. It takes a complex solution to answer a complex problem, and in many cases that is what we have with variable products.

Variable Universal Life Insurance

Although there is a type of product called simply *variable life insurance,* the vast majority of variable life insurance in existence is actually variable *universal* life insurance or VUL for short. A VUL policy combines annual renewable term life insurance with a *series fund.* The series fund in a variable product is has within it a series of sub-accounts, which for all practical purposes look, act, and behave as if each were its own mutual fund. Technically they are *not* individual mutual funds but each is priced separately, has a different investment objective and normally a different manager. The difference between them and an actual mutual fund that may well have the same name and a very nearly identical portfolio is that they are inside the series fund and that is in turn inside the variable universal life policy.

Because the series fund exists only inside the VUL, it is treated as *cash value* in a life insurance policy. Instead of shares, the sub-accounts have *units.* Those units are not subject to the requirement to distribute the interest, dividends, and capital gains each year, and so they don't!

Since they are not subject to the annual requirement to distribute taxable gains they don't do that either. Any gain stays in the value of the unit rather than appearing on an IRS form 1099.

Because of the non-distribution of realized gains and income, the value of a given unit reflects the actual performance of the portfolio. In other words, if you purchase a unit in a series fund within a variable product at $10 and later come back and find that the unit value has grown to $12, there has been a 20% gain in the sub-account. That is a lot different from a normal mutual fund. In a regular mutual fund, it is quite possible to find that the dollar valuation posted on your account has grown while the share price has declined. This strange effect comes from the distributions. If a regular mutual fund is purchased and the shares are bought at $10, and over the years there are $2 in additional fractions of shares bought with distributions, the share price may well still be at $10, but an additional $2 of value may have appeared in the form of new shares and fractions of shares. Fortunately, the series fund in a variable product offers a "what you see is what you get" view of the sub-account value.

Although there are many bells and whistles to a variable universal life policy, the basic function is going to be pretty much the same. When you purchase the policy you are applying for life insurance. Presuming that you need the life insurance and you qualify medically, the policy is issued with two elements, the term life coverage and the series fund.

The life insurance coverage integral to the policy is actually something called yearly renewable term (YRT) and changes in price per thousand dollars of insurance coverage per year. The YRT can either be *level* or *decreasing*. If it is *level*, then the total death benefit, consisting of a combination of the value in the series fund and the term coverage, *increases* with the series fund. In other words, with an *increasing death benefit* option, the payout to your beneficiary at your death is the face amount of the insurance policy *plus* the total value of the sub-accounts of the fund. If you elect to have a *level death benefit*, then the internal insurance will *decrease* as the cash value in the series fund builds so that the beneficiary would receive the face amount of the policy no matter how much of that dollar amount was pure term insurance and how much was fund value.

When you send in a *premium* to the life insurance company for a variable universal life policy, it does not go directly to pay the *cost of insurance* internal to the policy. Rather, it is deposited in the series fund. If there is a fee or commission or state tax on such a deposit, it will be deducted before it goes in the fund. As it arrives at the variable series fund, the money will be allocated to the various sub-accounts in accordance with the instructions on the application or any changes you have made or authorized. Note here that there was no deduction from your premium to pay for the monthly cost of insurance. At the corresponding day of the month nearest to the day of the month your policy was issued, the monthly cost of insurance is drawn from the series fund to pay for the term life insurance coverage.

One of the prime advantages of a VUL policy is that the Internal Revenue Code assumes a low rate of return on the cash value in a life insurance policy. In order to cover the cost of insurance and adminis- trative costs in a traditional whole life insurance policy, the policy- holder would need to contribute sufficient premium to not only pay for all of the charges but also develop a cash value equal to the face value of the policy by the maturity date (normally 95 or 100). That assumption allows the policyholder of a VUL to contribute a very sub- stantial amount of money to the policy, if desired, and still have it treated for tax purposes as cash value. The maximum annual contribu- tion increases if the policyholder is older or if there is more insurance coverage.

What that means to the VUL policyholder is that they may shelter from taxes a very large amount of money, beyond what is necessary to pay for the underlying life insurance coverage. That excess, and most of the gains in the policy, may be taken out either by annual with- drawals, commonly limited to 10% per year to avoid running afoul of the tax code, or by policy loan, which can be treated very much like an advance on the death benefit. Presuming that the VUL is properly set up and not over-funded, loans and withdrawals have the potential to be taken on a tax-exempt basis.

Life insurance, like a Roth IRA, has the advantage of allowing the owner to withdraw the principal first. Because the principal is consid- ered to be after-tax money, there is no taxation on the withdrawal. Once the principal is exhausted, a policy loan can be made from most policies at a near zero net interest rate. The loan, like the principal withdrawal, is not subject to current income taxes. Meanwhile, the monthly cost of insurance is being paid out of the series fund. Presuming you have gains in the underlying sub-accounts, you are actually using untaxed gains from that fund to pay for the monthly cost of insurance.

There are several limits to the amount of money that can be put in as premium for a VUL. First, there is a maximum amount, called a *single premium,* that can be deposited and still have it considered for tax purposes as a life insurance policy. However, if you were to deposit that amount in the first year the policy was issued, you would have commonly just created something called a *Modified Endowment Contract,* or MEC. A MEC is treated like an annuity when money is either withdrawn or borrowed. The growth inside the policy is still tax-deferred and the internal cost of insurance is paid from the cash value without a taxable event, but withdrawals and loans are partially taxed, unlike the non-MEC policy.

You can prevent the policy from becoming a MEC, and thereby retain the effectively non-taxable status of withdrawals and loans, by not exceeding the MEC or 7-Pay "guideline." That guideline is a dollar figure that represents the maximum contribution that can be made in a single *policy* year.

Basically, do not exceed the 7-Pay guideline in the first twelve months you have the policy. If you do not reach the 7-Pay limit in a twelve month period, any difference between what you actually contributed and that limit carries over to the second year and so on.

I recognize that all of this sounds horribly complicated, and it would be were it not for computers and software that can produce a report on all the dollar limits in seconds. It is also notable that a special license is required in most states before an insurance agent or securities representative can offer the policy. Unfortunately, the license does not normally require an extensive knowledge of the calculations and limitations I have touched on above. Here we have a wonderful tool that can allow a person or a family to fund their cost of insurance with untaxed earnings while providing the potential returns of a series of investment portfolios in the series fund. A major drawback to it is that there are at least three or four different tax laws limiting the amount and timing of contributions. It does take a bit of special training and an advisor who has done his or her homework to make these policies work up to their potential.

Finally, there is something called a *level pay guideline* which if exceeded for several years will cause the insurance company to return further premiums. If that total were exceeded in the first few years cumulatively, then it would no longer be treated as an insurance policy and would become taxable. Ideally, a variable universal life policy should be funded to at least the level pay guideline every year to obtain the maximum benefit. Because the internal cost of insurance does not rise with the amount of money contributed, the more money you deposit, the lower the insurance gets as a percentage of the total. In cases I have observed for fifteen years, when the policy is funded in that manner, the cost of insurance amounts to between one half and one percent per year! In fact, if you were to have funded any of the cases I have observed over the same fifteen years by earning money at your job, paying taxes on that earned income, then taking the remaining post-tax income and purchasing term life insurance while investing in one or more mutual funds and paying taxes on them, you would have had a substantially lower return than you did in a variable universal life policy. Of course, all that presumes that you had a decent set of fund mangers and a reasonable return in both the VUL and the mutual funds we are using for comparison.

One of the major drawbacks to variable universal life is that it commonly has a charge for total surrender of the policy that can, and often does, run fifteen years. The plus is that the charge only applies to the last money in the policy, and typically about 90% of the value above that charge amount is available in any one year. In other words, you could typically access about 80% of the value in the underlying series fund if it were needed without having to surrender the policy. The "surrender charges" would apply only if you closed or "surrendered" the policy.

If there are a number of good managers available in the VUL series fund, then staying in the investment for fifteen years only means that you are truly committed to the concept of investing. At just about any point, it is possible to transfer the values in the policy to another company utilizing Section 1035 of the Internal Revenue Code. Again, if you have chosen your life insurance company well and looked hard and long at the underlying series fund, that should not be necessary because the cost of insurance is pretty much a regulated commodity. So, the decision is based more on the managers available than the actual insurance anyway.

Let me give you another warning. I have not fully explained the complexities of a variable universal life insurance policy here. They are complex and sophisticated vehicles. Extensive software is normally available from the company that offers the policy to calculate the tax and insurance related issues. Hunting down the managers in the VUL Series Fund can also be quite an effort. In many cases, the same manager will be managing a regular mutual fund and his or her investment record may be examined in detail. Here again, my advice is to use a professional who has that information as well as a solid understanding of the issues surrounding not only the VUL but also life insurance in general.

There are a few critical things to understand about a VUL policy. First, you should know what managers and management companies are nested inside the policy. If you are going to build a tax exempt investment portfolio inside a VUL, then obviously the investment choices should be wide and of the highest quality. Next, you should clearly understand the cost structure of the policy. While that is not as important as getting a good net return from the underlying investment sub-accounts, it is an important factor. There will be an internal cost to each sub-account for management, and there will be an additional charge for being in the variable life insurance series fund.

The additional charge is commonly under 1% and is used, among other things, to pay the advisor that sets up and services the policy. Do not begrudge him or her the fee but insist that the advisor earn it! When you consider the 3% to 5% per year that taxes will cost you in an unsheltered mutual fund, the fee in the series fund looks quite attractive. While the cost of insurance is pretty much a regulated commodity, that too is good to know and understand.

If you do need life insurance, then the VUL has the potential not only to provide that insurance but also to give you what amounts to a very well-established tax shelter for a fairly substantial amount of capital invested. Another aspect of a life insurance policy that varies from state to state is the protection from creditors for the cash values. This issue is one that you should explore carefully before assuming it is there, but a VUL has the potential in many cases to provide legitimate protection against litigation losses.

A properly structured variable life insurance product also has a great deal of use in a trust. There is even a special kind of trust known as an Irrevocable Life Insurance Trust (ILIT) that has been developed specifically for that. Because trusts are highly taxable, using a life insurance policy, with its exemption from ongoing taxation, can be very valuable in a trust. One of the optimum uses of life insurance in a trust is the second-to-die life insurance policy in an ILIT. The cost of insurance on a second-to-die policy is amazingly low as the chances of two persons both dying in the same year are extremely remote. Because the policy pays when the *second* person dies, the cost of insurance in any one year is normally negligible. If there are expenses at the death of the second spouse, using such a trust and policy is excellent. Additionally, it is an ideal way to fund quite a number of things, like college educations, but we will discuss that in a later chapter.

Variable Annuities

Variable annuities are vehicles that, like variable life insurance policies, contain a series fund. Here though, the primary use for the vehicle was originally not to provide a death benefit but to defer the taxation on the underlying investment until such time as the owner or annuitant wished to use the money. Variable annuities then behave with regard to taxation very much like a non-deductible IRA, but with no upper limit on the amount that can be deposited.

While that aspect of the variable annuity is certainly still valid, the vehicle has evolved into quite another role. Variable annuity companies commonly offer a guaranteed minimum death benefit as part of the variable annuity. That guarantee varies from one company to another, but the basic promise is that in the event of the death of the annuitant, the annuity company would pay the beneficiary at least as much as was deposited in the annuity should the underlying fund value be below that figure. Companies also commonly offer a guarantee that this guaranteed death benefit would rise by a set percentage each year with 5% being a common number. Another optional benefit in some variable annuities is the right to have the guaranteed death benefit increased each year if the fund value is higher than the amount invested. Obviously if the value of a family's investment portfolio is a critical matter in the event of the primary income owner's death, then this guarantee becomes quite important.

Variable annuities have become one of the fastest growing types of investment vehicle in America during the last years of the 20th and early years of the 21st centuries. Considering that a large quantity of the money that has been deposited in these vehicles is in the form of IRAs, clearly the tax deferral aspect of the variable annuity is not the only thing spurring this growth. My personal experience with investors indicates that the guarantee to make the beneficiary whole in the event of the premature death of the owner/annuitant is the primary benefit that makes them so attractive.

I have witnessed several cases where the husband died after retiring, and the widow saw the monthly income from pension and government sources decline significantly. In one case, the couple had planned for the widow to supplement this drop in income through withdrawals from his IRA after his death. An analysis at the time the plan was prepared indicated that the retiree did not need life insurance because the combination of even a reduced pension and social security income in conjunction with the IRA would be sufficient to maintain the widow's standard of living. Unfortunately, the plan did not take into account that the values in the investment portfolio might have declined greatly with a major bear market! If the widow only had the IRA account value to draw from without considering a death benefit, she would have had to choose between selling her home and moving to a less expensive residence or risking the exhaustion of the IRA while she was alive. However, the guaranteed death benefit provision of the variable annuity where her husband had deposited his IRA enabled her to live at the standard of living they had planned. Because of his health record it would have been impossible for the husband in this case to obtain life insurance anyway.

There have been many articles condemning variable annuities for their "high" expenses. The added expense of a variable annuity indeed is often over 1%. However, if there is a need to defer taxation on a substantial investment portfolio and the purpose of the investment is to generate retirement income, a variable annuity may well be worth the expense. If there is a need to ensure that a minimum balance is available from a retirement account in the event of the death of the owner, again, a variable annuity may be the optimal answer.

The first variable annuities appeared in the early 1970s, and at least one has a well-known "no-load" mutual fund as one of the sub-account investment choices. As an experiment, I set up an historical illustration contrasting the performance of $100,000 invested in the regular mutual fund versus depositing another $100,000 into a near perfect clone of that fund inside the variable annuity. In order to pay the taxes on the mutual fund each year, I directed the Morningstar software I used for the illustration to pay out the dividends from the fund as cash, take the taxes due from that income and then reinvest the remaining money. I allowed the money to accumulate in both accounts for ten years and then began an identical systematic withdrawal, net of taxes.

The "no-load" mutual fund ran out of money after about fifteen years while the variable annuity with its substantially larger internal expenses still had well over the hundred thousand dollars that was initially deposited intact after the same time period. The difference was the taxation on the mutual fund that occurred each year. Over the time period from 1971 until 2001 when I terminated the illustration, the cost of taxes reduced the average annual compound return on the mutual fund by about 5% per year. The variable annuity, on the other hand, had an additional internal charge of 1.4% but no annual taxation except on that money actually withdrawn as income.

Over some of that time period, a lump sum withdrawal from the annuity would have been taxed at a higher rate than one from the mutual fund. Over other periods, the rate would have been the same. Either way, variable annuities are generally not a good idea if you anticipate needing a lump sum rather than a stream of income. What they are excellent for is tax deferral and death benefit guarantees. Additionally, the ease of transferring between sub-accounts at no cost and the ability to receive electronic deposits into your bank account through systematic withdrawals from the annuity are quite significant advantages.

When using regular mutual funds for systematic withdrawals, the mutual fund custodian often will not do withholding for taxes. That leaves it up to you to remember and calculate your taxes due to the IRS each quarter. One more advantage of variable annuities is that annuity companies are excellent at administering the calculation and withholding of tax on retirement accounts.

Variable annuities, like other investment vehicles, have their place and as long as they are used for the purposes for which they were designed, they have the potential for excellent service to an investor.

Brokerage and Advisory Accounts

It is certainly possible to hold the asset classes one needs to execute a financial plan in a brokerage account. Given that I have expressed my warnings about individual stocks as serious investment assets, unless your wealth is measured in the millions of dollars, the use of a brokerage account for trading stocks is to participate in "the losers' game." There are reasons other than the trading of stocks to own such an account, though. In many accounts, it is possible to hold several mutual funds from different fund families as surrogates for asset classes thereby creating the diversification that is the basis for a well-managed portfolio. It is also possible to rebalance these funds to keep your intended asset allocation mix.

The difficulty, however, in using a regular brokerage account for such goals is the fees that are charged for rebalancing. The transaction fees normally charged by the brokerage firm offset the convenience of being able to liquidate shares in one fund and purchase them in another. Here, the decision needs to be made on a case-by-case basis.

At the time of this writing, E-Trade, a discount brokerage firm, charges 1.5% per year to allow access to money managers, but has a minimum of $100,000 per manager. To have at least five managers, as I normally recommend, the minimum portfolio size would then be $500,000 with an annual charge of $7,500. Should you elect to use mutual funds to establish your portfolio, E-Trade will charge you around $25 per transaction unless it is one of the funds that pay E-Trade from its own account, in which case you may be assured that E-Trade will make that $25 anyway and perhaps more. Of course, if you find a manager who is in a fund that charges a commission, that will be paid to the fund if you use a discount brokerage firm like E-Trade. These costs inherent in mutual funds do not go away just because you make a purchase through a brokerage account.

There is also the issue of restricted access to the financial markets. For example, Charles Schwab & Co. has around 40 plus large company value funds in its One Source® list out of the 911 listed in the Morningstar database. A quick search for the large company funds with stable management and the highest ten-year rate of return revealed that none of them were in the One Source list.

Using a stockbroker to set up a financial plan portfolio is quite conceivably going to be hazardous to your financial health. Generally, brokers are paid through commissions and commissions are only paid when there is a transaction. It is thereby in the best interest of the stockbroker to move money. It is commonly in your best interest to minimize the movement of your investments and to stick with a good manager over a long time period. This conflict will create a strain in the relationship you have even with the best of stockbrokers. Some firms have gone to using a fee-based system to accommodate customers who do not wish to be pursued with "hot stock tips." The difficulty here is that a broker is not an Investment Advisor! The term "Investment Advisor" is restricted to those registered under the Investment Advisory Act of 1940 and requires the advisor to act in *your* best interest and to give you full and written disclosure of all fees, commissions, and conflicts of interest.

Unless you are going to take the time and the responsibility for your own account, and have someone who will watch your managers when you are unable or unwilling to do so (like when you are on vacation or ill), then it is in your best interest to find a properly registered and certified Investment Advisor. In many cases, that Advisor will recommend some type of advisory account. Sometimes that account may be held at a branch of a brokerage firm where there is normally a discount on the fees or the administrative fees may be included in the Advisor's annual fee.

The use of an advisory account will allow the Advisor to deduct the annual fees from your account on a regular basis either annually, quarterly, or perhaps monthly. Quite a large number of mutual funds that normally charge a substantial commission for purchasing their shares will waive that commission if the fund is purchased through an advisory account. Generally speaking, a properly registered and certified Investment Advisor can actually get you the investments you need in your portfolio and provide for the rebalancing and other needs of your financial plan less expensively than you can by yourself!

One of the greatest shocks that people have had upon seeing the analysis I have done of their existing portfolios is to note the fees and commissions they have been paying over the years. I certainly do not object to paying fees to a competent advisor, but the question always comes back to the net return. If one is paying a fee to an advisor, it is reasonable to expect to see an improvement in the overall return and management of the portfolio that is greater than the fee. If one is paying a broker to simply buy and sell securities without a plan, my experience indicates that the portfolio will do no better than one managed without the services of the broker. I do know that the portfolios I have seen that have had the services of a serious and properly qualified and certified Investment Advisor have had a substantially better record than either investor-managed portfolios or broker-traded portfolios. Unfortunately, I have yet to find an objective survey on the subject.

In the final analysis, using accounts or sub-accounts that allow you to automatically rebalance on a regular basis across appropriate asset classes, with little or no additional charge, has historically had a far greater effect on total performance than any other factor. Then, if you choose a series of managers in each asset class that have historically had the discipline and the systematic approach that has allowed them to exceed the performance of the underlying index, you have the best of all worlds. That leaves the most expensive issue to be discussed in the next chapter: taxes.

Chapter 17 – Managing the Risk Factors

Risk

A change in attitude is in order for most of us. We are greatly in love with the idea that things "should" go smoothly. Unexpected and unpleasant events or situations "should-not" happen or if they do, they "should" be resolved within the half hour allotted for a television show or at worst, the two and a half hours in which the hero normally resolves things in a movie.

Let's face it, we may have managed to bring much of our environment under control but it is going to be very unusual for a person or a family to go through their normal life span without some circumstance that could be made into a model for a Shakespearian tragedy! Kids get sick and sometimes stay that way. Local economies collapse as some major employer moves away or "downsizes." Divorce happens in at least one third of marriages. A moment's inattention as your cell phone rings can result in an auto accident followed by lawsuits and a virtual hell of issues. Even the act of building a house has often turned into a personal disaster of epic proportions! The risk of that last issue goes up with your net worth, as do many other risks. It is as if when you don't have too far to fall, you don't notice when you stumble, but when the top of the mountain is nearly in sight, the distance to the bottom is terrifying.

Risk is inherent in all that we do, but when it comes to investing, it sometimes appears that we completely lose sight of all that we know about risk and either totally ignore it or, and this is worse, believe it is everywhere but where it really is! After I outline a well-allocated portfolio of managed investment accounts to a couple, it is not at all unusual for one of them to ask the question, "Is this a high, low, or medium risk portfolio?"

That question reveals such a profound misconception of the term "risk" that I have often been rendered nearly speechless as I hear it! The word "risk" by itself means almost nothing. My normal response to them has been, "Risk of what?" If we do not know what the "risk" is *of,* then we have no way of understanding how to manage it. Risk *demands* an object. Risk of nothing is exactly that, no risk at all!

261

In our financial and investing lives we start off with the risk of being broke, but we have quite a lot of time to rectify that state of affairs. Along the way, we face the very serious risk of being too old or otherwise incapable of making a living. If we fall victim to either irrational speculation or a scam, we stand the chance of losing the investments we have accumulated toward our goals. We have the potential for a number of low probability but highly catastrophic things to happen to us. All of those are risk. Nearly all of them can be managed to the point that we can effectively forget about them. When people speak of "risk" in their investments though, what they seem to commonly mean is the short-term variability that is legitimately associated with any return above zero, after taxes and inflation.

Here is one of the most important things you could learn about risk: *If you consistently follow proven principles in any area of your life, the longer you do so, the more you lower the probability of failure and increase the probability of success.* The inverse of that statement is also true: *If you consistently violate proven principles in any area of your life, the longer you continue to do so, the more you raise the probability of failure and lower the probability of success.* In other words, sometimes you can beat the odds for a while, but eventually, those odds will catch up with you if you keep ignoring proven principles.

Smoking cigarettes increases the chance of a host of medical maladies, most of which are ultimately deadly. Inhaling semi-toxic smoke into one's lungs for extended periods of time is a pretty clear violation of the principle that ingesting poison is generally a very bad idea. Still, I have met many people who do it. When I can get them to be honest with me, I often hear them express the observation that they have been smoking for years without ill effect. One now deceased old friend of mine expressed exactly that observation as he was using his rotary saw to cut up asbestos shingles while puffing on a cigarette. A year later, he was dead of lung cancer. Smoking a cigarette for one day is a low risk act. Smoking cigarettes for forty years is an extremely high-risk behavior. The longer you violate the principle, the higher the risk of failure you assume.

The same thing can be said about driving recklessly, jumping out of airplanes or off bridges, or riding a motorcycle without a helmet. The odds are low that any one event or day will cause a catastrophic loss, but because all you have to do is lose just once to fail, the longer you do those things, the greater the probability of that failure eventually occurring.

In the world of investing the same principle applies. Putting money in a bank savings account carries an extremely low probability of loss in any given day or even year. Over a forty-year period, the chances of losing at least part of the purchasing power of that money in a bank account rises to near certainty. If, in this same example, the definition of success is to have enough income from that saved money to live comfortably for any significant period of time, then using a bank to accumulate money for financial independence is very nearly guaranteed failure. First the money is guaranteed not to appreciate, and second, the income, after taxes, will not be more than is necessary to adjust for inflation. Historically, a zero volatility, guaranteed position, like a bank account, has never returned more than is lost for inflation and taxes over an extended period of time.

The reverse of that is true of a well-diversified and allocated stock portfolio. Jeremy Siegal points out in his book *Stocks for the Long Run* that a broadly diversified portfolio of U.S. stocks has outperformed every other asset class in every twenty-year period over the last 200 years. On the other hand, that same well-diversified portfolio of stocks would have lost money in any *single* year about thirty to forty percent of the time.

Now we come to the question that started this, "Is a broadly diversified portfolio of stocks a higher or lower risk than a bank account?" The answer depends entirely on whether you intend it to be used as an emergency savings account or to provide for some long-term goal like retirement or to fund the future college education of a young child.

Time is the determining factor if we are using some reasonable and historically proven financial strategy. The true risk comes when we ignore the principles and try to get a zero "risk" investment that will still give us enough to live on or conversely, attempt to use an equity fund as a savings account for short-term needs.

Before I leave this subject, I want to emphasize that on the equity side of things I have said "broadly diversified" over and over. Using a portfolio that is not very well-diversified carries a very high risk, and the longer you keep it, the higher the risk becomes. Sooner or later, each and every company in which you might invest will, with certainty, fail. Company failures do not always come after warnings. As often as not, the failure of a publicly traded company comes as a great surprise to the majority of its shareholders. If it were not so, they would not have the shares.

For short-term needs and to cover the risk of needing to draw money in an unexpected situation, there is no substitute for *savings* accounts, be they money market funds or FDIC insured bank accounts. For long-term goals, such as retirement, there is no substitute for broadly diversified equity investments of some kind. The difference is *time*.

Bulls and Bears

History has demonstrated again and again that investors have a powerful tendency to get caught up in the elation of bull markets and the depression of bear markets. Both my personal observations and the results of studies have underscored that individual investors tend to have pretty miserable rates of return when compared with any of the major indices.

The reason identified by both the surveys and by observation is that amateur investors tend to buy high and sell low. When the market is "going up," the consensus gradually builds that buying into a given class of securities is a good thing. That consensus is pretty much hard-wired into our brains from the long-term experience that doing what everyone else is doing is far safer than heading off in a different direction. Unfortunately, markets work in the opposite direction of the other things in our lives and, as a result, will devastate your portfolio if you follow the masses.

The only reason a rising, or bull, market is a bull market is that there is more buying pressure than selling pressure. In other words, the more money that is offered to buy securities, be they stocks, bonds, or anything else, the higher the price of those securities will be. It is a simple matter of supply and demand. Thus, rising prices in a market or a security simply mean that there is more interest in buying than there is in selling. Obviously then, the market or a security will be at its highest point when the maximum number of people are trying to buy it.

The reality of market valuations, particularly in liquid securities markets like we see in stocks and bonds, is that a great number of the buyers will make their purchases at or near the very top of a "bull" market. That is when the buying pressure is the greatest because that is when the price is the highest. There also tends to be a real shortage of people wanting to sell at the height of a market mania as well. During the bull market that peaked in the year 2000, the highest inflows into stock mutual funds ever recorded took place in the last quarter of 1999 and the first quarter of 2000. It is no coincidence that the absolute top prices occurred in those same periods.

Conversely, the highest outflows in history occurred in the summer and early fall of 2002, exactly at the bottom of the bear market that followed. A great number of individual investors entered the stock market with their money at the top of the most dramatic bull market in U.S. history and then exited at the bottom of the most lengthy and severe bear market since the 1930s.

It is critical to understand that the reason the bull market was so high was that very inflow of money and the reason the bear market was so low was the outflow of money. *Buying* raises prices and *selling* lowers prices. The greatest inflow and outflow was from the S&P 500 index funds. The greatest losses, at least in percent terms, I have seen were in the accounts of investors who were using online discount stock brokerage firms. In many cases, they were trading vigorously at extremely low charges per trade until they nearly or completely ran out of money.

How can we avoid this trap of rushing to participate in a sector or asset class that is already overpriced? It is not intelligence that can save us here. Sir Isaac Newton, arguably one of the most intelligent men who have ever lived, lost his fortune in the runaway bull market in stocks now known as the "South Sea Bubble." Instead, the critical difference seems to be between those who were simply making a bet on some investment and those who had a plan, selected assets based on long-term performance models and then fully planned to hold those assets for a period of seven to ten years, or longer, if necessary.

Two elements come into play then. First, have a plan and follow it. Second, have a method to automatically keep you on that plan by reallocating your capital back to the original allocation either chronologically or at the point where elements of your portfolio have gotten out of balance by some pre-set amount.

Management Change
Back in Chapters 15 and 16 we identified the critical elements of the managers that we use in our investments. To reiterate that lesson, it is not things that create wealth but the people who manage them.

265

Unfortunately, good managers tend to go away. If you were to start investing at age 30 or even 40 and wanted your investments to first grow and then produce income for the rest of your life, you would be looking at a minimum of a forty year period of time.

If a manager got started right out of his or her education at about 25 and then had ten years experience, we are looking at someone who is at least 35 when we start to use their services. Presuming that manager was a good one, the manager would get some pretty good bonuses over the years. Said manager would then be quite wealthy in about ten to fifteen years, just about the time he or she had accumulated twenty to twenty-five years in the business. In my experience, thirty years is about as long as most of them will stick around, unless they have almost complete authority over what they do. So then, it is likely that you will have a maximum of ten to twenty years of use out of any given manager. In fact, five years is more often the time frame.

Because you will need good management in the scenario outlined above for about forty years, you will need to use between two and eight managers for each asset class over the life of your plan. If, as I normally recommend, you are using five managers (one per asset class), that means you will need a total of between ten and forty different managers over the course of time.

While the logic of what I have just stated is irrefutable, I have found it to be extremely rare that an investor even plans how and when he or she will leave an investment, much less where the investment should be placed when (note that I did not say "if") the management changes on the original investment.

The answer, here again, is pretty simple. First, have a back door. Know what it will take to get out of an investment position before you get in. Ideally, you should be able to leave one portfolio and jump into another within the same account and without any significant charges or fees. That will not always be possible, but understand what will be needed to change management before hiring the first manager.

The second, and even more important issue, is to continually update your plan for where you will move your money when you leave your current manager. If you are in a taxable position, by the way, the ideal time to leave one position and go to another is when the price is down. That will either generate a loss or limit the taxation. If you already have your next position planned out, then you are not leaving the market in a low spot and thereby taking the risk of missing the upward movement, but simply moving laterally to a (hopefully) better place.

Financial Failure of Associated Companies

A little appreciated risk factor in any investment portfolio or position is that of the custodian, advisor, transfer agent, or any of the other host of associated companies entering into financial failure. As I outlined earlier, I recently had to break the news to an elderly couple that the insurance commissioner of a distant state seized the insurance company in whose care they had placed their IRAs.

The same bad news could have been delivered to someone whose investments were held by a brokerage firm or even a bank or trust company. In the case of the bank, far too many people think that if they invest their money in the lobby of a bank then the money must be safe. With the advent of brokerage salespersons in the lobby, the FDIC letters should have, in my opinion, been removed from the bank doors. Unfortunately, I seem to be about the only person who advocates that approach.

In today's economic world, someone or some institution will be the actual custodian of any investment you have. Even if you elect to have certificates delivered to you that represent whatever you have chosen for your portfolio, you will still need to safeguard those certificates. Even a sophisticated stockbroker I knew lost his rather large retirement fund when the bank he was using as his custodian failed! Because he was using the trust department of the bank as the custodian for his IRA, he assumed that he was protected. He was profoundly shocked to learn that his portfolio was considered an uninsured credit to the bank holding company. In the end, he did receive a small portion of the account back, but to add insult to injury, in the middle of the bankruptcy of the bank holding company, his account lost its status as an IRA and he was liable for taxes on the entire amount!

His story is rather extreme and is the result of an attempt to create a sophisticated "self-directed IRA" so that he could tinker with out of the ordinary investments that had great prestige. Every year, no small number of investors find out about the risk of having their money outside of the protection of either the FDIC or the Investment Company Act of 1940. Brokerage accounts normally have insurance under the Securities Investors Protection Corporation (SIPC), but recovery of the securities can take quite a long time in the event of the brokerage company's failure. During that period, access to your securities is commonly restricted or forbidden. More, the SIPC is not responsible for what happens to the valuation on those securities while you are waiting to retrieve them.

In this area I am quite a coward. Plain Jane mutual funds and the series fund or sub-accounts inside variable products are protected from the creditors of the associated companies by federal law. That eliminates one whole level of risk from the equation. It still makes me uncomfortable when someone says to me "I have my money with (fill in the name of the well known company), and they are just too big and well-established to fail." I heard that about Executive Life of California, Monarch Life, Enron, MCI, and a host of other companies over the years. If you haven't learned this already, learn now: There are no companies that are too big or well-established to fail. If you have investments that are not protected from the creditors of the companies holding them directly or indirectly by U.S. statute law, you are taking what I believe to be unnecessary risk. The prestige or the supposed guarantees offered to entice you to do so are simply not worth it.

Personal Risk

This is a book about investing and investments, but before I leave the area of risk associated with investing, we have to talk about saving. One of the facts of life is that unexpected things will happen. Some of them may be quite pleasant and others may be catastrophic, but they will happen. Risks that appear totally unrelated to an investment portfolio can devastate it if you do not take the appropriate actions to prevent that from happening.

The sudden loss of a job requiring an expensive move to another location can result in the need to liquidate all or part of your retirement accounts. The Internal Revenue Code does not consider that to be a legitimate emergency and you stand to lose as much as half that retirement fund to taxes. Because lay-offs tend to be much more common in down markets, you may find yourself selling at or near the worst possible point in the market cycle.

How could that have been avoided? In a word: savings. Having a minimum of three months living expenses in a cash reserve has the potential to save your investment portfolio from devastation. If, for example, you find that job move will cost about $25,000, you can either take it from your savings positions or liquidate $50,000 from your retirement fund and split it with the IRS. If that liquidation occurred in your 40s, about 25 years ago, and your portfolio had done about as well as the broad market, you would be looking at a portfolio today that was a whopping $400,000 smaller than it could have been. By not having $25,000 in reserve, you stand to have lost around $25,000 *per year* in potential income *for the rest of your life!*

I explain my interest in getting my clients to save money regularly and automatically as insurance against the risk that they will liquidate investments and thereby destroy the potential for future wealth. Both they and I need that wealth to achieve success. Taking a trip across the country without a spare tire in your car would be considered foolish, but far too many Americans simply don't have a good savings position. Having that cash available is one of the best risk reducers for an investment portfolio that you can have.

Taxes, Fees, and other Distractions

Taxes

When I look at the historic return of an investment portfolio, I calculate the tax effect on the performance. If the entire portfolio is in some kind of a tax deferred account and no money has been withdrawn, then the before and after tax historic return will be the same. The rub comes when the retiree wants to begin using the retirement account to generate income.

For example, if a person were 50 years old, using an employer sponsored retirement plan, and was able to contribute $11,000 per year for fifteen years prior to retirement, at an 11.47% net rate of return he would have just under $400,000 when he retired. As he began to withdraw money to live on in the sixteenth year, let's say he wanted $31,500 net income. While that seems like a very reasonable withdrawal from his $400,000 retirement account, he will in fact probably need nearly $40,000 as a gross withdrawal presuming 20% taxation on the income.

While that is all a very nice financial planning calculation, the point I want to make here is not about returns but about the fact that if his retirement account got a nominal return of 11.47%, it would actually only be returning a real after-tax return of 10% or about 87% of the total return. This percentage will vary from one investor to another depending on how close they are to taking money from their account and what their tax status will be when they do it. However, even a tax qualified retirement account is only about 85% to 90% tax effective.

That loss in tax effectiveness is more than offset if the employer has a matching program. If the employer matches the $11,000 with $5,500, the required return on the portfolio would drop to a much more comfortable 9%. The lesson here is that employer sponsored retirement programs are generally a great idea if the employer matches, but after that they need to be evaluated on a case-by-case basis.

I have seen cases where a rental property investor has been steadily losing a couple of hundred dollars per month after the monthly payments for years. Finally, they were able to sell it for enough to pay off the mortgage and cover commissions and selling costs. Unfortunately, along the way, they had been taking depreciation deductions and now owe taxes on the money that was used to pay off the mortgage. One of the biggest reality shocks I have seen is when someone who has been holding a money-losing rental property for what must seem to be ages has to actually pay money to sell the property and then is astonished to find that he or she owes even more money to the IRS on the "loss."

A similar problem comes up when an investor decides to liquidate an IRA that was either deductible or was converted from a qualified retirement plan at a former employer. During "down" periods in the stock market, IRA owners have chosen to liquidate an IRA because of some other need, such as building a house. While there is a non-penalty liquidation allowed for a down payment on a home, it is only for the first house the IRA owner has ever had and has other limitations. IRA owners having some fuzzy knowledge about some kind of exemption for home purchases, may, and have, chosen to liquate that IRA. The shock comes when an IRA that has "lost money" generates a tax bill equal to as much as half the value of the liquidation!

The Internal Revenue Code that governs all these complexities is quite probably the single largest document in the world, unless you count it as part of the U.S. Code that comprises all of federal law. Here again, professional assistance is invaluable. Even many tax preparers and accountants are apparently unfamiliar with some of the provisions of the tax code with regard to investments and retirement accounts. For example, if an IRA ownership is transferred to a trust, in many cases that transfer will constitute a taxable event and be counted as "early withdrawal" for tax purposes! I have received written requests to make such a transfer from estate attorneys who were unaware of the consequences. The same issue arises if the owner of a retirement account elects to use it as collateral for a loan. Once again, any taxable amount in the account may be suddenly converted into "early withdrawal" if the retirement plan does not have loan provisions built into the plan document.

One of the issues in making a written financial plan rather than just buying whatever investment seems good at the time is that the creation of that plan forces both the planner and the investor to take a close look at the events that will occur when the invested capital is needed for some purpose and turned into *money*. Because that act must ultimately take place before any investor can realize a true gain and be able to convert the capital they have invested into something they actually wish to use, wisdom would decree that it be an important issue. Unfortunately in many, if not most, cases, that aspect of the investment process is not even considered until *after* the liquidation! That is when the shocks of taxation hit most visibly.

Tax shock at the end of the journey is not the greatest effect in most investors' portfolios though. If I start with the 100 largest funds in the Morningstar database that have existed for at least fifteen years and examine the return of the best performer, as of 10-31-2002, I find that it has a nominal average annual return of 12.45% for the past ten years.[5] According to Morningstar, ongoing taxation generated by distribution of the interest, dividend, and capital gains each year would have reduced that return to 9.5%. In other words, the real taxed return (presuming there were no actual withdrawals over the decade)

---

[5] Please note that I have *not* chosen the best performer over the ten-year period. I chose the best at 15 years which, as it happens, is number 12 for ten years. Another reason I chose that fund is that it meets my criteria for an investment account having had the same manager for the entire fifteen-year period.

was only 76% of the nominal return. Another way of looking at it is to note that the cost of taxation for the fund in a non-tax-deferred account would have been 3% per year.

Proponents of indexing point out that index funds have a lower number of internal transactions and thereby theoretically lower distributions and taxation. Comparing a very popular S&P 500 index fund over the same period shows a ten-year nominal average annual return of 9.8% and an after tax return of 7.14%. For the index fund, the net return was about 72% of the nominal return. Worse, the nominal return was only 78% of the managed fund! Now, before someone jumps on me about unfair comparisons, note that of the 100 largest funds with a fifteen-year or longer record, 66 were "equity funds." With number 1 being the best and 66 being the worst performer, the S&P 500 Index fund was number 56.

To get a handle on the results of that 3% per year tax charge, consider that a $10,000 investment ten years ago at 12.45% would stand at $32,329 at very nearly the bottom of the bear market and that same investment with the tax liability taken out each year would be $24,782. That $7,547 ultimate tax cost amounts to a 23% reduction in value.

If the investment was intended to create income in retirement, it may very well have been in the investor's best interest to have that money in a variable annuity. Even with an additional fee of 1.4% the net return would still have been 11.05%, presuming the same portfolio with the same manager were available in the annuity. With those qualifications, the variable annuity would have accumulated $28,522 at this point, after all fees. The drawback would be that if the investor wanted to convert the entire amount to cash immediately, the taxation would not be at capital gains rates but at regular rates. If he or she were in the 27% tax bracket, that taxation would amount to about $5,000 for a net, cash-in-hand liquidation of $23,522. However, that still handily beats the $19,930 the index fund would have returned net of tax for the same period.

Once again, I want to give a warning here that variable annuities are not all created equally nor will they always produce a real tax advantage in a ten-year period at liquidation. A variable annuity is simply a tax deferral vehicle in this case. It also has a higher annual cost, but that cost is commonly more than offset by the tax deferral.

That same investor today conceivably could have used a Roth IRA if the investor's income was low enough to qualify and if he or she were willing to take four years to invest the money. In order to calculate whether that was a good idea or not, we would have to take into account the fact that the money could not have been invested all at once and the majority of it ($7,000) would miss the first year's performance and so on. If we concurrently put the excess $7,000 into a taxable mutual fund so we don't miss being out of the market on the portion that doesn't qualify for the Roth, it would have actually taken us over five years to transfer all of the money into the Roth because of the growth in that fund! Meanwhile, the taxes were accruing on the non-Roth portion *and* there would be no tax loss at liquidation. It actually works out better in the variable annuity in most cases.

Tax planning is a critical issue in achieving financial success. Even though we have to make some educated guesses as to what the tax laws will look like ten, twenty, and thirty years from now, it is a pretty good idea to presume that something that is taxable now will remain taxable in the future. Planning to minimize that taxation, and adjust for it, is an even better idea.

Fees

There are elements of truth in the comments that fees make a difference. Unfortunately, the popular propaganda on the subject so thoroughly misidentifies the largest fees that it has sent people running directly into the mouths of the wolves!

If you examine the 30 best performing mutual funds out of the largest 100 over the past fifteen years, you will find that exactly half had "front-loads" of 5.75%, generally, and that the average expense ratio was 0.88% and as high as 1.61%. Shortening the time frame down to ten years made little difference.

While I can find no correlation between high returns, either before or after tax, and low expenses, I can find a very clear relationship between low returns and low internal expenses! It doesn't take a background in statistical analysis to note that the bottom performing 30 funds of the largest 100 have an average expense ratio of 0.63% and an average return of 9.8%. Compare that with the statistics for the 30 funds with the best ten and fifteen-year returns. The expense ratio was (as noted above) 0.88% with an average "front load" of 2.35%. The real kicker comes though when we look at the average return of these funds, a delightful 13.14% per year over the fifteen year period ending October 31, 2002, and 11.64% per year for the ten years ending on that date. This is quite a difference from the 9.8% average return from the low expense funds.

If I were a statistician I could now come forward with a claim that I have found a correlation between low expenses and low returns and high expenses and high returns! Strictly from the numbers, we could conclude that adding one-quarter percent to the internal expenses and about seven-tenths percent to the front load increases the return on large mutual funds by about one third! First, I assure you that this is not my conclusion, but it is the type of conclusion that can be, and often is, reached when the statistics are bent and twisted in advertisements for fund companies and in the media. Sadly, supposed well-educated academics jump on the same numbers to "prove" that the higher the expenses the lower the long-term return. If you are confused at this point, don't think you are alone.

There are only two critical data points that can be derived from the type of research that averages the performance of those funds. First, among the thirty best performers, the average manager tenure has been 14.4 years. For this survey I have eliminated funds that are less than fifteen years old and we are in fact seeing the actual manager tenure. The next data point of relevance, other than the high performance record, is that the top 30 funds are 86.5% invested in U.S. stocks.

Average Characteristics of the 100 Largest Mutual Funds By average annual Return over 15 Years				
Average Annual Return	Manager Tenure	Expense Ratio	Front Load	% U.S. Stocks- Foreign Stocks- Bonds
13.14%	14.4 Yrs.	0.89%	2.35%	86.5%- 4.0%- 1.2%
11.12%	13.3 Yrs	0.70%	3.21%	69.7%- 10.8%- 11.8%
9.8%	12.2 Yrs	0.63%	1.63%	9.8%- 13.9%- 70.0%
Source: Morningstar Principia Pro, 10-31-02. 100 largest mutual funds with inception date of October 1987, or earlier, broken into top, middle, and bottom thirty, ranked by 15-year average annual return excluding funds not available to the general public.				

From the table above, I could easily draw the inference that the higher the expense ratio and front-load, the higher would be the expected return. In fact, the evidence is there, at least among those 100 funds. Of far more relevance is the asset allocation breakdown. The funds with the highest returns invested mainly in U.S. stocks and only minimally in bonds and foreign stocks. Another correlation shows up in the manager tenure.

I actually question whether there is much that can be drawn from these figures except that: 1) U.S. stocks have had a higher performance than other asset classes; 2) the increase in purchase commissions and internal expenses did not seem to have a dampening effect on the performance; and 3) the longer a manager has been in place the more likely he or she is to have high performance. That last one should come as no surprise to anyone who has ever worked in a competitive corporate environment. If the manager did not perform well, the chances are slim that he or she would be allowed to continue managing for more than a decade.

Incidentally, if we expand the search to the 200 largest funds, the data progression remains pretty much the same. Among the top 50 performers, the managers have averaged 12 years of tenure, U.S. stocks comprise 83% of the portfolio, and the expense ratio is now 1.01% with a fifteen-year return of 13.59%. The bottom 50 performers have average manager tenure of 9 years, bonds comprise 84% of the portfolio with 0.5% in U.S. stocks, and the expense ratio is 0.69% with an average fifteen-year return of 7.19%.

To answer the criticism that all I am seeing here is the difference in return between stocks and bonds, let me point out that the numerical progression as we look at long-term performance moves smoothly through stocks, foreign stocks, and finally into bonds with regard to performance. Even in the world of nearly pure stock funds, the average internal charges increase as we move up the long-term performance chart, as do the manager tenures. The middle 50 have manager tenure of 11.2 years, an average return of 10.21%, and are comprised of 65.1% U.S. stocks and 19% bonds.

I honestly do not know whether there is some underlying principle that correlates low expenses with low long-term returns or whether it is just happenstance that they correlate the way they do. What I do know, and am more than a little comfortable with, is the fact that manager longevity and good return seem to be well-aligned. I am also quite comfortable that the return of U.S. stocks has been substantially better than either foreign stocks or any mixture of bonds.

All I have done here with regard to asset classes is confirm what Jeremy Siegel found in his book *Stocks for the Long Run*. The point in this exercise is to "prove" there is no meaningful relationship between low expense ratios and high returns. There is a strong correlation between good, long-term return and length of management tenure, at least in the world of the larger mutual funds.

While fees are not to be ignored, if the service as well as the return on your invested capital is good, then the fee is a minor issue. Even when measuring against the long-term return of an index, like the S&P 500, the issue of fees can be quite misleading. Presuming the surveys done over the years on average investor returns are correct, it is not the performance of the underlying fund investments that has most affected portfolio performance as much as the investors' behavior.

If a fee is paid to a legitimate investment advisor who in turn provides you with a sufficient education and guidance to keep you from bailing out of an asset class when it is down or overloading in one when it is up, then you have your money's worth. If he or she causes you to take a good long-term look at your goals and assess the situation you will face when you reach the point of taking money from your portfolio to live on, and if he or she causes you to buy the insurance and pay for the documents that provide for the protection and transfer of that wealth to your dependents and heirs, then the fee is one of the best uses you could possibly make of your money.

Portability

As a final point of some significance, your investments should be portable. By that I mean that you should not purchase investments that you cannot move to another advisory firm or physically take with you wherever you go!

Limited partnerships, proprietary unit investment trusts, proprietary mutual funds, and proprietary variable products have no business in your portfolio. Each of those are issued and held by a single brokerage firm, and as such, you are locked into the relationship with that company as long as you have the investment. The larger Wall Street brokerage firms like Morgan Stanley, Merrill Lynch, and others, often have a universe of proprietary products that not only are unable to be moved to another firm, but in many cases, would be unacceptable to a serious advisor anyway.

One of those, as an example, is a unit investment trust I recently examined that invested in the "Dogs of the Dow." I mentioned it earlier, but what I did not say was that the product was neither transferable nor was it able to be sold by the owner until it matured, or at least that is what the account holder was told by the broker. Worse, the product had an automatic rollover feature that paid the broker a commission on sale and immediately on purchase the next day. The account holder was told that if he failed to advise the company that he didn't want to rollover on the day it matured, he would be automatically reinvested for another year. In actuality, when he demanded to speak to the broker's branch office manager, the story suddenly changed. It still took him several days of demanding to have the investment liquidated.

Some mutual fund companies have the same attitude toward investors. As long as you are working with them and making purchases, they are friendly and helpful, but I have been called on to assist no small number of investors over the years that have been to the point of complete frustration with a "no-load" fund company that was effectively blocking their liquidation or transfer of assets. In some cases, we have had to give investors the name of a securities attorney as well as the means of contacting a federal regulatory agency, as we too were unable to break the logjam.

Generally speaking, if you are using an independent advisor who contracts through a broker-dealer rather than being an employee of some investment or brokerage firm, you will tend to get investments that are portable. Still, it is important that you ask and either get the answer in writing or make it clear that you are taking notes. Here is a point where reading the prospectus or other information carefully has value. The legalisms of some investment documents make it quite unclear if and how the product is portable. Asking an advisor what the procedures would be if you wanted to move the investment to another advisor in the event you were unhappy with this one or if something happens to him or her, is a valid question and should be well answered. As with all other such issues, don't just ask the question, take notes in writing, and let the advisor see that you are doing so.

Chapter 18 – Beyond the Grave: Planning for Those Who Survive Your Demise

A whole book could be written on this subject alone. The fact is *you are going to die!* It has been quite normal for people who are speaking to me about estate planning over the years to make the comment, "If I die…" Face it; we all are going to die, some sooner and some later. It has become sort of a cult in Western culture to deny death. In earlier times and more primitive cultures, we made a big thing out of death. Remnants of those traditions persist in the funeral service and, in some communities, the wake.

As we have become less community oriented we have also tended to banish the subject of death to the far corners of our awareness. We have instituted hospice institutions to house the dying, funeral homes for the ceremony, and the wonders of the skilled embalmer to make the corpse of the recently departed appear to be peacefully sleeping. In all of this, we have transitioned from a people who routinely witnessed death and the dead to one where the sight of a really dead-looking corpse is a shock and is considered to be a form of visual profanity. Death is no longer real to us. That we no longer consider it real does not make it less so.

Life Insurance

How much do you need?

We have instituted a form of insurance that reflects our denial of death: life insurance. In most types of insurance we name either the thing we will replace or the hazard we are insuring against. Fire insurance, for example, is to deal with the financial risk from a fire. Auto insurance is to replace or repair our automobile. Health insurance is designed to pay for returning us to health. Then, there is life insurance. It is more properly termed "death insurance" than life insurance and better thought of that way.

Death is a certainty and the only question is "What will happen financially *when* you die." If your death comes before retirement, or financial independence, then your income will probably cease. If there are people who were dependent on that income or your services to them, they are going to suffer a loss beyond the emotional pain at your absence. Because we are talking about financial matters here, that is what we will focus on.

Step one in determining your needs in this area is to look at what you earn and what part of it is needed to meet obligations and provide for someone else's standard of living. Then, consider what you were planning to do from your income or the investments your income would have funded in the future. For example, if you have children that you planned to send to a university, then the cost may have been planned from your investments, but if you are not around to fund those investments, they will need to replace the money from somewhere or else settle for a lesser educational opportunity.

Over on the emotional side, it is not unusual for a surviving wife to want to pay off the mortgage if her husband dies. In many cases, this is not a great financial move, but the emotional security that is gained from not owing a monthly payment to a mortgage company is sometimes a greatly needed support for a widow. Do not forget though, that the taxes and homeowner's insurance premiums are still going to come due, and they may well be a growing expense as the years pass by.

Another factor to consider is that your income has been going up over the years, in all likelihood. If that is a fact, then you may want your family to experience that same increase in income that you have been providing. If you do not want to calculate the compound interest rate at which your income has been rising, you can make an educated guess. If your *real* (after inflation) standard of living has been slowly rising over the years, then you may want to simply double your estimate of inflation. For example, if you estimate that inflation will run at about 2.5% into the future, then give yourself a 5% personal inflation figure.

Once you have determined what income your survivors will need from your estate, convert that number to an annual dollar amount. Let's say you determine that your spouse will need $70,000 to replace the income you were providing to meet your standard of living. Now divide that number by the *real* rate of return that your investment portfolio is likely to be able to provide. That number can range from 5% for a conservative portfolio to 8% for more aggressive widows.

Remember that it is not *your* investment approach we are considering here, but the investment approach of your survivor(s).

Seventy thousand dollars divided by 0.05 (5%) gives us an answer of $1,400,000. What we have just done is to determine how much capital it will take at a 7.5% return (5% real return plus 2.5% inflation) to generate $70,000 per year and adjust for inflation in a conservative portfolio. If we assume an 8% real return, then we are assuming that we can get 10.5% from the portfolio with 2.5% inflation.

Using a 6% real return reveals a need for $1,167,000. Let's say that you have an insurance policy provided by your employer that is convertible to an individual insurance policy (that is very important because if you lose your job after being stricken with some terminal disease, you will need that insurance) in the amount of $250,000. Let's also suppose you have a retirement portfolio with $300,000 in it. We then can deduct $550,000 from the $1,167,000. Just for income to support your dependents, you will need $617,000 in coverage from a commercial insurance company. If your family has additional needs, add them in as well. For example, because higher education costs are going up at about 7%, simply fund the total cost in your insurance planning. If your investigation shows that it will cost about $15,000 per year for that four-year university education, then add $60,000 to the total per child, bringing the need up to $677,000 with one child.

It is important to take the time here to carefully research the costs and income that will need replacing. University websites routinely give estimates of what a year or a semester will cost including room, board, books, and tuition. They also commonly provide an estimate of how much extra it will cost for a student to reside in the area and pay for the odds and ends that life requires. I would not take the viewpoint that "I worked my way through college and he (she) can do the same," if you have a bright child whom you want to take full advantage of a university education. Universities are packing about twice the information and education into four years than they were thirty years ago. If your child is going to get a degree in a difficult subject, it will be a full time, 12 hour per day job, at a minimum, to absorb the information you are paying for.

Don't skimp here. I have rarely seen anyone with too much life insurance, but I have seen many people with too little. It is not unusual for people to tell me they think they have too much life insurance on *their* life, but only rarely have I heard the beneficiary say that about the person whose life was the subject of the policy. In the vast majority of the instances where people have believed they are over-insured, the type of analysis that I have outlined above has revealed that they are actually rather under insured! It has been one of the more predictable issues, in my experience, that when I subtract the items that the survivor would pay for or fund with a lump sum, like educations, mortgages, or debt elimination, and then state the monthly income that would be available given the investment preference of the survivors, there follows a shocked silence. I can almost see the thoughts going through their heads as they consider how life would be with the very limited income that money would provide.

What kind of life insurance do you need?

An underwriter at an insurance company that focused on term insurance once confided in me that only very rarely did they have a death claim when compared with other companies. I asked why that was, and he explained that the later years of a person's life were when they were most likely to die and when the cost of the term insurance would rise dramatically. As a result, older people either got tired of paying ever higher amounts for insurance or were under sufficient financial stress in the case of a terminal illness that they would very commonly either cancel or fail to make the premium payment and thereby lose the policy before they died!

Some people have listened to the theorists who suggest that life insurance is not needed as people grow older and so advise buying term insurance that will decrease in coverage over the years. In fact, the need for life insurance only comes when a person dies. The older a person is, the more likely they will die in any given year. That tends to make insurance more expensive for older people, but it also is usually quite seriously needed in those years as well.

For example, if a couple is reasonably well off and has enough to retire on, but the spouse with the higher social security and perhaps a pension goes through a period of nursing home care prior to death, it may well be that those retirement funds will be partially depleted when he or she dies. The combination of the depletion of retirement fund and the decrease in income may well place a severe hardship on the surviving spouse just when declining health may become an issue for them as well. If the care giving survivor-to-be knows that the means are in place to replenish the retirement fund as well as provide a reserve, he or she can relax and focus on the relationship, rather than the finances, in the months or years prior to the death of the first spouse.

The better life insurance companies now provide some form of terminal condition rider that allows even the beneficiary to draw on the death benefit of the life insurance policy prior to the death of the insured person as long as a physician certifies the terminal condition. If you decide to use a variable universal life insurance policy to fund your life insurance needs (as I normally recommend), and you use the "increasing death benefit" option (as I normally recommend), the survivor can even draw money from the policy or take "loans" against the values in the policy that will be paid off at the death of the insured, income tax free!

All life insurance, if you are able to dig down deep enough, will be revealed as annual term life insurance. Each year, and in some cases each month, will be calculated separately. With each year of age there is a certain statistical probability of your death. Different "types" of life insurance exist to theoretically give you a choice as to whether and/or how you will pay for the underlying term insurance as your age increases and your annual probability of death rises.

In fact, some policies do that quite well while others confuse the issue to the point where the purchase of life insurance becomes an exercise in frustration and emotion. Rather obviously, the simplest solution is to purchase the lowest price pure annual term insurance available. As with most other things in the world of investing and money, the simplest solution is not always the best.

The Internal Revenue Code has, as I discussed in the section on variable universal life insurance, made a special provision for the cash value in a life insurance policy. As long as the policy is funded according to the Code calculations, that cash value can have gain from either interest or appreciation or both without current taxation on the build up in value. The purpose of that provision is to encourage people to have life insurance coverage that will be affordable in their later years and thereby prevent those dependent on them from becoming dependent on the government.

As a result of this provision allowing for a tax advantage in the cash values of a life insurance policy, it can be quite cost effective to accumulate value inside a policy to pay for the higher insurance cost in the later years. Unfortunately, the traditional whole life insurance policy that was quite effective in an era of deflation and regulated interest rates became very ineffective in the 1970s. A person who calculated a need for $35,000 of life insurance in the 1970s may well have found that in twenty years that need had increased to $250,000. In fact, that was the actual increase the Veterans Administration determined soldiers needed in Serviceman's Group Life Insurance over that period. Inflation was one factor in that change but a rising standard of living was just as important.

People who purchased life insurance in the early 1970s commonly had purchased several more policies by the mid-90s, even if they still had the original policy. Due to a combination of extended life expectancies, greater efficiencies in administration, and increased investment returns, the cost of insuring a life declined by more than 50% over that period. The fixed coverage and high cost per thousand doomed the old fixed life insurance programs.

Two kinds of life insurance emerged to replace the old whole life insurance policies. Because the whole life policy assumed a rather low guaranteed fixed rate of return, the life insurance companies had the opportunity to effectively take money they were borrowing from the policyholders at rates from one to three percent and reinvest it in bonds that by the late 1970s and early 1980s were paying double digit interest rates. Universal life insurance was introduced as an alternative to whole life. In the universal life policy, the interest rates were "floating" with a guaranteed minimum. Unfortunately, many of them were sold with the assumption that the then high rates of bond returns would continue forever. As interest rates declined, so did the interest paid in the policy, thus, many of the policies either lapsed or were surrendered as they ran out of cash value and the insurance companies demanded large amounts annually to keep the policy in force.

Term life insurance became popular at about the same time. The obvious advantage of term life insurance is that it is less costly in the early years because cash value does not build up in the policy. With term insurance, the policy owner pays only the current cost of the insurance, or perhaps the averaged ten-year or even twenty-year cost. For those not yet advanced in age, the required monthly or annual premium is quite low. Once again, age and time factored into the scene as the thirty year old who bought twenty-year term coverage in 1980 found it to be prohibitively expensive to renew that same coverage in the year 2000. Additionally, the 50 year old who is looking at the cost to renew the policy has a much higher probability of having some health problem than did that same person twenty years earlier. As states tightened their standards on such term policies and the market return on the insurance companies' portfolios tightened along with their underwriting practices, the renewal price climbed.

Finally in 1987, The Investment Act of 1940 was amended to include the underlying sub-accounts in the series fund that provided the cash value of a variable universal life insurance policy. Now a policyholder could, to the extent provided in the series fund, self-direct the cash value in a life insurance policy. Because the cash values, if the rules are followed, can have some rather significant tax advantages over non-tax advantaged investment vehicles, the variable universal life policies emerged to provide what could be potentially the most cost-efficient life insurance policy. Additionally, presuming some reasonable market return over the long haul, the policy could provide a substantial amount of excess gain to the policy owner as a means of providing for needs like college funding, retirement, or even a down payment on a retirement home.

Fundamentally, the decision of what kind of life insurance you need depends on what you want to accomplish in the future. If it is appealing to have what can be effectively a tax-exempt fund to pay for your term life insurance as well as fund your long term goals, if the market returns so support, then VUL is something you should explore. If you are barely making ends meet and need a lot of life insurance, there is no substitute for pure term insurance. In between, the interest rate guarantees of whole life or some form of universal life may be what you want. The important thing to remember is what an old insurance agent told me while I was still in the Army: "The best kind of life insurance to have is whatever you have when you die."

My last comment here on life insurance is related to that statement. A few years ago a man came into my office with a term life insurance contract that was about to expire. Sadly the man carrying the contract and on whose life the policy was issued also had recently had a severe heart attack. He had been warned that his probability of living more than about ten years was low and that he should avoid strenuous labor or stressful situations.

He asked me to look over his life insurance policy and see if anything could be done with it. In the twenty-year term policy was a provision that allowed for conversion to a new policy with the same company without medical question or examination. I called the number listed on the policy and found that it no longer existed. Then I did some research and found that another company had bought out the company that had originally held the policy.

I called the new company and discovered that they would indeed honor the conversion guarantee. Then came the shock. The only policy they would allow conversion to was a whole life policy that was so high in price that when I told the man sitting across from me he started laughing. He explained that the amount they were going to demand from him monthly was about the same as he was receiving in disability income! While I don't know the final outcome, I strongly suspect that he did not convert the policy and was forced to go on without the coverage he said he needed.

Once again the lesson here is that we often make financial decisions without considering the end result. Rather we dwell on the immediate cost to our long-term detriment.

Wills, Trusts, and Transfers

Wills

Because we all know we are going to die and we all know that whatever we own will need some form of documentation to transfer it to someone else upon our death, it would then be logical that most people would have created some form of "last will and testament." In fact, several articles I have read support what funeral directors and attorneys have told me over the years: most people do *not* have a current will when they die!

I have known people who knew their passing from this life was close at hand and have asked them if they have an up-to-date will that conforms to both state law and their desires. They have emphatically answered in the positive only to have it revealed after their death that the estate documents they had were neither prepared in accordance with the laws of their state of residence nor reflected their desires for their property. I could readily determine that there was a disconnect when we found the beneficiary designations on their life insurance, annuities, retirement accounts, and mutual funds were quite at odds with the instructions in their will.

If you have minor children, the issue becomes more complicated in that you will need to designate a guardian or guardians for your child or children. Additionally, you will need to designate a trustee and delineate a trust for the property that would otherwise pass to any minors. If you have people to whom you want to leave some or all of your estate but are concerned that they may or may not have the maturity to deal with what you want to leave them, then you need to create a trust that comes into existence at the time of your death to receive your property. That trust needs to be a well-written, legally binding document that gives clear and unambiguous instructions to the trustee. Of course, you will need to name a trustee, and an alternate trustee. You will probably need to go on to name even a successor trustee if you are starting out with trustee(s) who are not particularly young.

One example of how confusing things can be came from a will prepared by an elderly woman dying of cancer. She indicated that a certain chest she owned be given to one of her sons. What she did not indicate was whether the items *in* the chest at the time of her death were to go to him or to someone else. Quite a lot of confusion and hurt feelings resulted from that unclear bequest. That same, rather poorly thought out will stated that "I give my house to …" As she, at the time of her death, actually owned two houses, one of which she was renting to one of her sons, it was manifestly unclear what she wanted to happen.

In yet another example, a younger woman with a terminal condition whose husband had preceded her in death directed that a certain amount of money from her estate be given to her church. She also directed that her residence be given to her parents. At the time of her death, after her medical expenses were paid, the amount of money she directed be given to her church was not available in her estate unless the house she had directed be given to her parents was sold! Her mother, who was the executor of the estate, simply elected to not give the whole amount to the church so as to retain the house. The church, to which the now deceased woman had verbally promised the money as well as including it in the will, sued the estate. In the end, the house was sold and after legal expenses and paying off the mortgage in a very poor real estate market, neither the church nor the parents got a great deal.

I am a financial planner, not an attorney, so I may have a rather slanted point of view here, but I have found that after preparation of a well-thought-out financial plan, you have, at that moment, all the information and the state of mind that will best prepare you to create your estate documents. If your planner is a good one, you should be able to sit down with him or her and discuss what you want to happen in a series of contingencies. Unless your financial planner is also an attorney, he or she will not be able to, nor should, prepare the actual documents. What you will be able to obtain with your planner is a clear set of notes outlining what you want to happen in each scenario following your death. If you have used that financial planner to create your investment portfolios, then by bringing the planner into the document preparation process, you have a much higher probability of having your investments that pass by contract line up with what your will directs.

If you and/or your spouse have children that you do not share, it is important that you not make up a standard spousal simple will. In that simple will, it is the norm that the first spouse to die leaves everything to the surviving spouse. Because each of you will probably have a will that leaves all your possessions to *your* children and not to your now deceased spouse's children, what will have happened is the first spouse to die has disinherited his or her children! The solution, in that case, is that the first spouse to die leaves his or her property to a trust, normally with the surviving spouse as the trustee. The surviving spouse has the right of use of all the property and, if the trust allows, can liquidate the property and take the value for him or herself.

Finally, with documents and advice that will have a major effect on your life and financial situation, choose your advisor carefully. It is wise to choose an attorney who is experienced, who focuses on wills and estate planning, and who is part of a firm of attorneys. It is also not a bad idea to find one who is relatively young! Ideally, the attorney who prepares your will, or at least his or her firm, would be the one to probate it. That way, if there are problems that arise with the documents or some other aspect of what was done earlier, the firm that created the documents in the beginning will have to take responsibility for all of it.

Trusts

A trust is, in effect, a separate entity from the persons associated with it. In order to have a trust, there must be a *grantor* (who normally creates the trust by gifting property to it or leaving property by a will) one or more *trustees* (who will manage and control the trust), and one or more *beneficiaries* (for whose benefit the trust is managed and who will receive the trust benefits at some point). Additionally, and this is often overlooked, there often will be a *custodian* which actually holds some or all of the property of the trust.

The whole idea of a trust is to separate ownership of property from a person. For example, if you have a daughter to whom you wish to either gift or leave property at your death, but you do not want that property to become entangled with a present or future husband's property, you might leave or give it to a trust with the daughter as the beneficiary. Another option would be to have the property held in the trust but with the daughter as the trustee and her child or children (presuming she had a child or children) as the beneficiaries. You could make that trust a *revocable* trust and thereby allow the trustee (your daughter) to revoke parts of the trust for her own use as she saw fit.

A very good use for a trust occurs when a married couple each have children by previous marriages. As I mentioned above, it is not uncommon to see wills that effectively disinherit the children of the first spouse to die. In this situation, instead of leaving all property to the surviving spouse, each spouse leaves his or her property to a trust, thereby, each parent's property can go to his or her own children after the surviving spouse dies. Normally, the surviving spouse would be the trustee and have the right to take assets from the trust for his or her use to maintain a customary standard of living.

A common use of trusts in those states where probate is an onerous process is the *living* or *inter vivos* trust. The purpose of such a trust is two-fold. In the event of the incapacity of one spouse, the other automatically can take control of the couple's assets if they are in a properly structured trust. In the event of the incapacity of both, or of the surviving spouse, a third party, such as a relative, can take over the management without having to go to court and have one or both spouses declared incompetent. A living trust can also be used to reduce or nearly eliminate the cost and inconvenience of probate.

Here is where a trap lies. In many cases, creating the trust, transferring the property into the trust, and then maintaining the trust over the years actually amounts to a greater inconvenience and cost than simply probating the estate. If titled property (such as real estate) is placed in the trust, adequate proof must be on file at the courthouse with the deed and transfer documents clearly defining who has the right to sell the property. If real property is transferred to a trust without adequate documentation filed at the courthouse, then a "cloud" may be placed on the title when the time comes to finally sell it. Without a valid copy of the trust, there is no way a potential buyer can tell whether the person who is selling the property actually has the right to do so.

If property is in a trust, the formality of getting a court to sign off on the transfer at the death of one of the grantors is no longer required. Consequently, there are times when the trusteeship is not properly transferred or documented, leading to a potential situation where the trust becomes invalid but property is still owned by the (now invalid) trust. As you may guess that is a formula for a small nightmare and large legal fees to correct!

Perhaps the most important use of a trust is to provide income to care for a child who is incapable of caring for him or herself either due to age or incapacity. Once again, it is important to use an experienced and highly qualified trust attorney. I also strongly recommend you use an equally qualified and experienced financial planner to advise you on how set up the investment portion of the trust.

A couple came to my office to ask my guidance as they had just become aware that the wife's father, who was dying of cancer, had placed his estate in a trust and had designated her as the co-trustee at his death. The other trustee was to be her son. As I read the trust, I realized that some very real problems were about to arise. Both the wife and her adult son had a major goal of being able to pay for the college educations of *the son's* children. The "living" trust that her father had created made absolutely no provision for such a use. It was to become an irrevocable trust at his death and did not allow for liquidation of the assets for many years into the future. While the income was to be paid to the grantor's daughter and his grandson, the two trustees, the trust made no allowance for other distributions except for a list of unpleasant events such as total disability or death. In other words, the trust effectively prevented its use to pay for any support of the grantor's *great*-grandchildren!

My advice, which they followed, was to quickly get together with a qualified estate attorney. The attorney was able to modify the trust, and they were fortunate in that her father had a few hours of lucidity that very evening when he was able to comprehend what the trust had done and intelligently make changes. Neither the grandfather nor his attorney thought of the possibility that he might live long enough to have no need educate his grandson but rather his great-grandchildren!

Another common failing in that trust was that he had not maintained it. Quite a number of items of property were still listed in the trust that he had subsequently sold. Another long list of properties had been purchased along the way that he had failed to include in the trust! One rental property was owned by the trust, but the rent had been paid to him as a person for many years. In short, the trust had created a major mess.

Had the creator of that trust simply had a will that left everything to a trust (presuming he wanted to do that) with his daughter and grandson as co-trustees, he would have made life far simpler than it turned out to be.

At the risk of overstating this issue, trusts can be useful and valuable tools, but they require a great deal of thought and planning in advance of the visit to the attorney to draw up the legal documents. That is why I recommend an experienced financial planner who is properly registered as an *Investment Advisor*. Creating a trust is like building a house. If you do not know exactly what you want in a house before you use an architect, what the architect produces and the builder builds may well not even be close to what you really wanted! It is far less difficult and expensive to make a list and have a clear idea of what you want *before* drawing up the documents.

Chapter 19 – Choosing an Advisor

Do You Need an Advisor?

As late as the 1970s, it was quite possible in the world of investments for an amateur to compete effectively with the professionals. It did take some education, formal or self-administered, but it could be done. The understanding of investor, security, and portfolio behavior was extremely limited, and the information about publicly traded corporations was relatively simple and very much standardized.

Back then it was possible for an individual investor to personally research the information from a relatively large number of companies as efficiently as would a professional. It required being willing and able to read and understand the annual reports issued by those companies along with a daily reading of the *Wall Street Journal* and a weekly review of *Barron's*. This put the disciplined amateur on an equal footing with the professional.

Of course, there was the small problem of diversification. Even back before portfolio theory, dedicated amateurs understood that stocks should be held in a relatively large number of companies. The guidance was that a minimum of twenty issues (companies) should be included in one's portfolio and those should be from different industries. The commonly accepted rule was that having five industries with a minimum of four issues per industry was the very least diversification that would be acceptable.

To avoid the "odd-lot" charge that comes with buying stocks in less than multiples of 100 shares and at an average cost per share of $50, one would be required to have at least $100,000 to invest in order to have a minimally diversified portfolio. If we adjust for inflation since then, what we are talking about here is the equivalent of a portfolio of $1,000,000 today! That was just for the "stock" portfolio. The wisdom of the day dictated that one have at least 40% of one's investment portfolio in long-term bonds. Thus, another $670,000 would be required in today's dollars!

The problem with that formula today is that the information flow from companies and from the analyst community is overwhelmingly complex and the volume of information is staggering. The competition you face in the marketplace was once mainly others with little formal education in securities but is now true professionals.

Today, the manager of an investment fund commonly has a master's degree in finance and is a Chartered Financial Analyst (CFA). The inherent change in our economy and markets has accelerated to where another profession has emerged along with an education and designation. The Certified Financial Planner practitioner (CFP®) not only has the education and the experience but also gets at least fifteen hours of continuing education each year just to minimally keep up with the changes in tax and securities related laws and understanding investment concepts.

I was once convinced that I could manage a small stock portfolio as well as the professional portfolio managers. I tried, and found that I could not unless I had their resources and the time they had available to do it! Today, I am spending thousands of dollars per year on data just to find good *portfolio managers*! In order to compete with them, I would need tens of thousands of dollars to spend on data and many times that to spend on adequate staff to assist me.

My research into the cost of portfolio management indicates that a manager without a budget of at least $300,000 per year cannot hope to compete successfully in the marketplace. Simply put, unless a portfolio has at least $6,000,000 and the owner is willing to devote a full day's work to the portfolio every day as well as hire a staff to assist him or her, then that portfolio will be at a distinct disadvantage against the professionals.

Considering that the same portfolio could be managed by using professional managers in publicly available positions while paying a personal investment advisor a percent or so and *still* produce the return, why would someone choose to do it themselves?

Historically, a good advisor using a series of about five mutual fund managers has been able to manage such a portfolio for far less than an individual would need to spend to do it him or herself. That leaves the time free for the financially independent owner of the portfolio to do what he or she wishes.

Unless you are capable of thoroughly investigating several hundred publicly traded corporations by traveling to their headquarters and facilities across the country, you will not be able to gather sufficient information to make an investment decision without consulting the reports of some advisory agency or company anyway.

The bottom line is that in some manner, you *will* choose one or more advisors upon whom you are dependent when you invest. The question is whether you will do so consciously and carefully or whether you will have your advisors thrust on you unaware.

Every advisory agency has some conflict of interest. Using an advisor who is an employee of some agency is dangerous, particularly when that agency receives most, or all, of its income from the very companies it is supposed to objectively rate. The reliability of reports made up for mass distribution with little or no charge is certainly questionable. The value of advice you receive without cost is generally about what you paid for it. Worse, the value of the advice you get is generally near zero by the time you receive it. An upgrade or downgrade of a company by any of the major advisory firms will create a movement in that company's stock price literally in seconds. By the time the public has received and digested the new report, the stock price has commonly already moved on that news, leaving the individual investor "holding the bag."

If, however, you choose to use one of the tens of thousands of available mutual funds, you must first trust some advisor to recommend a fund to you or to report accurately on the fund. Second, you are entrusting your money, your capital, to the manager of that fund.

Even before you actually invest, it is critical to create a clear and well thought out plan and keep that plan up to date if you want to be successful. That can be done without an advisor, but most who attempt to do so will actually use *Quicken* or some other software that was created with a set of assumptions supplied by an advisor. Whether or not those assumptions are correct, or if they apply to you, is a major unknown. The question is really not whether you will use an advisor if you plan to invest for a goal, but whether the advisor is working for you or for a corporation that is only interested in selling something to you, and of course whether or not that advisor is competent.

Hiring a competent and professional investment advisor is going to cost you something, but the cost should be tiny compared with the improvement in investment performance you can gain from his or her advice.

Credentials

The first thing to look for when searching for an advisor is the licensing status. At a minimum, the person or persons offering service to you should be registered at both the state (where you live) and federal levels. Your state securities commission should know of this person through that registration. The other organization, at a minimum, that should be aware of your advisor's existence is the NASD[6]. Those unpronounceable letters stand for the National Association of Securities Dealers, the national regulatory body that governs the sale of most securities in the United States.

The one registration that I believe anyone who is giving advice on investments should have is that of either *Registered Investment Advisor* (RIA) *or Investment Advisor Representative* (IAR). Investment Advisors, be they RIAs or IARs, are regulated by the state securities commissioner and, in some cases, by the Securities and Exchange Commission. Unfortunately, they are not regulated too well unless they are registered through what is known as an "umbrella RIA." As I will explain below, I believe that it is in your best interest for your advisor to be registered with and supervised by *both* agencies as well as a supervising corporate headquarters with deep pockets!

Your state may have a website through which you can investigate the person offering advice, but the NASD has one of the best for doing this research and it can be found at www.nasdr.com/2000.asp. Once you arrive at the site and clear the necessary screens where the NASD discloses and disclaims at great length, you can search for the individual representative. I would not get too involved looking at the firm the advisor belongs to, as many of them have literally thousands of representatives and you may well be seeing a lot of "stuff" that has nothing to do with the person you are seeking.

---

[6]The NASD was once officially titled "The National Association of Securities Dealers" but has since split itself into different organizations. "NASD" as I use it here refers to the NASD-R or the organization that is empowered to regulate security sales to the public in the United States under the supervision of the Securities and Exchange Commission (SEC). The SEC and the various state securities commissioners regulate Investment Advisors, while the NASD and to a lesser extent, the states, regulate the security broker-dealers and their representatives who sell securities to the public.

On the NASD website, you will find the licensing status as well as any complaints that may have been lodged against the person. You will also find a link to investigate the advisor's registration as an Investment Advisor if they are directly registered with the Securities and Exchange Commission. At a minimum, *if you do not find the person and/or firm that is offering you advice on either the state or NASD websites, you are not dealing with a properly registered person. If a person who is not so registered attempts to advise you, I strongly recommend you not use that person's services. What you may have encountered is either a con-man (woman) or someone so ignorant of the issues that he or she doesn't even know they are breaking the law!*

In my opinion, one of the most critical issues is whether the person is registered as an *Investment Advisor* or is just some form of salesperson. If you are dealing with a "financial advisor," "account advisor," "account executive," or any other of the multitude of titles sales organizations come up with, then you *are* dealing with a salesperson. I have no bone to pick with salesmen or women, but it is critical that you, the potential customer, understand what you are dealing with and take any advice offered in that light. What the Securities and Exchange Commission has ruled is that *advice given purely as a part of the sale or attempted sale of a security to a member of the public does not constitute investment advice and does not subject the giver of such advice to the provisions of the Investment Advisory Act of 1940.*

That means the person giving you advice about purchasing an investment product is not obligated to give you full disclosure of either what you will be paying or any conflicts of interest *unless they are registered and acting as an Investment Advisor under that act!* That is perfectly rational because the law assumes that there is an adversarial relationship between a salesperson and a purchaser. The rules of the NASD call for "full and fair" communications, but I can assure you that the verbal sales pitch of most any securities salespersons (e.g. stockbrokers) would never pass muster with the regulators.

The NASD licensing process requires that the licensee prove that he or she is familiar with its rules and regulations as well as the underlying nature of the securities being offered. There are several levels of licensing at the NASD and they do make a difference.

The lowest level is the NASD Series 6, allowing the sale of mutual funds and variable products. To be very frank, it is the "newbie" level license in the securities profession. A Series 6 license is both easy to get and very limiting in what it allows. While there are certainly professionals with only a Series 6 license, if you have a financial situation or a portfolio that is beyond a few simple mutual funds, this is not the person you should be working with.

Additionally, all licensed securities representatives will have either an NASD Series 63 or Series 66 license. Those licenses are uniform for all states and entitle the representative to be state-licensed to sell securities. Each securities salesperson in a given state is required to be licensed in that state to sell securities. If you live in one state and the salesperson is in another state, then he or she is required to become licensed in the state where you live to offer you securities.

The next level is the NASD Series 7, general securities salesperson, which authorizes the advisor to sell most securities. Above that is the NASD Series 24 license for a Registered Principal. This is someone who is held to a higher standard and is required to both understand the regulations extremely well and take responsibility for the representatives under his or her supervision.

While there are "fee-only" investment advisors who are not licensed at all with the NASD, using them involves some risk. Purely from the aspect of being an investment advisor, the testing requirements in some states are non-existent. If your advisor is licensed through a large corporate broker-dealer, then that corporation is financially responsible for the activities of the advisor. If you are dealing with an independent investment advisor who is not contracted through a large broker-dealer as a representative, you may well find yourself standing in line behind a lot of other investors if something untoward happens to your investments! Additionally, the non-NASD licensee must work through some broker-dealer who must actually be registered with the NASD unless you are executing the investment purchases yourself. That involves some conflicts that are only now being recognized.

If the total money under management and/or customer base of the advisor is less than $25 million, registration with the state is all that is legally required for a fee-only investment advisor. If an advisor is registered with the state only, you may be dealing with a very competent person who has just chosen to do business on a very small scale, but it is more likely you are dealing with the second or third string. While there are many independent advisors who will loudly disagree with me on this point, I firmly believe that the advisor you choose should be registered through an "umbrella RIA." Those who are so registered are officially "Investment Advisor Representatives" or "IARs." Advice from an IAR is subject to the same strict guidelines as that from an RIA. The difference is that the IAR is responsible to, and under the regulation of, that corporation's compliance department. I am a great believer in checks and balances. Otherwise, securities advisors and salespersons down at the level where meetings go on with the public are not well supervised by the regulatory agencies. The regulations are there, but there are just too many offices and too few regulators. The method our nation has determined to be best in this area is to let the industry "self-regulate" under supervision of the NASD and SEC.

With an advisor who falls under an umbrella RIA, the NASD regulations require that a Registered Principal inspect the advisor's files at least once a year. Additionally, all correspondence to and from that representative relating to securities must be reviewed and cleared by a Registered Principal. All sales are supposedly reviewed and cleared by a principal as well. The way enforcement more often works, though, is when a member of the public files a complaint or a lawsuit. It is often then that the mechanism really swings into action. When a complaint is filed or some judicial or arbitration action finds against a securities salesperson, the supervising corporation and the representative are thoroughly investigated and commonly hit with substantial fines as well as whatever judgment a court or arbitration panel awards to the investor.

If an advisor is an *independent* RIA, and not registered as a representative of a corporate broker-dealer with the NASD, then it may be years between inspections of his or her files, if they are inspected at all. The limitations on what the advisor says and writes to the general public, while strict, is not nearly as strict as under the NASD. Perhaps the most uncomfortable issue for me, though, is that the completely independent advisor simply has no one looking over his or her shoulder! NASD registered representatives often refer to the "compliance department" as the "sales prevention department." Fortunately for the general public, they are often right! In the interest of protecting the corporate parent from litigation liability, the compliance department is in the business of considering each and every action in light of how it would look to the federal and state regulators as well as the court system.

The minimum requirement I would recommend in the way of credentials is that the person you employ be licensed with the NASD and that they be contracted as an Investment Advisor Representative. In the worst-case event that you are dealing with someone who is a charlatan and a crook, at least you will have a corporation with deep pockets to go after in order to get your money back.

While I mentioned this earlier in the book, it is worth repeating that in the very recent past, many millions of dollars have been given to "independent" investment advisors who had a host of great references and brilliant reputations, yet all of that did not replace the millions of dollars that are now lost to fraud and incompetence. The victims range from plain old common folk with a few tens of thousands of dollars to movie stars with hundreds of millions.

The similarities between the losses are many. The very personable advisor claims that his or her independence allows the investor to gain an advantage over those who are associated with regulators and corporations. Apparently, the returns are absolutely astonishing from year to year, seemingly giving validity to the claim of the maverick advisor. What ultimately comes of these schemes is named quite appropriately after our old friend, *Ponzi*.

Certifications

What we have done so far is discuss only the regulatory and licensing requirements. The fact that a person is licensed and regulated and possibly quite honest is no indication that he or she has a clue about what they are doing. It is similar to the issue of driving a car. A sixteen year old may well be properly licensed and have adequate insurance coverage as well as be from a responsible and respectable home. That does not mean that he or she is someone in whose hands you would willingly place your life!

Recently, there have been a plethora of organizations that have stepped forward to certify those who would give investment advice. Among those, there are three or four that have generally come to be accepted as most likely to guarantee at least minimal competence in offering advice to investors.

The first designation is commonly associated with the life insurance industry and requires that the certified person first qualify as highly proficient in that area. It has the rather complex name of

Chartered Financial Consultant or ChFC. If you go to the website: http://www.amercoll.edu, you will be able to research the school that confers this designation. As you would surmise, if your prime interest is associated with life insurance, a person with this designation is probably going to provide the best expertise.

Another designation is the Chartered Financial Analyst (CFA) and it is awarded by the Association for Investment Management and Research (AIMR). Its website is: http://www.aimr.com. CFAs are specialists in the analysis of individual securities and in building portfolios. Most mutual fund, pension fund, and corporate investment managers are either so certified or on the way to having this designation. While I would not consider the lack of a CFA after a portfolio manager's name a serious negative, the presence of those three letters is a definite plus. CFAs are the ones to seek out if you do not want general financial planning but a true portfolio manager. Generally, you will find them managing pension and trust funds.

When it comes to general financial planning and working with families and individual investors, the designation of choice is that of Certified Financial Planner®. That certification is issued and maintained by the Certified Financial Planner Board of Standards http://www.cfp.net. A person designated as a CFP practitioner is certified as being proficient in all aspects of personal financial planning and has had at least three years in the profession before using the designation. The CFP Board is also a regulatory organization that can remove the right of a person to use the designation. A CFP designee is expected to act as a fiduciary when creating or executing a financial plan. In other words, the CFP mark after a planner's name means that when you are dealing with him or her on matters pertaining to that plan, they are required to act in your best interest, reveal any conflict of interest, and give you full disclosure of fees and charges.

Note though, that the mere presence of letters after a person's name mean only that the person has passed tests verifying that they have the knowledge to do the job right. It does *not* mean that they will. For example, if you are dealing with a stockbroker who has the CFP certificate hanging on the wall and the CFP mark on his card but he does not prepare a financial plan for you and work within the parameters of that plan, then you are simply dealing with a stockbroker with fancy letters after his name! As mentioned earlier, there is no

<

requirement for a stockbroker to act in your best interest. In fact, he may be under legal obligation to act in the best interest of his employer, the brokerage firm!

Again, the absence of those letters behind the name of your advisor does not mean that he or she is not the one you should use. I have worked with a CPA in Connecticut, for example, who is a registered representative and acts as an IAR when dealing with clients. She is one of the most knowledgeable and honest advisors I know. At the other extreme are CFA, CFP, and CPA designees who are clearly employed by a corporation to sell their wares. While CPAs are one of the most respected professional groups in the nation, it did not keep them from conveniently overlooking or helping to hide phenomenal losses at corporations where they had taken on the role of employee.

Before I leave the subject, I want to make one more clear distinction. Generally, a person who is solely a Certified Public Accountant has had very little training in investment management or financial planning. Some states have even made it illegal for a CPA to be paid for investment advice. Similarly, a CFP designee has had little or no training in preparing tax returns or accounting. I would not recommend a person who was merely certified as a CPA to give you investment advice any more than I would recommend a CFP to represent you before the IRS or to prepare your tax return. Each of the designations represents an area of expertise, and it is wise to not get them confused.

After several decades of observation and participation in the business of offering investment and financial planning advice to the public, I have come to some conclusions. First, using an advisor who has at least a certification or a master's degree in some financial area lets you know that the person has taken the time, money, and energy to become knowledgeable about the subject matter, and that substantially increases your chances of getting the right advice. Second, and most important, using an independent advisor who is properly registered with the SEC and state authorities and who has a contractual relationship with a deep-pocketed corporation offers a great amount of protection.

Knowledge About Valuation and Asset Classes

There are many in the financial profession who will sell you whatever they are hired or have chosen to sell without regard to whether it is appropriate. A long time ago, someone told me that if all you have to work with is a hammer, pretty soon everything starts looking like a nail!

Investment management has progressed in much the same manner as medicine. Thirty years ago I used an independent family doctor on some occasions, but more often relied on home remedies. Today, with the advent of thousands of wonder drugs as well as procedures that were unheard of decades ago, using a Primary Care Provider who will refer me to specialists at a medical center is a minimum requirement. In other words, just as we could use our family doctor in the past but now need far more sophisticated medical care, using the local stockbroker did fine in the 1960s but today we would get left in the dust without access to someone with the sophisticated data and skills.

Values

After considering credentials, certifications, and knowledge, you may reasonably conclude that you have sufficient insight for making your choice. There is one more consideration though, and this one is critical. One of my biggest failings in life has been the mistaken belief that other people whom I trusted had the same basic values as I did. In fact, many people do not share my value system at all and, in many cases, I have been shocked at what some trusted person did when I should have known in advance that would be their behavior.

My definition of "truth" is that which "is." The difficulty with that definition is that it leaves very little room to make predictions about the future. It also means that before I can state that something "is" or "is not", I have to do a little research to make sure that what I am saying is in fact the best information on the subject. Unfortunately, the securities and financial industry is not exactly overflowing with people who have that attitude. Whether it is newspaper commentators, talking heads on cable T.V., or salesmen for "guaranteed promissory notes," there are plenty of people who will make statements as if they are the absolute truth on things about which they know next to nothing.

Those statements are often not considered lies by the people who make them. That helps to explain why a person listening to them can be impressed with the sincerity with which the misleading or untruthful statement is made. One of the first signs that a person does not share my standard for truth is the word "gonna." As soon as I hear "This (fill in the blank) is gonna go up!" I know that we are in different worlds when it comes to the definition of truth. I am often amazed not only that people will make a definite statement about the value of an investment in the future, but that otherwise reasonable people will ask me something like, "When will the market go back up?" My standard response is, "If I knew, you couldn't afford to ask me."

If you have ever gotten the call late at night from the commodities salesperson who wants you to buy silver or gold or some other speculative non-producing item, you are familiar with the enthusiasm and sincerity with which they can insist that "You have got to get in now, at the bottom. This stuff's gonna go up fast, and you will be crying that you missed the greatest opportunity in your life!" In the case of the boiler-room telephone con-man, you may be sure that he well knows that is a lie, but because he neither knows nor cares what the truth is, he can lie with great enthusiasm.

More dangerous is the untruth of pure ignorance. In con games, as in many a sale of limited partnerships, promissory notes, viaticals (interests in life insurance policies of terminally ill persons), dot-com initial public offerings, speculative real estate, and many other "hot issues," the salesperson may have really believed in the product. I well remember the days of real estate and oil limited partnerships in the early 1980s. The wholesalers who came around to speak to the brokers at the regional branch where I worked were extremely sincere when they told us that oil was "gonna go up" for the next twenty years. They were as sincere and enthusiastic as the real estate partnership salesmen who told us about "cap-rates" and the scarcity of land in cities, and how their partnership company had returned twenty to thirty percent per year over the last several years.

More recently, the Beardstown Ladies promoted their book with its front cover claim of over 23% per year returns and asserted the truthfulness of those returns on national television. I really don't think they were intentionally lying any more than the limited partnership salesmen. They were convinced that what they were offering was completely sane and correct. The representatives of Enron were probably completely sincere when they visited pension fund managers around the country to sell the bonds and interests in the limited partnerships from Enron too!

How do you dodge the supposed advisor who either sincerely believes he or she is being truthful while they pass on to you the lies they have been fed? How do you dodge the charlatan for that matter? The simple answer is to ask them questions. If a person claims that you are entitled for some reason to some kind of an insider deal that the general public is not going to see, *run!* Recently a major "hedge fund" collapsed whose investors included a list that sounded like the Who's Who of Hollywood. The principal director of the fund had even received an academy award for his role in producing and directing a film. Unfortunately, he was far more astute at creating images than he was at assessing reality. He used his relationships with celebrities to gather in hundreds of millions of dollars. The story he presented was that in his fund he was not restricted by those nasty governmental regulations that limited the mundane mutual funds, so he could exercise his genius to create returns that only the rich and famous were entitled to enjoy. The rich and famous obviously had not read Charles MacKay's *Extraordinary Popular Delusions and the Madness of Crowds* or they would have recognized the same line used by John Law in the process of nearly destroying the financial base of the nation of France!

Greed and fear are the devices of the untrustworthy. Analysis, caution, and integrity are the hallmarks of those to be trusted. Presuming you are working with an advisor who is registered with the NASD, you may visit the NASD website and find any complaints that have been registered against the representative. You can call or write your state security commission and check there too. While anyone who has been in the business of advising investors has probably had at least some complaints, if any of them were found to be valid or if there are a lot of them, you have been warned.

Another thing that you should not be afraid to ask is about the personal life of the advisor. How many times has he or she been married? Has there ever been a filing for bankruptcy? How many and what complaints have been lodged against him or her? What plans are there for the future of the business? What is the succession plan in the case that he or she is unable to continue in business? Will he or she "sell" your account to another advisor? When you ask those questions, *make notes!* It is amazing how uncomfortable people who are not telling the complete truth get when the person on the other side of the table is making notes.

While this sounds too simple to work, simply asking the advisor who is being interviewed for his or her definition of "truth" is sometimes an eye-opener. If you find a person who has a set of values and is comfortable talking about them, you may have found a real jewel! Ask the advisor what he or she does to verify that the investments they recommend are what they say they are. Ask what specific investigation the advisor has done personally to verify the character and role of the manager. In essence, what you are trying to do here is investigate the character and integrity of the person who wants to be hired to assist you in managing your portfolio.

Next, after he or she suggests some investments, investigate the investments. If he or she has said that a given manager has a record of a certain rate of return over a specific period of time, go to the web and do a search for the investment and the manager by name. Examine the relevant facts of the record of the manager and take a look at those returns as well as any commentary you can find. You may find things you are uncomfortable with, but that should not deter you. What you then have is the ammunition you need to determine the character of the advisor. When you see the advisor the next time, ask about the negatives you found about the recommended investments. The advisor should be aware of the negatives and preferably has mentioned them.

Here is where you find out about character. When the advisor is challenged about the negatives you found, there will be a reaction. If he or she is actually knowledgeable about the investment product, then the response will be a reasoned and thorough response that addresses those items you have raised and explains them thoroughly. It may be that you have found something of which the advisor is unaware. If so, that is not a killer. A good advisor will either immediately turn to a reference or offer to get back with you with an answer. Investment advisors are not perfect, but if one is confident and has done the required "due-diligence" or homework on the investment, then he or she will be able to give you a reasoned response.

I often have recommended investment products that are not well-spoken of in some popular periodicals. Well-read people have often objected on the basis of an article by Jane Bryant Quinn or some other luminary. I am honestly quite happy to hear such a complaint. That person who has read up on the issues at least will be able to appreciate my reasons for choosing some given investment vehicle. The more knowledgeable my clients are, the easier it is for me to do my job. That is true of all good investment advisors. If you make yourself reasonably knowledgeable about the issues on which you are being advised, you will soon know whether you are dealing with a salesperson or an honest advisor.

Remember, too, that the ability to write a column for a newspaper or a magazine does not make the writer an expert in any subject. Some of the silliest investment advice I have ever heard has appeared in the columns or articles of widely read publications.

Fees and Commissions

Here is a subject so overworked that it has become one of the least understood of all the areas of investment advice. One of the amazing things to me is that highly sophisticated board members of university trust funds, insurance companies, and pension funds are ready and willing to pay substantial fees for investment advice and management, while many unsophisticated investors are convinced that fees detract from performance.

It comes back to that simple question of whether you believe that you can do it yourself. I took some bad (free) advice and skimped on the planning fees when we built a house. That was some of the most expensive free advice I have ever encountered! Only after being burned did I research and find that every dollar spent on professional planning would have saved me over $100 in building costs. I also learned, that had I used a firm that included architects and engineers and which was willing to manage the building process, I could have saved a tremendous amount of time, money, and aggravation. In the interest of saving on fees, I added about 30% to the cost of our house!

Good advice will not cost you... it will save you! Recently, I had the opportunity to review two portfolios with very nearly identical amounts of money invested for the same period of time, one using a highly qualified personal investment advisor and the other managed by the same person on their own. The portfolio invested with the advice and direction of a qualified financial planner was worth about eight times the original investment over an 18-year period while the other portfolio, positioned with the best advice that could be gleaned from investment magazines, the Internet, and the TV talk shows, had not quite doubled in the same period.

In other words, the rather dull and counterintuitive portfolio used at the advice of the professional advisor, and on which fees had been paid every year, had experienced about a 12% average annual compound rate of return. The relatively fun and exciting ride of the personally directed portfolio had returned about 4%. In the best tradition of such things, that 4% return was about what the investor could have gotten from a money market fund or a short-term bank CD over the same period.

Some of the best performing and best thought-out portfolios I have seen (outside those I have created) have been "load funds." Even as the magazines and broadcast media have drummed the paying of "front loads," about half of the best performing long-term funds charge a commission to purchase them. Does that commission improve the performance of the fund? The unqualified answer to that question is "no." On the other hand, if that commission was paid to a fund salesperson who honestly worked to keep the investor in a good portfolio, then we need to change the question and the answer.

If the person to whom the commission was paid worked to keep the investor in the fund, and it was a reasonable, even mediocre fund, the commission *did* improve the performance, not of the fund, but of the investor!

Fees are important. They are important in that you are paying for something and it is critical that you know both how much you are paying and what you are buying. The most important thing you need to know about fees and commissions is that to the degree that you are told what you are being charged, you can trust the person doing the telling. If someone tells you not to worry about the fees because the "company will pay him," that is another signal to run for the nearest exit. There is no such thing as a free lunch.

Any return that is quoted to you should be "net" of or after fees have been subtracted. I have seen quite a number of portfolios where the reported return was modest but reasonable, until I realized that what I was seeing was not the actual return to the investor, but either a "gross" return or, worse, a "hypothetical" return of an index. In some cases, the "fee-only" investment manager had carefully detailed out the theoretical performance of a series of indices on the front of the report while the actual return to the investor was buried deep within! As you may guess from the placement, the actual return was less than desirable.

If that same investor had been paying higher fees but had a better return, would that have been bad? I don't think so. The bottom line is that a good investment advisor, commissioned or fee-charging, is going to be paid, and if he or she is good, hopefully paid well. The question is not what you are being charged, although that should be clearly and prominently revealed, but what you are getting in return for the fee. Don't forget that the average equity fund investor got only about a 4% average annual compound return from the beginning of 1984 through the beginning of 2002 while the broad indices were turning in double digits. The difference between the two returns was not poor performance of the investments, but irrational behavior by the amateur investor.

The Final Analysis

In the end, there is only one thing that counts. Did you achieve your goals? If you don't know what those goals are, then the chances are that you will not achieve them. A good financial planner should spend the time it takes with you to help you determine exactly what you want your capital to achieve. He or she should provide you with a written analysis of those goals, of your existing portfolio, and of a proposed way to reach those goals. He or she should provide you with the rationale behind the assumptions of the plan and explain what it will cost and what you will receive in return.

Your planner should explain to you the issue of variance or volatility in the investments you have and the investments he or she is recommending. Your planner should address the taxes that will be due on your investments and what effect they will have on your return. All of this should be in writing.

Finally, the opportunity should be given to you to examine the document prior to making a decision about your investments. If you have all of that, then you may well have received the best treatment you will find anywhere. There will always be differences of opinion on what approach to use in investing, but if you have found someone who will give you the personal attention that allows you to determine what success means to you and then lays out a reasoned and researched plan to take you there, you have in front of you something that only very few investors will ever see.

It may be possible for you to do it yourself, but the record is not good. It is the same story in every profession. If you are good enough to do better than the professionals, then why are you not a professional in that area yourself?

If you have been able to set clear goals and convert them into objectives; if you have taken your present position and determined the rate of return that it will take to get to those objectives with what you plan to invest along the way; if you have then examined the asset classes available to you and selected several that together have the best probability to get you there; if you have found the managers and investment vehicles that will allow you to invest in those asset classes, using exceptional managers from different companies; if you have researched and determined the best way to limit taxation and cost as you rebalance from one asset class to another; and if you have been able to set up your estate to take over your investments and property in such a manner as to minimize the difficulty for those who survive you, then you may not need an advisor. If you have fallen short of that standard, the best investment you ever make may be the time you spend interviewing and consulting with a properly credentialed, certified, and knowledgeable investment advisor/financial planner.

Printed in the United States
1197900003B/1-48